S0-ACB-679

The Look of Distance

Landscape with the Fall of Icarus, by Pieter Bruegel. Courtesy of the Musées Royaux des Beaux Arts de Belgique, Brussels.

The Look of Distance

Reflections on Suffering & Sympathy in Modern Literature—Auden to Agee, Whitman to Woolf

WALTER J. SLATOFF

Ohio State University Press : Columbus

Library of Congress Cataloguing in Publication Data

Slatoff, Walter J. (Walter Jacob), 1922–
The look of distance.
Includes index.
1. English literature—20th century—History and criticism. 2. Suffering in literature. 3. Sympathy in literature. 4. American literature—History and criticism. I. Title.
PR479.S93S58 1985 820′.9′353 85-10447
ISBN 0-8142-0385-X

(Copyright notice continued on page vi)

To Zoë and Megan

(Copyright notice continued from page iv)

CONTENTS

❖

Acknowledgments

For their various gifts of help and encouragement, I wish to thank Mary Ahl, Murray Beja, Jonathan Bishop, Tom Burke, Allan Emery, Johann Hannesson, Winston Hannesson, Lamar Herrin, James McConkey, Paul Sawyer, Don Slatoff, and Joan Slatoff. Above all, I wish to thank my wife, Jimmy, who contributed far more than I can possibly acknowledge.

I am grateful also for a Humanities Research Grant from the College of Arts and Sciences of Cornell.

THE LOOK OF DISTANCE

I ❖ Introduction

THIS BOOK IS AN EFFORT TO TALK ABOUT SOME MATTERS THAT have deeply concerned me for nearly a lifetime of reading and teaching, and to do so in a way that will not do violence either to the kinds of experiences I talk about or to the nature of my engagement with them. In general, there is a disturbing gap between the conventional modes of discourse about literature and literature itself. When the subject is suffering and sympathy, that distance seems not only uncomfortable but indecent. My own engagement has been largely in the form of a debate with myself—about particular literary works, particular characters, and particular issues—and my deepest effort as a teacher has been to persuade my students to take part in that same debate rather than to sell them a thesis or survey a body of material. Inevitably, it seems to me now, the book has taken on a similar form.

Put most broadly, the debate is about whether the reading and teaching of literature can be decent occupations in a universe so much ordered by suffering as this one and about the appropriateness of various responses to suffering—by authors, fictional characters, and readers, including the readers of this book. Put more personally, it is about whether in my reading and teaching I am performing something ugly, voyeuristic, and evasive or am doing one of the best and least harmful things I know how to do. Subordinate questions have to do with the relative merits of too much compassion as against too little; with the relations between compassion and self-crucifixion; with the appropriate distances between humans, between humans and other animals, and even between gods and men; with the possibilities of human connection and the curious ways people have found to remain simultaneously together and apart; and with what might be called "moral aerodynamics": the motions of highfliers like Icarus, Jesus, Vittorio Mussolini, and Joyce, and the impacts of all sorts of things—from boys to bombs to violets—that can fall from the sky. As may be evident already, it is a debate about tones as well as ideas and feelings, for suffering is not adequately acknowledged by solemnity alone.

Obviously these are not questions that are subject to answers or even ones that yield much light when approached directly. What light this book does provide is generated chiefly, I believe, from the motions of its own flight, its moment-to-moment journey through and above the landscapes (and seascapes) it crosses, rather than a place it arrives at. And I urge my readers to attend not only to the human inhabitants we encounter but to the various birds, animals, and flowers as well, especially to their use and misuse, whether it be Zeus's use of a swan to rape Leda, Conrad's use of the horse that Stevie Verloc wishes to take to bed with him, William Carlos William's use of an injured dog for singing away his pain, my own use of eagles, deer, and roses, as I seek to hold my book together and to conclude it. I hope the reader will not merely observe my debate with myself, which from a distance may seem excessive, but will join in, at which distance it may seem more necessary, even quite urgent. What I am hoping really—and I know it is much to hope—is that my reader will be able to think of what follows more as a poem than a treatise: will read it with something of the kind of moment-to-moment engagement a poem compels; will, as he and she encounter the recurrent characters and images, the shifts in my own tones and distances, and the transactions between sky and earth, trust the resonances as much as the reasons, the modulations as much as the meanings.

I like to think that despite its essentially ruminative nature the book does accumulate toward something. In my most confident moments, I believe that it accumulates the way a poem accumulates, or even a symphony, and that upon finishing it the reader will experience some sense of comfort or closure along with the lacerations I mean to inflict. In less confident moments, I am content to view the book as a kind of anthology with commentary, in which the things I talk about gain resonance by virtue of the unconventional company they have come to keep. Have come to keep because, for reasons not pertinent here, my reading and teaching have followed lines in which American and non-American writers, fiction and poetry, old and new, even fiction and reality have not been able to keep their usual distances. There is no question but that this breeds confusions—for me and my reader both—as well as what I hope is illumination. I hope readers will be patient when the light seems more muddy than bright, when they know more about the particular writer or work than I do, and when I have neglected to mention some favorite text of theirs that is relevant to my subject. Indeed, the subject is so pervasive in literature that I imagine it could be explored using an almost entirely different set of texts. I hope, in fact, someone will want to do just that. In defense of my willingness to mix real and fictional characters, I will say here only that my own world is peopled with both; and that although I understand it is frequently important to distinguish between the two, I find they are neither so unlike one another or independent of one another as is often thought.[1]

I hope too that the reader will understand that the lengthy summaries and quotations I provide are as much the substance of this book as my own commentary and will allow them their proper weight—which is greater than mine. They are included in part, but only in part, because the works I discuss are such an idiosyncratic selection that few readers can be expected to have read, much less remembered, very many of them, and because the book is to some extent a dialogue between a large number of writers who do not ordinarily speak to one another: a dialogue that I have arranged and participate in but that to be worth much must exist in their languages as well as my own. I hope, therefore, that as he reads about the dilemmas of Major Scobie or Lily Briscoe or Agee's young Richard, for example, or about the ways Mr. Ramsay and his children struggle to remain together and apart, or about the plight of Agee's tenant farmers, or even briefly views a hunted slave or a cholera victim in a Whitman catalogue, my reader will attend to them in the way he might while reading the works in which they appear as well as to what I have to say about them. Except on rare occasions, the quotations and summaries are not included as examples to prove or illustrate arguments. They are parts of the arguments, their contents part of my contents, and the reader must permit them to be part of his experience of the book. There is more at stake than this, however. I want my readers as much as possible to experience or reexperience the writings in the light of my subject; even more, I want them to become afflicted, at least provisionally, with the compassionate views, however excessive, of some of the characters, to attend with more than customary care to what I shall later term "the Stevies, Miss Lonelyhearts, and Major Scobies of the world and of one's own heart." And to let them remain present while more sensible voices are holding sway. I want them also to witness again, rather than merely to recollect, the terrible ambivalences over separateness and connection that afflict so many of the characters here, to witness again, rather than merely to recollect, the flights, descents, and martyrdoms that must be part of this account. If this is too much to ask so early, I might add that in view of the underprivileged status of literary texts (to say nothing of their contents) in some recent modes of criticism, there is a special need for some of us to work toward their reconstruction.

A few further comments about my hopes and intentions may be helpful to some readers. I did not consciously set out to write a sequel to my *With Respect to Readers: Dimensions of Literary Response*, a book in which I argued that teaching and criticism should take more account of individual reader's responses; and I would certainly be disappointed if what follows were to be viewed mainly as the illustration of a theoretical position or as an exercise in what has come to be called reader response criticism (or perhaps the word should be "horrified," to express my dismay at the extent to which such criticism has blacked out the responses of actual readers and become an arena for theoretical controversy—one more darkling plain with "neither joy, nor love, nor light" on which, shall we say, theorists clash with professional delight). I would be content, however, to have it seen in part as an extended offering of one reader's responses to a number of writings that have engaged his deepest attention; and as such it may serve as an answer to those who expressed a wish for a fuller and more personal demonstration of the kind of activity I urged in the earlier book. I would be even more content if it is viewed as the exposure of a *way* of responding to literature, a way that offers the reader some of the freedoms and opportunities afforded by current modes of criticism but without depriving the text of its more traditional powers and integrity. It is a way that enables a reader to exercise his sympathies, allows a story to become (as a colleague put it who read this book in manuscript) "an occasion for coexistence imaginatively with a fictional person's way of feeling"; it allows one to be educated or angered by a text, to let a text speak for one, to quarrel with it or simply to be in awe of it—in short, to respond in all the ways a live individual reader as opposed to a theoretical one might wish to respond to a text. It allows, finally, what I have meant to be true in these pages, the act of reading and writing to be a way of bearing witness, or to use the language of Martin Buber to which I turn at the end, a way of being "attentive" and presenting ourselves with less than our usual armor.

Although I do not want to seduce myself into a lengthy discussion of the present critical scene, I must say a word or two, however insufficient and unfair, about where I think my way fits in. Professional literary study has always been a somewhat armored (not to say combative) activity in which distance, dispassionateness, impersonality, and methodology have been the favored positions—in many classrooms as well as most critical and scholarly books and journals. There are obvious reasons for this, and obvious benefits have come from it. But the losses have also been great, for the very adoption of such postures wards off many gifts that literature offers and blunts many of its powers. Not only its power to move, excite, and trouble its readers but its offering of certain kinds of truth—those imparted by the mysterious and irreducible innards of metaphor and by the moment-to-moment experience of reading—above all, those truths that come into being only when armor and distance are removed or when the reader permits himself to read as nearly as possible with what

Coleridge has called the whole of one's soul. Until the early part of this century, however, there was, I believe, a tacit recognition of this disjunction between the acts of studying and reading and a sense that the study would contribute somehow to fuller readings. I fear that understanding has progressively diminished. For some critics and scholars, as for many social scientists, truth became more nearly equated with what was presumed to be scientific precision. More and more ways were found to classify literary texts or to convert them into instances or examples of something or other—a period, a style, an archetype, a political or sexual stance. The New Criticism and its various descendents rescued texts, and continue to do so, from certain kinds of distortion and emasculation by insisting on their autonomy and examining them carefully and closely. But by viewing them essentially as sets of internal relations or as objects in a network of other literary objects, such criticism also dehumanizes them. When we remove a text, whether explicitly or implicitly, from the context of author and reader, we obscure the fact that whatever the theoretical rationales and whatever the layers of static or disguise, literary works are forms of communication, often quite wonderful ones, between human authors and human readers. And by so doing we help prepare for those current intellectual gymnastics in which all those poems, stories, novels, and plays that have given us so much are *only* texts, not different presumably from other texts or verbal constructs—graffiti, military manuals, lectures, critical discourse. No different, but apparently better off demystified and deconstructed (deprived of mystery and torn down?) to make sure we will not be tricked into loving or learning from them. Of course we can train ourselves and others to look at literature that way, look at anything that way—love, sex, loyalty, hope, and even cries for help—if we like. We can define a person as a text and erase him, or as a biochemical construct and maybe clone him. Of course we are clever enough to play games at the borderline between sense and nonsense and to dance at the edge of the abyss. We have become clever enough, in fact, to deconstruct the planet, but why do we have to go on proving it? I am being strident and unfair, I know, and I must confess that some of my nicest and smartest students are fascinated by the poststructuralist scene and have profited from it. I, myself, like, and have learned from, colleagues who are part of it. But I am also very frightened. If we deny to words and literary works their power to move and mystify us; if critics and writers remain infatuated by pronouncements about the fictionality of fiction; if we refuse to let words create fictional worlds for us to respond to as though they were real; if all that lies before us is semiotics and a landscape of texts to decode, what an empty prospect, what a terrible bore. I have had a sense in the past year or so that there is a movement away from such textifying and from other extremes of critical distance and dispassionateness, one that allows a reader to respect (yes, even to "privilege" or submit to) literary texts and in which critics neither muffle their own voices nor use them to despoil, but rather seek to make audible their personal stakes in the writings that engage them. If I am right, though this book was not written for that purpose, I hope it will help swell and shape that tide.

For those who do not like to set out on a journey without a map, I can add here to the Table of Contents that Part One of this work presents and examines the ways a variety of authors and fictional characters respond to sufferings, both great and small, and worries especially about some excesses and insufficiencies of compassion. Part Two looks at the aspect of human behavior perhaps most intimately related to suffering and sympathy—the distances, both physical and psychological, we occupy in relation to one another, and considers a variety of lonely embraces people use to manage their profoundly ambivalent needs for connection and separateness. I argue that such embraces are especially attractive to artists and have much to do with the origin and shape of literary creations. Part Three wonders mainly about various forms of singing about suffering (the ways art makes pain palatable) and about the voyeurisms such singing compels.

The ending of my title—Auden to Agee, Whitman to Woolf—has been somewhat worrisome to me and some friends and editors: for its improper suggestion that this work might be a survey of all that lies between those writers, as if such were possible, for its seemingly facile assonance and alliteration, and for the awkward length it gives the title. I decided to retain it for several reasons. First, because I hope the pairings will clearly announce my intent to cross between nations and genres and sexes; second, because the four writers have for a long time occupied especially compelling positions in my thinking. Auden and Agee present profoundly though not totally opposed postures toward suffering, and they do quite literally appear at the beginning and ending of this work. Whitman and Woolf are wonderfully different and alike in the ways they embrace the mysteries of separateness and connection, including that final distance, death. Finally, I remain awed by the mysterious way those two central attributes of poetry—assonance and alliteration—can coincide with my own thought and reduce the distance between four so apparently separate men and women.

The opening phrase of my title—The Look of Distance—as many readers will recognize, is drawn from Emily Dickinson's poem "A certain slant of light." I intend the phrase to have all the meanings my reordering of her words have given it, and that set of meanings better than any other sums up the concerns of the book. But the phrasing in her poem and the poem as a whole must also belong to my text.

> There's a certain Slant of light,
> Winter Afternoons—
> That oppresses, like the Heft
> Of Cathedral Tunes—
>
> Heavenly Hurt, it gives us—
> We can find no scar,
> But internal difference,
> Where the Meanings, are—
>
> None may teach it—Any—
> 'Tis the Seal Despair—
> An imperial affliction
> Sent us of the air—

When it comes, the Landscape listens—
Shadows—hold their breath—
When it goes, 'tis like the Distance
On the look of Death—[2]

Part One

II ❖ Some Varieties of Armor and Innocence

THREE PERSPECTIVES AND VOICES HAVE MUCH INFLUENCED my thinking about distance and compassion and very much govern the shape and texture of this book. The first, Auden's poem "Musée des Beaux Arts," is so central, in fact, both in its argument and imagery, that this entire book could be viewed as a commentary on the poem.

MUSEE DES BEAUX ARTS

About suffering they were never wrong,
The Old Masters: how well they understood
Its human position; how it takes place
While someone else is eating or opening a window or
just walking dully along;
How when the aged are reverently, passionately waiting
For the miraculous birth, there always must be
Children who did not specially want it to happen, skating
On a pond at the edge of the wood:
They never forgot
That even the dreadful martyrdom must run its course
Anyhow in a corner, some untidy spot
Where the dogs go on with their doggy life and the
torturer's horse
Scratches its innocent behind on a tree.

In Breughel's *Icarus*, for instance: how everything turns
away
Quite leisurely from the disaster; the ploughman may
Have heard the splash, the forsaken cry,
But for him it was not an important failure; the sun shone
As it had to on the white legs disappearing into the green
Water; and the expensive delicate ship that must have seen
Something amazing, a boy falling out of the sky,
Had somewhere to get to and sailed calmly on.[1]

Eventually I shall want, above all, to weigh the content of this poem, the extent to which Auden and the Old Masters are right or "never wrong" about the position of suffering, and we shall meet a great many witnesses to that martyrdom and fall. But first, what shall we say for Auden's own position? It is certainly a civilized and reasonable one. Auden (or, to be more precise, the narrator of the poem) is not unmindful of the suffering nor is he callous toward it. He is aware of the distance between the sufferers and those whose centers of attention are elsewhere. To a degree the poem reminds us of that distance, attends to it, and implies that the ironies of such distance are worth pondering. At the same time, however, the poem and its author also keep their distance. They too avert their eyes from the details of the dreadful martyrdom in that untidy corner. They do not render the screams of the tortured person or the precise ways in which that person's flesh was torn. Nor do they remind us of the probably more sanitary police stations, prisons, concentration camps, or reeducation centers in which such martyrdoms continue to occur, places to which it is unlikely dogs have access and where the torturers will be awaited not by horses but by a car or jeep, with a bumper in place of a behind, capable neither of innocence nor guilt. They note the forsaken cry of Icarus and the white legs disappearing into the sea but say nothing of the inside or outside of the fragile head as it must have smashed against the water. It would not be fair to call the author complacent, but neither does he seem troubled or even anxious. Unlike some of the writers we shall be looking at, he is not rubbing his own guilty behind against a tree. In fact, one of the things he is not aware of—at least he does nothing to make us aware of it—is that he has a behind, either innocent or guilty. And though the poem is not heartless, Auden is at pains to keep his own heart under wraps.

Auden would probably be glad to hear this said, for he is generally suspicious of those, especially poets, who let their hearts hang out, and has made some devastating comments on that subject. Here is one that connects very closely with the poem:

> There are events which arouse such simple and obvious emotions that an AP cable or photograph in *Life* magazine are enough and

> poetic comment is impossible. If one reads through the versified trash inspired, for instance, by the Lidice Massacre, one cannot avoid the conclusion that what was really bothering the versifiers was a feeling of guilt at not feeling horrorstruck enough. Could a good poem have been written on such a subject? Possibly. One that revealed this lack of feeling, that told how when he read the news, the poet, like you and I, dear reader, went on thinking about his fame or his lunch, and how glad he was that he was not one of the victims.[2]

This is an interesting statement. It seems at first to insist that, like the figures in the poem, we are all relatively indifferent to the suffering, and that our utterances, especially our poems, should reflect or confess that indifference. Yet it is Auden who has remembered the Lidice Massacre and said that such events do arouse such simple and obvious emotions (by which he must mean horror, pity, or sympathy) that poetic comment is impossible. And when he turns to our lack of feeling and our self-concern, I think he at one and the same time is protesting his indifference too loudly and is leveling a judgment against the inadequacy of his and our indifferent responses. It is hard to decide in what direction the weight of the passage finally falls. And it is hard to decide whether he is more troubled by the pretenses of emotion or by the lack of feeling.

Some further passages from the same work are illuminating though perhaps equally indeterminate in final emphasis.

> The girl whose boy-friend starts writing her love poems should be on her guard. Perhaps he really does love her, but one thing is certain: while he was writing his poems he was not thinking of her but of his own feelings about her, and that is suspicious. Let her remember St. Augustine's confession of his feelings after the death of someone he loved very much: "I would rather have been deprived of my friend than of my grief."[3]

Here both Auden and Saint Augustine are suspicious about self-indulgences of the heart but in their very expression of that suspicion assert their high valuation of love and imply that hearts should cherish friends and lovers.

Or again, when he writes that "the poet is capable of every form of conceit but that of the social worker:—'We are all here on earth to help others; what on earth the others are here for I don't know,' "[4] he is attacking the expressed concern for the welfare of others but does so by emphasizing the real insufficiency of such concern, at least among professional do-gooders, its latent contempt for others. But since all these explications, I suspect, do Auden too much and too little justice and do not really capture his curious patterns of concern and evasiveness, let me, for the moment at least, give him the last words:

> The present state of the world is so miserable and degraded that if anyone were to say to the poet: "For God's sake, stop humming and put the kettle on or fetch bandages. The patient's dying," I do not know how he could justifiably refuse. (There is, of course, an inner voice which says exactly this to most of us, and our only reply is to be extremely hard of hearing.) But no one says this. The self-appointed unqualified nurse says: "Stop humming this instant and sing the Patient a song which will make him fall in love with me. In return I'll give you extra-ration cards and a passport"; and the poor Patient in his delirium cries: "Please stop humming and sing me a song which will make me believe I am free from pain and perfectly well. In return I'll give you a penthouse apartment in New York and a ranch in Arizona."
>
> To such requests and to the bribes that go with them, the poet can only pray that he will always have the courage to stick out his tongue, say, like Olaf the conscientious objector in Cummings' poem—"There is some s. I will not eat,"—and go on humming quietly to himself.[5]

The second voice and vision, one that for a long time has haunted my own consciousness and that will very much haunt the pages of this book, is the voice and vision responsible for the following passage in George Eliot's novel *Middlemarch:*

> Nor can I suppose that when Mrs. Casaubon is discovered in a fit of weeping six weeks after her wedding, the situation will be regarded as tragic. Some faintness of heart at the real new future which replaces the imaginary, is not unusual, and we do not expect people to be deeply moved by what is not unusual. That element of tragedy which lies in the very fact of frequency has not

> yet wrought itself into the coarse emotion of mankind; and perhaps our frames could hardly bear much of it. If we had a keen vision and feeling of all ordinary human life, it would be like hearing the grass grow and the squirrel's heart beat and we should die of that roar which lies on the other side of silence. As it is, the quickest of us walk about well wadded with stupidity.[6]

As with the Auden poem, it is the content of the passage—that roar and that wadding—that will most absorb me. But it is worth pausing to observe that here too, just as in the poem and passages of Auden, the author is revealing and urging more compassion than her statement may at first seem to intend. Though her own tone is judicious and somewhat detached, it is also sympathetic; and though we are not expected to be "deeply moved" or to view Mrs. Casaubon's situation as "tragic," George Eliot has, herself, indicated that there is an element of tragedy (which she can perceive) that might move us deeply if our emotion were less coarse and we had a keen enough vision and feeling and if we were not so "well wadded with stupidity." In this way she has not only permitted but encouraged her readers to try to respond with more sympathy, anguish, and involvement than her own tone seems to have manifested. Despite her warning that too keen a vision, too much compassion, would be unbearable, might even destroy us, she is asserting the validity and desirability of such a vision. In fact, much of *Middlemarch* is an attempt to cut through the "wadding" of her characters and readers, an effort to make heard that roar behind the silence.

The third perspective is a particular instance of individual wadding (or hardness of hearing, to use Auden's metaphor) that has flabbergasted me for many years. That perspective is the one revealed when Vittorio Mussolini writes that the explosion of a bomb in the midst of a group of Ethiopian horsemen was like a rose bursting into bloom, and most amusing.[7] It is hard to know whether he is reporting his actual perception of the moment or his recollection of it in a moment of later tranquility or whether he is oblivious of the shocking quality of his simile or is striving for it. I am not sure it matters much. In some respects the matter is simply one of distance. He was watching the event from an airplane, at a distance from which he literally could not hear the cries of pain or see the torn and bleeding flesh, of either the men or the horses. Had he been among them, it is unlikely he would have thought of a rose. If nothing else, the odor would have been quite different. Quite certainly he would not have found it amusing. Had he been on the ground watching from a distance of twenty yards, even as an enemy, the noise and sight of the thrashing limbs would no doubt have left him feeling less flowery. Depending upon the size of the bomb, a large metallic thorn might have pricked his finger or perhaps torn one of his eyeballs. There is no telling what a rosy bomb will do. Had he been a mile up in the sky, he might only have seen a puff of dust or smoke and wondered what it was. But from where he was, he was reminded of a rose. No one in Bruegel's painting or Auden's poem seems to have occupied quite the distance Mussolini chose.

Probably they were right to leave such a witness out. For there cannot be many whose wadding is so curiously constructed as to permit quite so complacent, not to say amused, transmutation of suffering into beauty. Still, one cannot simply commit him to that nightmare realm in which we hold at a distance our knowledge of the Neroes and Caligulas, and of Ilse Koch, who made lampshades from the skin of the people in her concentration camp.

For one thing, he is in the company of so many writers, to say nothing of gardeners, who have done some form of violence to the rose by likening it to so many things it is not like and by using it to savor their own scents. More seriously, though, he is one of a large company of writers whose response to suffering could be called aesthetic. Few of them are quite so complacent, and for many the aestheticism is a way of containing and expressing their pity or compassion; but as we shall see, writer after writer has leaped gracefully between beauty and pain. Indeed, much of literature could be defined as a transmutation of suffering into aesthetic form and therefore from a hostile view be regarded unfairly only as another form of wadding. Then, too, in Mussolini's defense, we can say that there is a vantage point, a distance that nearly all of us have occupied at least for moments, from which the entire spectacle of human suffering and endeavor can appear beautiful, calm, or orderly, from which the torment and death of an Oedipus or a Lear appears as a species of beauty, and even a cloud of lethal dust becomes a richly growing mushroom. There is a distance too from which our entire endeavor, from Icarus to Einstein, from Christ to McCarthy (either one), must seem absurd. It may be, in fact, that there is in the distance only distance or perhaps a Cosmic Joker or that we are to all the gods as flies to wanton boys, who kill us for their sport. Or it could be that since He is made in our image, He too is merely "hard of hearing" or well wadded with stupidity.

Such remarks as these, though, involve an armoring of myself that feels evasive and insincere, and does not alter my sense of horror at Vittorio Mussolini's remark and at the peculiar degree of distance and deafness it reveals.

With these three perspectives as partial reflectors, let me turn toward the responses to suffering of several young men, and to some responses of my own toward them. The first is the response of a very young one—Nick Adams in Hemingway's "Indian Camp."[8]

Young Nick, who is then about seven or eight years old, has gone at night with his doctor father and his Uncle George to a settlement of Indians where a woman has for two days been having great difficulty in giving birth to a baby. After being rowed across the bay by some Indians and walking through the woods, they enter a shanty in which the woman is lying on a wooden bunk. Above her in the upper bunk is her husband, who had cut his foot very badly with an ax three days before. As they enter the room, the woman screams.

> Nick's father ordered some water to be put on the stove, and while it was heating he spoke to Nick.
>
> "This lady is going to have a baby, Nick," he said.
>
> "I know," said Nick.

"You don't know," said his father. "Listen to me. What she is going through is called being in labor. The baby wants to be born and she wants it to be born. All her muscles are trying to get the baby born. That is what is happening when she screams."

"I see," Nick said.

Just then the woman cried out.

"Oh, Daddy, can't you give her something to make her stop screaming?" asked Nick.

"No. I haven't any anaesthetic," his father said. "But her screams are not important. I don't hear them because they are not important."

The husband in the upper bunk rolled over against the wall.

While the father successfully performs a cesarean operation on the woman, who is held by Uncle George and three Indians, Nick stands by with a basin. We are told that it all "took a long time." It is not clear how much of the operation Nick was able to bring himself to watch, but after the baby is delivered Nick looks away "so as not to see what his father was doing," does not look at what his father puts in the basin, and as the father sews up the incision "did not watch. His curiosity has been gone for a long time."

Nick takes the basin to the kitchen while his father bends over to look at the woman, who is "quiet now" and apparently nearly unconscious, and then brags a little: "That's one for the medical journal, George. . . . Doing a Caesarian with a jack-knife and sewing it up with nine-foot, tapered gut leaders." A moment later he thinks to look at the baby's father.

"They're usually the worst sufferers in these little affairs," the doctor said. "I must say he took it all pretty quietly."

He pulled back the blanket from the Indian's head. His hand came away wet. He mounted on the edge of the lower bunk with the lamp in one hand and looked in. The Indian lay with his face toward the wall. His throat had been cut from ear to ear. The blood had flowed down into a pool where his body sagged the bunk. His head rested on his left arm. The open razor lay, edge up, in the blankets.

"Take Nick out of the shanty, George," the doctor said.

There was no need of that. Nick, standing in the door of the kitchen had a good view of the upper bunk when his father, the lamp in one hand, tipped the Indian's head back.

We are told nothing more about what happened until the father and son are walking back toward the lake in the early dawn, and the story concludes in this fashion.

> "I'm terribly sorry I brought you along, Nickie," said his father, all his post-operative exhilaration gone. "It was an awful mess to put you through."
> "Do ladies always have such a hard time having babies?" Nick asked.
> "No, that was very, very exceptional."
> "Why did he kill himself, Daddy?"
> "I don't know, Nick. He couldn't stand things, I guess."
> "Do many men kill themselves, Daddy?"
> "Not very many, Nick."
> "Do many women?"
> "Hardly ever."
> "Don't they ever?"
> "Oh, yes. They do sometimes."
> "Daddy?"
> "Yes."
> "Where did Uncle George go?"
> "He'll turn up all right."
> "Is dying hard, Daddy?"
> "No, I think it's pretty easy, Nick. It all depends."
> They were seated in the boat, Nick in the stern, his father rowing. The sun was coming up over the hills. A bass jumped, making a circle in the water. Nick trailed his hand in the water. It felt warm in the sharp chill of the morning.
> In the early morning on the lake sitting in the stern of the boat with his father rowing, he felt quite sure that he would never die.

I hesitate to comment much upon so delicate and modest a transmutation of suffering and death into a conviction of personal immortality, except to say that I do not think there can be many readers who feel other than affection toward the boy or would want to point out to so young a child how far he had turned from the suffering of others toward self-enchantment. The impact of the final sentence depends, of course, upon our remembering the screams and the bloody throat and upon our knowledge that the boy, like all of us, must die. And if we have come to the story in its context in the collection of stories *In Our Time*, we cannot have forgotten the screams and dead mothers and babies that fill the preceding story, "On the Quai at Smyrna," one of Hemingway's most gruesome renderings of human savagery and anguish. But the irony falls lightly. The weight of our attention at the end is mostly upon the boat and lake and bass and rising sun and rowing father, and upon that still hopeful child. Surely our wish is that while he is growing up, he will be able as much as possible to keep that unhappy episode out of his mind, will, in Auden's or Eliot's terms, remain somewhat hard of hearing.

When I think of that story, however, I usually think of another young man about whom I feel quite differently, Ivan Velikopolsky, in Chekhov's "The Student."[9] This young man is twenty-two.

Ivan, "the son of a sacristan, and a student of the clerical academy," is returning home from a day of shooting in the forest and begins to feel cold and gloomy as the good weather gives way to an unusually chilly evening. It seems to him that the cold "had destroyed the order and harmony of things, that nature itself felt ill at ease," and he remembers that as he left his house

> his mother was sitting barefoot on the floor in the entry, cleaning the samovar, while his father lay on the stove coughing; as it was Good Friday nothing had been cooked, and the student was terribly hungry. And now shrinking from the cold, he thought that just such a wind had blown in the time of Ivan the Terrible and Peter, and in their time there had been just the same desperate poverty and hunger, the same thatched roofs with holes in them, ignorance, misery, the same desolation around, the same darkness, the same feeling of oppression—all these had existed, did exist, and would exist, and after the lapse of a thousand years would make life no better.

On his way, still three miles from home, he stops to warm himself by a campfire at the "widows' gardens," so named because they were kept by two widows, a mother and daughter. "The widow Vasilisa, a tall, fat old woman in a man's coat was standing by and looking thoughtfully into the fire; her daughter Lukerya, a little pock-marked woman with a stupid-looking face, was sitting on the ground, washing a caldron and spoons." Lukerya is further described as a woman "who had been crushed by her husband" and as staring silently at the student with "a strange expression like that of a deaf mute."

Vasilisa and the student chat for a few moments, and the student, who is warming his hands at the fire, comments that the Apostle Peter had warmed himself "at just such a fire . . . so it must have been cold then, too. Ah, what a terrible night it must have been, granny! An utterly dismal long night!" Then obviously carried away by the analogy, the student goes on to elaborate:

> "If you remember at the Last Supper Peter said to Jesus, I am ready to go with thee into darkness and unto death. And our Lord answered him thus: I say unto thee, Peter, before the cock croweth thou wilt have denied Me thrice. . . . Then you heard how Judas the same night kissed Jesus and betrayed him to his tormentors. They took Him bound to the high priest and beat Him, while Peter, exhausted, worn out with misery and alarm, hardly awake, you know, feeling that something awful was just going to happen on earth, followed behind. . . . He loved Jesus passionately, intensely, and now he saw from far off how He was beaten. . . ."
>
> Lukerya left the spoons and fixed an immovable stare upon the student.
>
> "They came to the high priest's," he went on; "they began to question Jesus, and meantime the labourers made a fire in the yard as it was cold, and warmed themselves. Peter, too, stood with them near the fire and warmed himself as I am doing."

The student goes on to describe how Peter was questioned about his connection with Christ by a woman and the laborers around the fire and three times denied any acquaintance with him, and concludes his story:

> "And immediately after that time the cock crowed, and Peter, looking from afar off at Jesus, remembered the words He had said to him in the evening . . . [and] went out of the yard and wept bitterly—bitterly. In the Gospel it is written: 'He went out and wept bitterly.' I imagine it: the still, still, dark, dark, garden, and in the stillness, faintly audible, smothered sobbing. . . . " (ellipses all in the original)

After these words "the student sighed and sank into thought." Vasilisa "suddenly gave a gulp, big tears flowed freely down her cheeks, and she screened her face from the fire with her sleeve as though ashamed of her tears, and Lukerya, staring immovably at the student, flushed crimson, and her expression became strained and heavy like that of someone enduring intense pain."

Without further words, the student says good-night to the widows and walks on in the darkness and cold. As he walks along, he thinks about Vasilisa and muses that "since she had shed tears all that had happened to Peter the night before the crucifixion must have some relation to her" and he goes on to expand that thought:

> If Vasalisa had shed tears, and her daughter had been troubled, it was evident that what he had been telling them about, which had happened nineteen centuries ago, had a relation to the present—to both women, to the desolate village, to himself, to all people. The old woman had wept, not because he could tell the story touchingly, but because Peter was near to her, because her whole being was interested in what was passing in Peter's soul.
>
> And joy suddenly stirred in his soul, and he even stopped for a minute to take breath. "The past," he thought, "is linked with the present by an unbroken chain of events flowing one out of another." And it seemed to him that he had just seen both ends of that chain; that when he touched one end the other quivered.

As he continues toward home, his elation continues to grow and the story concludes:

> . . . He thought that truth and beauty which had guided human life there in the garden and in the yard of the high priest had continued without interruption to this day, and had evidently always been the chief thing in human life and in all earthly life, indeed; and the feeling of youth, health, vigour—he was only twenty-two—and the inexpressible sweet expectation of happiness, of unknown mysterious happiness, took possession of him little by little, and life seemed to him enchanting, marvellous, and full of lofty meaning.

I have taught this story many times, usually to students just two or three years younger than the one in the story, and I have always been surprised at how sympathetically they have viewed him and at how much they resist my judgment of him, which is very harsh. I cannot forget, as he does, his earlier sense of the endless continuum of "desperate poverty and hunger, the same thatched roofs with holes in them, ignorance, misery, the same desolation around, the same darkness, the same feeling of oppression." Even if I attribute some of the gloominess of that portrait to the same youthful exaggeration that informs his final elation, there is enough depiction of pain and poverty within the story to attest to its essential truth: his barefoot mother, his coughing father, the two widowed women, one in a man's coat, the other, "pockmarked," "stupid looking," "crushed by her husband," "the desolate village" (still described as desolate just as he begins his joyful epiphany), the "cruel wind." Nor can I forget the image of Lukerya at the end of the story of Peter, sitting on the ground "staring immovably at the student," "her face flushed crimson," her expression "strained and heavy like that of someone enduring intense pain." Nor the image of Peter weeping "bitterly—bitterly," and again "bitterly." I do not think the student is right that the old woman had wept "because Peter was near to her, because her whole being was interested in what was passing in Peter's soul." It seems more likely she wept in some far more complex response to the full story, including the agony of Jesus and Peter's denial of Him, and from some deeper sense of the relation of the two gardens. If she identified with anyone, it would hardly be with Peter, who stood by the fire warming himself as the student was doing, but with the laborers and the woman who noted that Peter had been with Jesus and who heard him deny it. I cannot help noticing also that the student has not only identified himself explicitly with Peter but focuses his story not on the suffering of Jesus but on the plight of "poor Peter," "exhausted, worn out with misery and alarm," "confused," finally weeping "bitterly—bitterly." His rhetoric is all reserved for Peter: "I imagine it, the still, still, dark, dark garden, and in the stillness, faintly audible smothered sobbing. . . . " Can one escape thinking that the student is another Peter, denying both the suffering of Christ and the suffering immediately surrounding him? But worse than Peter, who at least weeps bitterly over his betrayal, the student becomes joyful. He feels so full of exultation at the chain of connection between past and present that *he* has set quivering, that *he* can turn all the suffering and tears, in both gardens, into truth and beauty and think that such truth and beauty "which had guided human life there in the garden and in the yard of the high priest had continued without interruption to this day, and had evidently always been the chief thing in human life, and in all earthly life, indeed." Indeed! And finally, having so manipulated Christ and Peter and the two widows, he can go toward home with a "feeling of youth, health, and vigor," an "inexpressible sweet expectation of happiness," and a sense that life is "enchanting, marvellous, and full of lofty meaning." Finally, I cannot forget that the boy is a student at the clerical academy who has spent most of that day, Good Friday, shooting. Little in the story suggests he will mature into anything other than one more clergyman who spends his life denying Christ.

I know I am being too hard on the young man, for although the story itself allows and even encourages my reading of it, it does not support my angry judgmental tone. In a sense I am responding to the story as though it had ended with a final paragraph that read something like this:

> Back in the garden the two widows huddled closer to their fire, which no longer gave much warmth against the growing bitterness of the wind. Vasilisa still sobbed from time to time as though the weight of her own and Jesus' burden had somehow come together in her heart, and the expression on Lukerya's pockmarked face remained as it had been when the student left them, strained and heavy like that of someone enduring intense pain.

Chekhov is far more tolerant, or at least charitable, for not only does he do nothing in the last two paragraphs to remind us of the suffering the student has left behind, both in actuality and in his mind, he inserts into his final sentence the kindly "he was only twenty-two."

Should I not, then, at least feel something of the sympathy I feel for Nick Adams and be glad that Ivan too can throw off the weight of suffering in favor of the sense of his own youth, health, and vigor. I wish I could, and think I should, especially because I am, in effect, accusing him of indifference to suffering and yet wishing, myself, that he was suffering more. Yet I cannot overcome my harsher view of him. That is partly because twenty-two does not seem quite so young an age, partly because, unlike Nick Adams, he has manipulated the suffering and sufferers, and partly because he is so profoundly oblivious to the facile movements of his own consciousness. Nor can I keep myself from inflicting my view upon my students, and thereby darkening a bit perhaps their youthful optimism and happy forgetfulness of suffering.

And I cannot keep from briefly presenting here another vision that Chekhov offers for our contemplation, that of Ivan Ivanych in "Gooseberries." This Ivan is an elderly veterinarian who over the years has become so horrified by his brother's piggish and blind complacency that he becomes incapable of watching anyone's happiness without an "oppressive feeling bordering on despair." After spending an evening with his brother, he says to himself:

> How many contented, happy people there really are! What an overwhelming force they are! Look at life: the insolence and idleness of the strong, the ignorance and brutishness of the weak, horrible poverty everywhere, overcrowding, degeneration, drunkenness, hypocrisy, lying—Yet in all the houses and on all the streets there is peace and quiet; of the fifty thousand people who live in our town there is not one who would cry out, who would vent his indignation aloud. We see the people who go to market, eat by day, sleep by night, who babble nonsense, marry, grow old, good-naturedly drag their dead to the cemetery, but we do not see or hear those who suffer, and what is terrible in life goes on somewhere behind the scenes. Everything is peaceful and quiet and only mute statistics protest: so many people gone out of their minds, so many gallons of vodka drunk, so many children dead from malnutrition—And such a state of things is evidently necessary; obviously the happy man is at ease only because the unhappy ones bear their burdens in silence, and if there were not this silence, happiness would be impossible. It is a general hypnosis. Behind the door of every contented, happy man there ought to be someone standing with a little hammer and continually reminding him with a knock that there are unhappy people, that however happy he may be, life will sooner or later show him its claws, and

> troubles will come to him—illness, poverty, losses, and then no one will see or hear him, just as now he neither sees nor hears others. But there is no man with a hammer. The happy man lives at his ease, faintly fluttered by small daily cares, like an aspen in the wind—and all is well.[10]

Ivan has been saying all this in a comfortable sitting room to his friends Burkin, a high school teacher, and Alyohin, a gentleman farmer, and he goes on to lament that he is an old man now, unfit for action, capable only of grieving inwardly, becoming irritated, and lying awake at night with his thoughts. "Oh, if I were young!" he exclaims several times, pacing up and down the room excitedly, and then pressing Alyohin's hands, he implores him not to let himself "be lulled to sleep! As long as you are young, strong, alert, do not cease to do good! There is no happiness and there should be none, and if life has a meaning and a purpose, that meaning and purpose is not our happiness but something greater and more rational. Do good!" All this he says "with a pitiful, imploring smile, as though he were asking a personal favor." The story does not report how Alyohin receives this plea; it ends with the three men sitting for awhile in silence and then going off to bed.

As always in Chekhov, there is much that complicates our response—both to Ivan and his point of view. Among other things, he more than anyone else in the story seems able to enjoy life and even to sleep well (if I read the end of the story correctly); and the story itself suggests there is much in life, including the lovely maid Pelageya, to be enjoyed. At the same time, Ivan's vision is never deeply undermined; and near the very end of the story, Chekhov compels us to measure our response against that of Alyohin, who "did not trouble to ask himself if what Ivan Ivanych has just said was intelligent or right" and who is pleased because Ivan was "not talking about groats or hay, or tar, but about something that had no direct bearing on his life."

I myself have no settled response to the story. At times Ivan's seems a silly view to take. How absurd to be pained by the sight of a happy man or happy families because others are suffering, especially if, as is true in Ivan's case, one has no clear idea of what to do about the suffering. How futile to implore the sleepy and uncomprehending Alyohin merely to "Do good!" How dangerously the vision veers away from a concern with the plight of the sufferers toward a wish to inflict pain on those who ignore it, a wish that "behind the door of *every* contented, happy man" there would be someone with a hammer "*continually* reminding him with a knock that there are unhappy people" (emphasis mine), as though the discomfort alone were of value.

Yet how close or loud must the suffering be for happiness to be properly viewed as ugly or inappropriate. Only within eyesight or earshot? Only when it occurs within our own family, or town, or neighboring town? Only when it has not happened behind our backs, which after all are always turned toward some victim, intentionally or otherwise? Only when we witness the crucifixion? Shall we say that we ought not be troubled by suffering unless we know how to alleviate it or can make some effort to do so? And if we once begin to take on others' pain, when, where, and for what reasons shall we stop short of taking on the pain of the whole world? Obviously these are not directly answerable questions, but they help account for an obsession like Ivan's and for my own compulsion to become that someone with a hammer as I urge my own students to question the happiness of Chekhov's young student and remind them of the suffering he has forgotten, and as I write this book. I say not *directly* answerable because I like to think that the effort we are engaged in here may be a way of answering as well as asking.

Such questions also help account, though by no means entirely, for the behavior of another young man on Good Friday whose story takes us deep into the labyrinths that open for those who are perhaps insufficiently wadded against pain. He appears in a story by James Agee, who will appear quite frequently in these pages and who eventually will help bring them to an end.

The protagonist of this story, or short novel, *The Morning Watch*, is a twelve-year-old named Richard who is a student at a religious boarding school. It is a school very much like the one Agee attended, just as the boy is quite obviously patterned after the youthful Agee himself. Most of the story takes place between the hours of about three-thirty and dawn on Good Friday, and it is almost entirely concerned with Richard's determined and self-conscious efforts during those hours to maintain an acute and proper consciousness of Christ's sufferings during those same hours. He finds this very difficult because his mind keeps wandering: into a concern with his own physical and spiritual state and with what the other boys are feeling and thinking and about his relation to them, into speculations about the meanings and associations of various words in the prayers, into memories of his father's death, and above all, into prideful ruminations and fantasies. The story begins:

> In hidden vainglory he had vowed that he would stay awake straight through the night, for he had wondered, and not without scorn, how they, grown men, could give way to sleep on this night of all the nights in their life, leaving Him without one friend in His worst hour; but some while before midnight, still unaware that he was so much as drowsy, he had fallen asleep; and now this listening sleep was broken and instantly Richard lay sharp awake, aware of his failure and of the night.[11]

The failure is particularly upsetting to him because throughout the nearly forty days of Lent although "he had not managed perfectly to keep either his public or his secret Lenten Rules . . . he had been sufficiently earnest and faithful, and sufficiently grieved in his failures" that his feeling about the Passion had grown deeper and more rewarding than he had ever known before, and he was now coming into the heart of it "with heart and soul prepared and eager" (p. 29).

Lying in bed, he imagines deeply what Christ had already undergone in those hours while he slept and is yet to undergo; and for the first of many times, we watch him chastise himself: "Could ye not watch with me one hour? No Lord, his humbled soul replied: not even one: and three times, silently gazing straight upward into darkness he struck his breast while tears of contrition, of humility and of a hunger to be worthy, solaced his eyes, and awakened his heart" (p. 22). He continues to envision the events leading up to the Crucifixion: Christ standing "peaceful before Pilate, the one calm and silence amid all that tumult of malice and scorn and guile and hatred," Peter "in fury and in terror" denying his Lord, "the bitter terrible weeping . . . soon now the sentence and the torment, the scourging, the mocking robe, the wreathed, wretched Crown: King of the Jews." And he prays silently, "in solemn and festal exaltation": " 'O God . . . make me to know thy suffering this day. O make me to know Thy dear Son's suffering this day' " (pp. 22–23).

Meanwhile, "by a habit of their own" his hands have been searching and testing his sheet, and he is relieved to discover that he had wet his bed so little that by morning nobody would know. He then becomes occupied with the events in the dormitory as Father Whitman awakens Hobe and Jimmy, the other boys who are scheduled, as he is, for the four o'clock watch. These events include some unselfconscious cursing by the other boys ("*Quit* it you God damn—"; "Yeah fer Chrise sakes *shut up*"; "God All Mighty Christ, can't even wake nobody up in this friggin school—") in which Richard is, at first, glad he has not participated and then uneasy because "that was like being thankful you were not as other men and that was one of the worst sins of all; the Pharisee" (pp. 25–33). As the boys walk down the stairs, Richard, "by trying hard . . . was able to restore whole to his mind the thorn-crowned image of his Lord" but it was not "very little different from a pious painting he knew: the eyes rolled up in a way that seemed affected, and . . . the image meant little to him" (p. 31).

In the chapel he struggles, not very successfully at first, to focus his mind upon his religious duties but finally begins to pray with considerable seriousness, thinking carefully of each word. He manages reasonably well to control his usual ruminations over the word *inebriate* in "Blood of Christ inebriate me" and somewhat less well the literal and sexual images generated by "within His wounds hide me" and then falls into lengthy introspection over "that with Thy Saints I may praise

Thee" and "the burden of [my iniquities] is intolerable," neither of which he is ever able to say with what he considers adequate sincerity. "It wasn't anywhere near intolerable, no matter how much it ought to be," he thinks and wonders "how can you say things when you only ought to mean them and don't really mean them at all" (p. 59). With respect to saintliness, his problem is more serious and complex (as it is for Agee throughout his life and as it is in the general realm this book is exploring).

At first he thinks "it was wrong for people to ask to be saints. . . . Or even just to be *with* the saints, if that was what it meant. To just barely manage through God's infinite mercy to escape burning eternally in the everlasting fires of Hell ought to be as much as any good Catholic could pray for" (p. 58). Then it occurs to him that perhaps "this prayer had been written by a saint or by someone near sainthood, who was able to mean every extreme thing that was said. . . . But in that case it was a prayer which was good only for saints and near saints to say, not for ordinary people, no matter how good they hoped to be. Nobody's got any business even hoping he can be a saint, he told himself" (p. 60). Upon thinking this, he remembers with terrible shame that he himself had for a while cherished exactly that "inordinate ambition" and "with a cold and marvelling, compassionate contempt for the child he had so recently been," he loses himself in memories and thoughts about his quest of a little over a year before "when he was only eleven."

This section of the story is worth reporting in considerable detail, for better than any other account I know, it renders the kind of adolescent state of consciousness that both generates, and remains embedded within, some of the more interesting adult sensibilities that take special cognizance of human suffering. It is a state of peculiar susceptibility nourished by loneliness, in which pride and humility, self-infatuation and self-loathing, compassion and self-pity, the desire to be truly worthy and childish dreams of glory, self-knowledge and self-deception, mix with one another in an amazing bath of yearning, fear, and fervor. I want to linger here, also, because

I think that the adult Agee, in the final fullness and failure of his achievement, may represent the farthest a twentieth-century writer may travel toward saintliness without denying the complexities he has acquired through being a creature of his own time.

For the eleven-year-old Richard, it was a state in which

> the image and meaning of Jesus and the power and meaning of the Sacraments and of the teachings of the church, all embodied and set forth in formalities of language and of motion whose sober beauties were unique, and in a music which at the time moved and satisfied him as no other music could, had first and, it had seemed irreducibly, established upon his heart and mind their quality, their comfort, their nobility, their sad and soaring weight; and entering upon his desolation of loneliness, had made of suffering a springing garden, an Eden in which to walk, enjoying the cool of the evening. It had become a secret kind of good to be punished, especially if the punishment was exorbitant or unjust; better to be ignored by others, than accepted; better still to be humiliated, than ignored. (P. 61)

Now, kneeling in the chapel, he remembers how he had pretended not to know his lessons in order that his teachers might think ill of him; how he had abandoned his solitary wanderings in the woods when it had occurred to him that "for all their solitude and melancholy" they were more pleasant than unpleasant; how he would sing "*Jesus, I my Cross have taken* . . . already anticipating the lonely solace of tears concealed in public" (pp. 62–63) and "*all to leave and follow thee; destitute, despis'd, forsaken; thou from hence my All shalt be*" feeling "nobody else wants me" and doing "his best to believe it, even of his mother" (p. 63); and how he had even worked "to intensify his always all but annihilating homesickness" (p. 64) by asking permission to visit his mother when he knew it would be refused and had sometimes spent hours watching his mother's cottage "relishing the fact that only he knew of the miserableness of that watch" (p. 64).

During Lent of that year, he had experimented with extra fasting, and when that proved nearly impossible in the school dining room, he had tried self-mortification instead:

> He had gone into the woods and eaten worms, but this had disgusted him, and he had been even more disgusted when, on one occasion, he had come near tasting his own excrement. It had suddenly struck him as very doubtful indeed that Jesus would ever have done any such thing, and he had thrown the twig deep into the bushes and had carefully buried the filth. Efforts to scourge himself had been moderately painful but not sufficiently effective to outweigh the sense of bashfulness, even of ridiculousness, which he felt over the clumsiness of the attempt, in relation to the severity of the intention. So he had been reduced, mainly, to keeping very bitter vigil over his thoughts and his language and over his sensuous actions upon himself, and to finding out times and places in which it would be possible to kneel, for much longer than it was comfortable to kneel, without danger of getting caught at it. (Pp. 68–69)

During one such episode on his knees, while "absorbed in grateful and overwhelmed imagination of Christ Crucified" and sincerely wondering how he could ever do enough for Christ who had done so much for him, he suddenly supplants Christ's image with his own and "saw his own body nailed to the Cross and, in the same image, himself looked down from the Cross and felt his weight upon the nails, and the splintered wood against the whole length of his scourged back; and stoically, with infinite love and forgiveness, gazed downward into the eyes of Richard, and of Roman soldiers, and of jeering Jews, and of many people whom Richard had known" (p. 70).

In the very act of remembering these past vanities with "affectionate scorn," the twelve-year-old Richard drifts into somewhat comic musings about the difficulties he might have if he actually tried to nail himself to a cross and then into images of himself tied to a cross made of one of the school's gridiron bedsteads while his mother and various teachers and students and finally nearly everyone in the community watch him with amazement and respect.

Upon realizing this new "contemptible silliness," Richard feels an "insupportable self-loathing" and, "scarcely knowing his action, struck himself upon his breastbone, groaning within his soul, *the burden of them is intolerable.*" With this he realizes "in gratitude and a new flowering of vainglory, that he had been surprised into contrition so true and so deep that beside it every moment of contrition he had ever known before seemed trivial, and even false, and for an instant he questioned the validity of every Absolution he had ever been granted." In a moment, however, he finds himself worrying about whether his action of striking his breast was noticed and would be thought affected, and drifts into speculations about the sincerity, affectedness, and self-consciousness of another boy kneeling in front of him who seems to be praying with peculiarly visible intensity and physical posturings. When he returns, again with a new contrition, from these musings, he wonders "whether he would ever learn, from committing one sin, how not to commit another of the same sort even in the very moment of repenting it; and he felt that it was strange, and terrible, that repentence so deep and real as he knew that his had been, could be so fleeting" (p. 82).

As one might expect, he does not learn; and his struggle with his egotism, his wandering mind, and self-consciousness goes on and on until once again, after having forced himself to kneel painfully throughout the second watch, he succeeds in vividly imagining the moment of crucifixion:

> one hand, against splintering wood, and the point of a spike against the center of the open hand, and a great hammer, and the spike being driven through, breaking a bone, tight into the wood so that the head was all buried in the flesh and the splintered bone, and then to be able to say, *Father forgive them for they know not what they do.* And that's just one hand, he reminded himself. How about both hands. And both feet. Specially both feet crossed on each other and one spike through both insteps. How about when they raise up the Cross with you on it and drop it deep in the hole they dug for it! And imagining that moment he felt a tearing spasm of anguish in the center of each palm and with an instant dazzling of amazed delight, remembering pictures of great saints, shouted within himself, *I've got the wounds!* and even as he caught himself opening his palms and his eyes to peer and see if this were so he realized that once again this night, and even more blasphemously and absurdly than before, he had sinned in the proud imagination of his heart. *O my God,* his heart moaned, *O my God! My God how can You forgive me!* (Pp. 106–7)

After this new self-betrayal and a few last minor lapses into pride over his own contrition, he feels a dry, tired, and quiet emptiness in which he is able to pray and to think of the sacrifice of Jesus with a humble sorrow. At a few minutes after five, he leaves the chapel "light and uneasy and at peace within. There was nothing to do or think or say" (p. 120).[12]

Oh my! It is hard to decide how much to pity Richard for the awful burden he has of carrying such a consciousness and how much to envy him the richness of the internal drama of which he is participant and observer, how much to feel as does the woman narrator of Doris Lessing's *Memoirs of a Survivor,* how terrible it is to be young, and how much to mourn the loss of such wonderful youthful intensity that so often comes with age.

In some respects, of course, Richard's dreams of glory are not unlike those of any other child who wants to emulate some heroic figure (Sir Lancelot, Robin Hood, Joan of Arc, John Wayne, Superman, or Kojak) whose exploits seem to have impressed the world, and thereby to appear worthy in his own eyes and to astound his elders. Even the imaginary and actual subjection of the self to pain and ignominy is a common enough part of such fantasies, for somehow the human psyche very early learns to define full triumph in relation to the ordeal undergone in attaining it. (No doubt it is partly this that has made Christ so attractive an image, for apart from anything else, He emerges triumphant after an ordeal that is not only death-defying in all the usual senses but includes the infliction of death itself.)

At the same time, Richard's effort is riddled with special problems and paradoxes that set it apart. His real or deepest quest is to prove himself worthy in his own eyes, and such worthiness as he has defined it must include a conscious humbling of himself that takes no pride or satisfaction in that effort or achievement, an effort toward saintliness that cannot permit the presumption that it is such an effort, and an effort to imagine as fully as possible the suffering of Christ without feeling himself to be like Christ, to put himself in Christ's shoes, so to speak, without wearing them. The first two dilemmas, I suppose, could be termed occupational diseases of sainthood and the continual wrestling with them a lifelong obligation of all but the least self-conscious saints. I put it in this mildly flippant way not to belittle the seriousness or validity of such concerns (occupational diseases, whether black lung disease, ulcers, or boredom, *are* serious matters) but because they are concerns that are directed at self-definition rather than at the fate of others. The third dilemma seems more desperate, for it may be the most insidious problem of any serious effort to apprehend the predicament of another person. It is, after all, precisely at the moment when Richard has brought himself to the fullest and most immediate imagining of the Crucifixion—the spikes being driven through both of Christ's hands and both of his feet, breaking the bones, and the pain "when they raise up the Cross with you on it and drop it deep into the hole they dug for it" (pp. 106–7)—that he feels "a tearing spasm of anguish" in the center of each of his own palms and slips again into the arrogance and blasphemy of imagining his own sainthood. It is insidious not so much because of that final vainglorious slip (which anyone can outgrow) but because of the nearly inevitable way in which any truly intense apprehension of another's suffering must be experienced as a movement within the self. In taking on the pain of another, we cannot help but make it *our* pain. And *our* pain hurts *us*. This is obviously a special problem for writers, and readers too, and we shall have to ask eventually whether any act of imaginative seizure—indeed, any act of empathy—can avoid some such inflammation of the self, especially if it occurs in conjunction with the view that one is obligated to feel discomfort as a validation of one's sympathy.

A further terrible question is whether anyone afflicted with a truly intense quest to be worthy can attend to any of his other tasks with the same devotion he gives to measuring his degree of success in that endeavor. Richard pleads with God: "Let me not feel good when I am good. Let me just try to be good, don't let me *feel* good. Don't let me even *know* if I'm good" (p. 110). And yet a moment later, he feels a pride about this new humility and then new shame at that pride. What is quite obviously at stake is his own worthiness. Perhaps it is to avoid such a dilemma that some saintly beings have chosen a strictly ordered seclusion in which to perform solely for God.

Like Ivan Ivanych in "Gooseberries," and utterly unlike the young Ivan in "The Student," Richard is thoroughly convinced that any proper response to the suffering of another must involve an appreciable discomfort of one's own, and even more, that one's degree of concern is to be measured by that same discomfort. (And as is no doubt clear, I myself am not immune to such a notion.) Though it is a strange notion in many respects, and, as we have seen and will continue to see, it can lead to all sorts of foolishness and self-indulgence, it must also be an enormously compelling and understandable one, or else the image of the crucified Jesus could not have done the work it has or even begun to compete with the image of the gentle nursing madonna or the scales of justice. Or perhaps it is merely that we know a good deal about the behavior of those who seem to feel no discomfort at all about the suffering of others. Or perhaps, like Proust, when we "have had occasion to meet with, in convents, for instance, literally saintly examples of practical charity, they have generally had the brisk, decided, undisturbed, and slightly brutal air of a busy surgeon, the face in which one can discern no commiseration, no tenderness at the sight of suffering humanity, and no fear of hurting it, the face devoid of gentleness or sympathy, the sublime face of true goodness."[13]

It is time though to look at some less comforting examples of those who do not turn leisurely away from the suffering.

III ❖ Furious Compassions; Pity and Contempt

I AM HESITANT TO WRITE WHAT FOLLOWS BECAUSE THE experiences of some of the characters I shall be talking about could lead almost anyone to conclude that too much compassion is worse than too little, and I am not ready to believe that. It may be more terrible, more immediately injurious to the self and even to others, but it is not worse. It would not be an affliction in a world in which there was sufficient compassion. I am hesitant too because it is difficult to know what tone is appropriate for talking about such characters, especially difficult because the same problem quite obviously afflicts the authors who present them to us. Yet each of these characters must be present at any reading of Auden's poem and any gathering of the thinly padded.

> For he was difficult to dispose of, that boy. He was delicate and, in a frail way, good looking, too, except for the vacant droop of his lower lip. Under our excellent system of compulsory education he had learned to read and write, notwithstanding the unfavorable aspect of the lower lip. But as errand boy he did not turn out a great success. He forgot his messages; he was easily diverted from the straight path of duty by the attractions of stray cats and dogs, which he followed down narrow alleys into unsavory courts . . . or by the dramas of fallen horses whose pathos and violence induced him sometimes to shriek piercingly in a crowd, which disliked to be disturbed by sounds of distress in its quiet enjoyment of the national spectacle.[1]

In such a tone of voice, Conrad introduces Stevie Verloc of *The Secret Agent,* a young boy who is afflicted with a particuliarly acute sensitivity to suffering. And in this passage we can already hear behind Stevie's ineffectual shriek a voice that seems, itself, far from immune to the "pathos and violence" in the drama of the fallen horses or pleased with the complacency of the crowd, though one that does not give much help if we are wondering what would be an appropriate response to such "quiet enjoyment" of pain. Stevie is the younger brother of Winnie Verloc, who has married the seemingly equable and generous Mr. Verloc, whom she does not love—married him chiefly because she believes he will be able to provide a home and protection for that not very competent young man, toward whom she has maternal feelings. Winnie, who does not believe "things bear very much looking into," helps her husband run a shop that sells pornography but does not know that he is really an undercover agent both for a repressive foreign power and the London police. In connection with that work, he pretends to belong to a group of anarchists. All of them live in a London that Conrad presents mostly as a gray, squalid, and monstrous town; and the entire story is related in a tone that Conrad has defined as combining both pity and contempt but also as one that emerged from "a mood as serious in feeling and thought as any in which I ever wrote a line" (Author's Note, p. 12).

At the age of fourteen, before his sister's marriage, while working as an office boy, Stevie is discovered setting off fireworks on a staircase, a matter that Conrad says "might have turned out very serious." He goes on:

> An awful panic spread through the building. Wild-eyed, choking clerks stamped through the passages full of smoke; silk hats and elderly businessmen could be seen rolling independently down the stairs. Stevie did not seem to derive any personal gratification from what he had done. His motives for this stroke of originality were difficult to discover. It was only later on that Winnie obtained from him a misty and confused confession. It seems that two other office boys in the building had worked on his feelings by tales of injustice and oppression till they had wrought his compassion to the pitch of that frenzy. (P. 22)

Again the tone invites both sympathy and distance and an odd mix of feelings about an active response to suffering. How foolish and inappropriate to fight injustice with firecrackers, but how delicious those "silk hats and elderly businessmen . . . rolling independently down the stairs." Stevie is dismissed, of course, after what Conrad with fine scorn calls "that altruistic exploit" and is set to washing dishes and shining shoes in the lodging house of his guardians. Stevie's sensibilities are further inflamed by his reading of anarchist publications and overhearing of the ranting of anarchists like Karl Yundt, "who seemed to sniff the tainted air of social cruelty, to strain his ear for its atrocious sounds" (p. 51), and of whom Conrad writes further (and further mixes his and our feelings about altruistic action):

> The famous terrorist had never in his life raised personally as much as a little finger against the social edifice. He was no man of action; he was not even an orator of torrential eloquence, sweeping the masses along in the rushing noise and foam of great enthusiasm. With a more subtle intention, he took the part of an insolent and venomous evoker of sinister impulses which lurk in the blind envy and exasperated vanity of ignorance, in the suffering and misery of poverty, in all the hopeful and noble illusions of righteous anger, pity, and revolt. (P. 51)

Stevie's response to such inflammation is usually no more than an aimless, disturbed excitement, although on one occasion after reading of an officer nearly tearing off the ear of a recruit, he is discovered by his sister "shouting and stamping and sobbing" (p. 61) with a carving knife in his hand." 'He can't stand the notion of any cruelty'," she tells her husband. " 'He would have stuck that officer like a pig if he had seen him then' " (p. 61).

The most detailed and interesting exposition of Stevie's response to suffering (and Conrad's too, perhaps) occurs when he and his mother and grandmother are riding in a carriage drawn by an "infirm" and underfed horse and driven by a maimed driver with a hook in place of his left hand, a man whose "enormous and unwashed countenance flamed red in the muddy stretch of the street" (p. 134). Early in the trip, with breast heaving, Stevie gets out the words " 'Don't whip'," and we read:

> The man turned slowly his bloated and sodden face of many colours bristling with white hairs. His little red eyes glistened with moisture. His big lips had a violet tint. They remained closed. With the dirty back of his whip-hand he rubbed the stubble sprouting on his enormous chin.
>
> "You mustn't," stammered out Stevie, violently, "it hurts."

> "Mustn't whip?" queried the other in a thoughtful whisper, and immediately whipped. He did this, not because his soul was cruel and his heart evil, but because he had to earn his fare. (P. 135)

A few moments later, Stevie frightens everyone by suddenly getting out of the cab. When questioned he can only stammer, "Too heavy. Too heavy"; and when coaxed by his mother to get back in the cab, he does so "with a face of despair."

After a long, jolting ride, they arrive at their destination and the cabman is paid. And here I must summarize and quote at length both to convey the full tone and import of what follows and to provide a basis for my own commentary:

> Stevie was staring at the horse, whose hind quarters [his innocent behind] appeared unduly elevated by the effect of emaciation. The little stiff tail seemed to have been fitted in for a heartless joke; and at the other end the thin, flat neck, like a plank covered with old horse-hide, dripped to the ground under the weight of an enormous bony head. The ears hung at different angles, negligently; and the macabre figure of that mute dweller on the earth steamed straight up from ribs and backbone in the muggy stillness of the air. (Pp. 141–42)

Striking Stevie lightly on the breast with his iron hook, the cabman asks the boy how he would like to "sit behind this 'oss up to two oclock in the morning," and as Stevie's vacant expression turns slowly to dread, continues to lament his fate: "You may well look! Till three and four o'clock in the morning. Cold and 'ungry. Looking for fares. Drunks." At which point Conrad interrupts:

> His jovial purple cheeks bristled with white hairs; and like Virgil's Silenus, who, his face smeared with the juice of berries, discoursed of Olympian Gods to the innocent shepherds of Sicily, he talked to Stevie of domestic matters and the affairs of men whose sufferings were great and immortality by no means assured.
>
> "I am a night cabby, I am," he whispered, with a sort of boastful exasperation. "I've got to take out what they will blooming well give me at the yard. I've got my missus and four kids at 'ome."

> The monstrous nature of that declaration of paternity seemed to strike the world dumb. A silence reigned, during which the flanks of the old horse, the steed of apocalyptic misery, smoked upwards in the light of the charitable gaslamp. (P. 142)

When the cabman grunts and adds "in his mysterious whisper, 'This ain't an easy world,' " Stevie's feelings, we are told, finally burst out "in their usual concise form. 'Bad! Bad!' " Stevie continues to stare at the emaciated ribs of the horse,"self-conscious and sombre, as though he were afraid to look about him at the badness of the world" and the cabman responds, " 'Ard on 'osses, but 'dam sight 'arder on poor chaps like me.' " After which Conrad offers this remarkable passage:

> "Poor! Poor!" stammered out Stevie, pushing his hands deeper into his pockets with convulsive sympathy. He could say nothing; for the tenderness to all pain and misery, the desire to make the horse happy and the cabman happy, had reached the point of a bizarre longing to take them in bed with him. And that, he knew, was impossible. For Stevie was not mad. It was, as it were, a symbolic longing; and at the same time it was very distinct, because springing from experience, the mother of wisdom. Thus when as a child he cowered in a dark corner scared, wretched, sore, and miserable with the black, black misery of the soul, his sister Winnie used to come along, and carry him off to bed with her, as into a heaven of consoling peace. Stevie, though apt to forget mere facts, such as his name and address for instance, had a faithful memory of sensations. To be taken into a bed of compassion was the supreme remedy, with the only one disadvantage of being difficult of application on a large scale. And looking at the cabman, Stevie perceived this clearly, because he was reasonable. (P. 143)

We witness then at some length the cabman's departure. We learn that he "made as if to hoist himself on the box, but at the last moment, from some obscure motive, perhaps merely from disgust with carriage exercise, desisted" and that he instead approached the horse, "lifted up the big, weary head to the height of his shoulder with one effort of his right arm, like a feat of strength," and whispered, secretly, " 'Come on.' " And we watch as "limping," he leads the cab away, "the scrunched gravel of the drive crying out under the slowly turning wheels, the horse's lean thighs moving with ascetic deliberation" and as "the slow cortege reappeared, lighted up for a moment, the short, thick man limping busily, with the horse's head aloft in his fist, the lank animal walking in stiff and forlorn dignity, the dark low box on wheels rolling behind comically with an air of waddling. They turned to the left. There was a pub down the street." Unable to share in the wonderfully intricate distancing of such description, Stevie stands alone, "his hands thrust deep into his pockets, glar[ing] with vacant sulkiness."

> At the bottom of his pockets his incapable, weak hands were clenched into a pair of angry fists. In the face of anything which affected directly or indirectly his morbid dread of pain, Stevie ended by turning vicious. A magnanimous indignation swelled his frail chest to bursting, and caused his candid eyes to squint. Supremely wise in knowing his own powerlessness, Stevie was not wise enough to restrain his passions. The tenderness of his universal charity had two phases as indissolubly joined and connected as the reverse and obverse sides of a medal. The anguish of immoderate compassion was succeeded by the pain of an innocent but pitiless rage. (P. 144)

I suppose it is ungrateful to complain about so brilliant a piece of writing and so sharp an indictment of that conjunction of immoderate compassion and rage which afflicts so many more people than it is comfortable to think about—so many even when one excludes the self-righteously indignant, about whose compassion one has doubts, and those who exhibit what George Eliot describes in *Daniel Deronda* as "that rashness of indignation or resentment which has an unpleasant likeness to the love of punishing." Still, I find myself uneasy about Conrad's treatment of the episode and of Stevie in particular, uneasy because Conrad here so directly inflicts those most tormenting questions we have already been taunted with—what does constitute a proper (or not "immoderate") compassion and what can or ought one do about the suffering of human and other living creatures—and yet permits himself and his reader such a privileged relation to them.

Confronted with the actual suffering of the cabman and his horse, Stevie's desire to ease their pain reaches the point "of a bizarre longing to take them in bed with him," about which Conrad comments that "to be taken into a bed of compassion was the supreme remedy, with the only disadvantage of being difficult of application on a large scale." Conrad is perfectly right, of course; and while I read the passage, I am enough seduced by its tone to smile, though wryly, at Stevie's bizarre and hopeless wish. Not a complacent smile perhaps, but still one that helps blunt my own awareness of what Conrad has told me earlier in the paragraph about Stevie's suffering as a child. I am seduced also into sharing with Conrad a distance that keeps me from wondering too actively what wisdoms, solutions, and conducts of my own allow me to smile at Stevie or to feel in any way superior to him. I would rather not be encouraged to put on that much armor. And I wish Conrad were not quite so skittish when in the paragraph that follows he hints at the possibility that Stevie's compassion may, in fact, have caused the cabman to lift the horse's head and to lead him instead of climbing into the cab. Why the so careful, he "made as if to hoist himself onto the box, but from some obscure motive, perhaps merely from disgust with carriage exercise, desisted"?

Out from under the spell of the tone, I cannot help wondering what permits Conrad to say that Stevie turns "vicious" or knows a "pitiless rage," for these are not the appropriate terms for anything we actually observe Stevie doing or feeling. What he does, in fact, go on to do as best he can is to explore the problem of poverty and suffering, an exploration that Conrad continues to permit himself and us to enjoy mostly, though not entirely, from a distance, an exploration, that the book itself never really conducts.

When Stevie is rejoined by Winnie and they go off to seek a bus, they come upon the horse and cab in front of a public house. The appearance of the horse is "so profoundly lamentable, with such a perfection of grotesque misery and weirdness of macabre detail" that Mrs. Verloc "with that ready compassion of a woman for a horse (when she is not sitting behind him), exclaims vaguely, 'Poor brute!' " Without the benefit of that parenthesis which allows the narrator and reader to turn away ("quite leisurely") from the horse to the pleasures of light mockery, and sexism as well, Stevie stops suddenly, ejaculates " 'Poor! Poor! . . . Cabman poor, too. He told me himself!' " and is overcome by the contemplation of "the infirm and lonely steed."

> Jostled but obstinate, he would remain there, trying to express the view newly opened to his sympathies of the human and equine misery in close association. But it was very difficult. "Poor brute, poor people!" was all he could repeat. It did not seem forcible enough, and he came to a stop with an angry splutter: "Shame!" Stevie was no master of phrases, and perhaps for that very reason his thoughts lacked clearness and precision. But he felt with a greater completeness and some profundity. That little word contained all his sense of indignation and horror at one sort of wretchedness having to feed upon the anguish of the other—at the poor cabman beating the poor horse in the name, as it were, of his poor kids at home. And Stevie knew what it was to be beaten. He knew it from experience. It was a bad world. Bad! Bad! (Pp. 145–46)

Stevie goes on muttering and gets out finally: " 'Bad world for poor people.' " To which his sister responds: " 'Nobody can help that.' " Pained by this information, Stevie walks along gloomily for a while and then brightens up and suggests confidently that perhaps the police can help. When his sister explains that the "police aren't for that," his "face lengthened considerably. He was thinking. The more intense his thinking, the slacker was the droop of his lower jaw. And it was with an aspect of hopeless vacancy that he gave up his intellectual enterprise" (p. 147). This is an extremely curious and perhaps revealing remark (it is really the narrator who has given up, who nowhere in the book ever wrestles with the question whether anybody can "help that," who views with nearly equal scorn almost the full spectrum of those who want to change things and those who do not, and who is about to rise and run from some particularly crucial questions); for Stevie does not give up his questioning. In the very next paragraph, we are told that "unlike his sister, who put her trust in face values, he wished to go to the bottom of the matter" and asks angrily, " 'What are they for then, Winn? What are they for? Tell me.' "

Conrad prefaces her answer: "Guiltless of all irony, she answered yet in a form which was not perhaps unnatural in the wife of Mr. Verloc, Delegate of the Central Red Committee, personal friend of certain anarchists, and a votary of social revolution." She says: " 'Don't you know what the police are for, Stevie? They are there so that them as have nothing shouldn't take anything away from them who have' " (p. 147). (For those guilty of irony, what form should the answer take?)

Stevie, who "had always been easily impressed by speeches," is "impressed and startled now," and he asks at once, anxiously: " 'What? . . . Not even if they are hungry? Mustn't they?' " " 'Not if they were ever so,' " Mrs. Verloc responds, "with the equanimity of a person untroubled by the problem of the distribution of wealth, and exploring the perspective of the roadway for an omnibus of the right colour. 'Certainly not. But what's the use of talking about all that, you aren't ever hungry' " (p. 148).

At this point she cries out to Stevie to stop a bus, and the scene ends with Stevie "tremulous and important with his sister Winnie on his arm, [flinging] up the other high above his head at the approaching bus, with complete success."

Stevie never progresses any further in his effort to understand the causes or solutions for suffering. Soon after this scene, he is used by Mr. Verloc to carry dynamite as part of an absurd effort to blow up the Greenwich Observatory. Stevie trips over a root and himself is blown to pieces, into such small pieces that his remains must be gathered up with a shovel.

Such is the fate and such is Conrad's treatment of the only character in the book who seems capable of compassion for anyone beyond the limits of his own family. It provides a peculiarly depressing addition to what is in all other respects a peculiarly depressing book. Peculiarly depressing not only because of the number of despicable characters and the generally ugly portrait of all aspects of London scenery and life and because the book suggests no remedies for the ills it dramatizes, but because the few generous impulses Conrad allows his characters lead, without exception, only to greater ugliness and pain. Still, without the presence of Stevie I would have been reading a book in which compassion was so conspicuous by its absence that I could have believed I was to see it as a possibly saving virtue. Instead I am made to regard it too as a hopeless, and even absurd and dangerous, gesture. More than this, through Stevie's perceptions my own compassion is stimulated and then cut off short. Let me give one further brief illustration that sharply outlines this dilemma.

The only other specific person, besides the cabman, who is shown as a recipient of Stevie's compassion is a Mrs. Neale. She is introduced in this way: "Mrs. Neale was the charwoman of Brett Street. Victim of her marriage with a debauched joiner, she was oppressed by the needs of many infant children. Re-armed, and aproned in coarse sacking up to the armpits, she exhaled the anguish of the poor in a breath of soap-suds and rum, in the uproar of scrubbing, in the clatter of tin pails" (p. 153). While she is scrubbing the kitchen floor of the Verloc house, Stevie enters the room, and she groans "lamentably, having observed that he could be induced easily to bestow for the benefit of her infant children the shilling his sister Winnie presented him with from time to time."

> On all fours amongst the puddles, wet and begrimed, like a sort of amphibious and domestic animal living in ashbins and dirty water, she uttered the usual exordium: "It's all very well for you, kept doing nothing like a gentleman." And she followed with the everlasting plaint of the poor, pathetically mendacious, miserably authenticated by the horrible breath of cheap rum and soap-suds. She scrubbed hard, snuffing all the time, and talking volubly. And she was sincere. And on each side of her thin red nose, her bleared, misty eyes swam in tears, because she really felt the need of some stimulant in the morning. (Pp. 155–56)

Lest one still be unduly swayed by the pathos of her predicament, Conrad goes on to have Mrs. Verloc observe, "with knowledge": " 'There's Mrs. Neale at it again with her harrowing tales about her little children. They can't all be as little as she makes them out. Some of them must be big enough by now to try to do something for themselves. It only makes Stevie angry.' " Her words are confirmed by a thud as of a fist striking the kitchen table, and we are told that "in the normal evolution of his sympathy" Stevie had become angry and felt someone should be made to suffer when he discovered that he had no shilling and could not at once relieve Mrs. Neale's " 'little un's' privations." Mrs. Verloc goes into the kitchen and stops "that nonsense" firmly but gently. "She was well aware that directly Mrs. Neale received her money she went round the corner to drink ardent spirits in a mean and musty public house—the unavoidable *via dolorosa* of her life. Mrs. Verloc's comment upon this practise had an unexpected profundity, as coming from a person disinclined to look under the surface of things. 'Of course, what is she to do to keep up? If I were like Mrs. Neale I expect I wouldn't act any different' " (p. 156).

Here Conrad does offer the charity of his "*via dolorosa*" and his endorsement of Mrs. Verloc's final remarks, although qualified by the distances of an allusion in a foreign language and a surrogate voice.

But again, as with his earlier insistence about Stevie's desire to punish others when his compassion is frustrated, I am puzzled by Conrad's report that Stevie felt someone should be made to suffer because I see no evidence of it in the scene or elsewhere. If anyone is punishing others for the suffering he is unable to ameliorate, it would seem to be Conrad, whose scorn is such a merciless whip throughout the book.

But my sharpest uneasiness is over the ease with which Stevie's compassion is dismissed. Here, as with the horse and cab, Stevie has a clear and uncomplicated wish—to relieve the suffering. That he has no efficacious method for doing so is true, but that is hardly a great or absurd failing in a world (within the book and without) in which no one seems to have any better methods. What is Conrad's wish?

As is true of his treatment of the cabman and the horse, he

is clearly aware of Mrs. Neale's suffering and of the unpleasantness of her work, and he takes pains to make that suffering vivid for the reader. Yet in both cases he treats himself and us to some luxurious distancing metaphors: turns the "maimed" and "sodden" faced driver into a "jovial" cheeked Silenus discoursing "of Olympian Gods to the shepherds of Sicily" (p. 142) and the overworked scurbwoman into "a sort of amphibious and domestic animal living in ashbins and dirty water" (p. 155). And in both cases, he reminds us more than twice that his characters' most pressing concern is not their little children but the solace of a drink.

In these knowledges and perspectives, we are presumably superior to Stevie, who knows only his simpleminded compassion. Why superior? How have we and the narrator earned our distance, to say nothing of our armoring scorn. A more intelligent Stevie might have become only one of us, or he might have learned, as did the boy in *Morning Watch,* to complicate his compassionate urges with intimations and circumlocutions pertaining to his own saintliness. In either case the cabman and Mrs. Neale go on with their distressing lives, finding assistance only in drink

In an Author's Note written thirteen years after the book was published, Conrad defends himself against those critics who objected to the book because of the "sordid surroundings and the moral squalor of the tale" by saying that "the whole treatment of the tale, its inspiring indignation and underlying pity and contempt, prove my detachment from the squalor and sordidness which lie simply in the outward circumstances of the setting" (p. 8). And he goes on to say:

> I had to fight hard to keep at arm's length the memories of my nocturnal walks all over London in my early days, lest they should rush in and overwhelm each page of the story as these emerged one after the other from a mood as serious in feeling and thought as any in which I ever wrote a line. . . . Even the purely artistic purpose, that of applying an ironic method to a subject of that kind, was formulated with deliberation and in the earnest belief that ironic treatment alone would enable me to say all I felt I would have to say in scorn as well as pity. (P. 12)

In many respects, as is apparent in the passages quoted, the mixture of scorn and pity works to brilliant and powerful effect. Among other things, it implies throughout that there must be other modes of consciousness and behavior, ways of feeling and being, superior to those we are observing. But scorn is a seductive and habit-forming frame of mind, and I think it comes finally to dominate the book more than it should, especially toward the end, and especially in the treatment of Winnie Verloc after she has killed her husband. Even when the scorn and pity seem perfectly in balance, there is something evasive about the narrator, just as there is something evasive in Conrad's Author's Note, which pronounces his detachment from certain aspects of his subject but does not in any way explore the nature of the invovlement (complicity?) that he is deliberately trying "to keep at arm's length." With respect to such scorn and pity, I want finally to challenge the author of *The Secret Agent* with his own demonstration in his novel *Victory* of the destructive effect of the cynical and despairing father of Axel Heyst, that old man who preaches that all hope and action are pointless and on his deathbed responds thus to his young son's quite desperate "Is there no guidance?"

> "You still believe in something, then?" he said in a clear voice, which had been growing feeble of late. "You believe in flesh and blood, perhaps? A full equable contempt would soon do away with that, too. But since you have not attained to it, I advise you to cultivate that form of contempt which is called pity. It is perhaps the least difficult—always remembering that you, too, if you are anything, are as pitiful as the rest, yet never expecting any pity for yourself."
>
> "What is one to do, then?" sighed the young man, regarding his father, rigid in the high-backed chair.
>
> "Look on—make no sound," were the last words of the man who had spent his life in blowing blasts upon a terrible trumpet which had filled heaven and earth with ruins, while mankind went on its way unheeding.[2]

There is a side of Conrad in that book, too, that is fascinated by the old man's position. And it is possible to see the son's tragedy as resulting from a failure to remain sufficiently detached and distant and to see the viciousness of other characters in the book as a confirmation of the father's view of the world. But it seems quite clear that the book finally shows the father's attitudes to be responsible more than anything else for the tragedy and forces us to give nearly full assent to the last words of the son: " 'Ah, Davidson, woe to the man whose heart has not learned while young to hope, to love—and to put its trust in life!' "[3]

I would like to remind Conrad also, as well as some interpreters of the story, that what saves the captain, ship, and crew in his own story "The Secret Sharer" is the captain's hat, which he gives to Leggatt, his other self, not as a cynical onlooker and not in any mixture of scorn and pity, but as a Stevie Verloc might, from seeing himself plainly in Leggatt's position, "wandering barefooted, bareheaded, the sun beating on my dark poll" and from "my sudden pity for his mere flesh."[4]

I am not sure it is fair to inflict Nathanael West's *Miss Lonelyhearts* upon anyone who is not already acquainted with it. Not that it isn't a remarkable book, perhaps even a classic of its kind; but except to those few who can find it funny, it is likely to be a peculiarly tormenting book, even among what must already look like the reading list of a literary licker of lepers or licker of literary lepers (just beginning to think about the book makes me write something like that!). But both the author and title character must be permitted their confrontation with Auden. The first chapter is titled "Miss Lonelyhearts, Help Me, Help Me," and the book begins:

> The Miss Lonelyhearts of the New York *Post-Dispatch* (Are you in trouble?—Do-you-need-advice?—Write-to-Miss Lonelyhearts-and-she-will-help- you) sat at his desk and stared at a piece of white cardboard. On it a prayer had been printed by Shrike, the feature editor.

"Soul of Miss L, glorify me.
Body of Miss L, nourish me.
Blood of Miss L, intoxicate me.
Tears of Miss L, wash me.
Oh good Miss L, excuse my plea,
And hide me in your heart,
And defend me from mine enemies.
Help me, Miss L, help me, help me.
In saecula saeculorum, Amen."

Although the deadline was less than a quarter of an hour away, he was still working on his leader. He had gone as far as: "Life is worthwhile, for it is full of dreams and peace, gentleness and ecstacy, and faith that burns like a clear white flame on a grim dark altar." But he found it impossible to continue. The letters were no longer funny. He could not go on finding the same joke funny thirty times a day for months on end. And on most days he received more than thirty letters, all of them alike, stamped from the dough of suffering with a heart-shaped cookie knife.

On his desk were piled those he had received this morning. He started through them again, searching for some clue to a sincere answer.[5]

The reader must immediately join him in reading three of the letters. The first, signed "Sick-of-it-all," begins: "Dear Miss Lonelyhearts—*I am in such pain I don't know what to do sometimes I think I will kill myself my kidneys hurt so much*" and goes on to explain that the writer has had seven children in twelve years and was so sick after the last two that her husband "*promised no more children on the doctor's advice as he said I might die but when I got back from the hospital he broke his promise and now I am going to have a baby and I don't think I can stand it my kidneys hurt so much.*" She cannot have an abortion "*on account of being a Catholic and my husband so religious. I cry all the time it hurts so much and I don't know what to do*" (p. 2).

The second, signed "Desperate," is from a sixteen-year-old girl who was born without a nose. "*I have a big hole in the middle of my face that scares people even myself so I can't blame the boys for not wanting to take me out. My mother loves me, but she cries terrible when she looks at me*" (p. 2). The third is from a fifteen-year-old boy who fears his thirteen-year-old deaf and dumb sister will have a baby because a "*man came on the roof and did something dirty to her.*" He is afraid to tell his mother because he fears "*she will beat Gracie up awfull . . . and last time when she tore her dress they locked her in the closet for 2 days*" (p. 3).

Understandably, Miss Lonelyhearts has enormous difficulties in knowing how to answer such letters. In addition to what might flippantly be called the "normal" problems that anyone would experience confronted with such a task, Miss Lonelyhearts has some special ones. He is afflicted with a general feeling that both he and the world about him are cold and dead. It is "a world of doorknobs" (p. 9) and his own innermost recesses, both spiritual and sexual, are often an "icy fatness." The main thing (apart from sexual friction) that offers him a sense of life is a feeling of excitement about Christ. Even "as a boy in his father's church, he had discovered that something stirred in him when he shouted the name of Christ, something secret and enormously powerful" (p. 8). But he also, and with some reason, fears this excitement and sometimes regards it as "hysteria, a snake whose scales are tiny mirrors in which the dead world takes on a semblance of life" (p. 9). This obsession is also highly self-conscious, confused, and often theatrical. He removes an ivory figure of Christ from the cross where it had been and nails it to his bedroom wall with large spikes, but "instead of writhing, the Christ remained calmly decorative" (p. 8). When his fiancee has reacted to his anger at her innocent complacency by reaching for his brow and asking " 'What's the matter. . . . Are you sick?' ", he shouts at her, "accompanying his shouts with gestures that were too appropriate, like those of an old-fashioned actor. 'What a kind bitch you are. As soon as anyone acts viciously, you say he's sick. Wife-torturers, rapers of small children, according to you they're all sick. No morality, only medicine. Well, I'm not sick. I don't need any of your damned aspirin. I've got a Christ complex. Humanity. . . I'm a humanity lover. All the broken bastards . . . ' He finished with a short laugh that was like a bark" (p. 13). A moment later, his anger unappeased, he pats her shoulder "threatingly" and asks, " 'What's the matter sweetheart . . . Didn't you like my performance?' " (p. 13).

As may be clear even from this brief passage, the confusion and theatricality do not entirely invalidate Miss Lonelyhearts' point of view, and whenever we are tempted to see his obsession entirely as illness, we are stopped by the extent to which this allies us with the second of Miss Lonelyhearts' special afflictions, his editor, the brutally cynical and sterile Shrike. Totally lacking in any sympathy either for Miss Lonelyhearts or the letter-writers, he is little more than a "machine for making jokes." For him Miss Lonelyhearts is a "leper licker," Christ is "Miss Lonelyhearts of Miss Lonelyhearts" or "Christ Dentist . . . Preventer of Decay," and the letters only something upon which to exercise his wit. He goes so far as to invent a party game called "Everyman his own Miss Lonelyhearts" in which he passes out the letters to his drunken guests who are to try to answer them and relishes reading parts of them aloud as he passes them out. His cynicism helps drive Miss Lonelyhearts toward a mad religious fanaticism, and he accelerates "his sickness by teaching him to handle his one escape, Christ, with a thick glove of words" (p. 33). He has advised Miss Lonelyhearts to give his readers stones. " 'When they ask for bread don't give them crackers as does the Church, and don't like the State, tell them to eat cake. Explain that man can not live by bread alone and give them stones. Teach them to pray each morning: "Give us this day our daily stone" ' " (p. 5).

Miss Lonelyhearts, however, can no longer bear to go on giving his readers stones, has given them "so many, in fact, that he had only one left—the stone that had formed in his gut" (p. 5). Or as he tries to explain to Betty when she suggests he give up the job and "work in an advertising agency or something":

> "You don't understand, Betty, I can't quit. And even if I were to quit, it wouldn't make any difference. I wouldn't be able to forget the letters, no matter what I did. . . . Perhaps I can make you understand. Let's start from the beginning. A man is hired to give

> advice to the readers of a newspaper. The job is a circulation stunt and the whole staff considers it a joke. He welcomes the job, for it might lead to a gossip column, and anyway he's tired of being a leg man. He too considers the job a joke, but after several months at it, the joke begins to escape him. He sees that the majority of the letters are profoundly humble pleas for moral and spiritual advice, that they are inarticulate expressions of genuine suffering. He also discovers that his correspondents take him seriously. For the first time in his life he is forced to examine the values by which he lives. This examination shows him that he is the victim of the joke and not its perpetrator." (P. 32)

Here and elsewhere West seems to attach some value to the sincerity of Miss Lonelyhearts' compassion and pain, and he keeps reminding the reader of the world's suffering in various ways, including the reproduction of further agonizing letters. As does Miss Lonelyhearts, we must find Shrike's and Betty's obtuseness nearly intolerable and must share his anguish and sense that something ought to be done. So it is with the weight of some stone in our own gut that we must witness the way Miss Lonelyhearts botches up everything he touches, even in his dreams.

In one of his dreams he and two college roommates drunkenly try to sacrifice a lamb to God. While the roommates hold the animal, Miss Lonelyhearts chants, "Christ, Christ, Jesus Christ" and tries to kill it with a butcher knife. He botches the job so badly that the knife breaks and the mutilated lamb crawls off into the underbrush, at which the boys flee. After a while Miss Lonelyhearts begs them to go back to put the lamb out of its misery. When they refuse, he goes back alone, crushes its head with a stone, and leaves "the carcass to the flies that swarmed around the bloody altar flowers" (p. 10).

In an equally dreamlike and drunken but waking episode, Miss Lonelyhearts and another reporter stumble upon an old homosexual sitting on the toilet in the comfort station of a little park and force him to accompany them to a bar where they try to elicit his life story. When they first take hold of him and he goes soft in their arms and begins to giggle, Miss Lonelyhearts has to resist a desire to hit him. When he refuses to tell them his story and begins to cough violently, Miss Lonelyhearts feels as "he had felt years before, when he had accidentally stepped on a small frog. Its spilled guts had filled him with pity, but when its suffering had become real to his senses, his pity had turned to rage and he had beaten it frantically until it was dead" (p. 17). Finally, when the old man continues to insist that he has no story and begins to sob, Miss Lonelyhearts cries out, " 'Tell it, damn you, tell it' " and begins to twist the old man's arm. When the other reporter tries to tear him away, he refuses to let go. "He was twisting the arm of all the sick and miserable, broken and betrayed, inarticulate and impotent. He was twisting the arm of Desperate, Broken-hearted, Sick-of-it-all, Disillusioned-with-Tubercular-husband." The old man begins to scream, and somebody hits Miss Lonelyhearts from behind with a chair.

Toward the end of the book, while seeking to cultivate humility, he becomes involved with two of the people who have written him letters: a Mrs. Doyle, with "legs like Indian clubs, breasts like balloons and a brow like a pigeon" who virtually rapes him, and her husband, a cripple whom she despises and mistreats. One consequence of his efforts to help them is a scene in which Mrs. Doyle sends her husband out for some gin and sits on his lap. He tries to fend her off, but she keeps pressing her mouth against his, making him feel "like an empty bottle that is slowly being filled with warm, dirty water." When she opens her dress and tries to force his head between her breasts, "he parted his knees with a quick jerk that slipped her to the floor. She tried to pull him down on top of her. He struck out blindly and hit her in the face. She screamed and he hit her again and again. He kept hitting her until she stopped trying to hold him, then he ran out of the house" (p. 50.).

The other consequence is that Mr. Doyle believes his wife when she tells him that Miss Lonelyhearts tried to rape her and determines to take vengeance. By the time he seeks to execute it, however, Miss Lonelyhearts has gone through a period of rock-like calm that nothing, including Shrike and Betty, can disturb, into a state of fever in which the rock has become a furnace. Here with some deletions is the way West offers the reader his final stone:

> He fastened his eyes on the Christ that hung on the wall opposite his bed. As he stared at it, it became a bright fly, spinning with quick grace on a background of blood velvet sprinkled with tiny nerve stars.
>
> Everything else in the room was dead—chairs, tables, pencils, clothes, books. He thought of this black world of things as a fish. And he was right, for it suddenly rose to the bright bait on the wall. It rose with a splash of music and he saw its shining silver belly. . . .
>
> "Christ! Christ!" This shout echoed through the innermost cells of his body.
>
> He moved his head to a cooler spot on the pillow and the vein in his forehead became less swollen. He felt clean and fresh. . . .
>
> The room was full of grace. A sweet, clean grace, not washed clean, but clean as the innersides of the inner petals of a newly forced rosebud. . . .
>
> He was conscious of two rhythms that were slowly becoming one. When they became one, his identification with God was complete. His heart was the one heart, the heart of God. . . .
>
> Suddenly the doorbell rang. He climbed out of bed and went into the hall to see who was coming. It was Doyle, the cripple, and he was slowly working his way up the stairs.
>
> God had sent him so that Miss Lonelyhearts could perform a miracle and be certain of his conversion. It was a sign. He would embrace the cripple and the cripple would be made whole again, even as he, a spiritual cripple, had been made whole.
>
> He rushed down the stairs to meet Doyle with his arms spread for the miracle.
>
> Doyle was carrying something wrapped in a newspaper. When he saw Miss Lonelyhearts, he put his hand inside the package and stopped. He shouted some kind of warning, but Miss Lonelyhearts continued his charge. He did not understand the cripple's shout and heard it as a cry for help from Desperate, Harold S., Catholic-mother, Broken-hearted, Broad-Shoulders, Sick-of-it-all, Disillusioned-with-tubercular-husband. He was running to succor them with love.
>
> The cripple turned to escape, but he was too close and Miss Lonelyhearts caught him.
>
> While they were struggling, Betty came in through the street door. She called to him to stop and started up the stairs. The cripple saw her cutting off his escape and tried to get rid of the package. He pulled his hand out. The gun inside the package exploded and Miss Lonelyhearts fell, dragging the cripple with him. They both fell part of the way down the stairs.

Upon finishing the book one wishes one could feel one had read merely the case history of a peculiarly incompetent Christ, of a man with a peculiar coldness of body and soul, a peculiar susceptibility to rage, and a peculiar inability to set things right. Then, at least, one might comfort oneself by imagining a more effective savior. But West allows us no such luxury. Miss Lonelyhearts *is* a peculiarly disabled and disabling hero, but West neither suggests how he could have done better nor gives any clear indication that a less neurotic Miss Lonelyhearts could, in fact, have been more effective. Moreover, he is the only character with any nobility at all, and his feeling of compassion is the only thing in the book not made to look ugly or ridiculous. And even if there is enough tonal distance, at times even scorn, toward Miss Lonelyhearts to keep us from identifying with him, we are drawn into some kind of complicity with him because the story is told more from his point of view than anyone else's and because we too have been forced to read the letters. What *does* one say to Desperate, Broken-hearted, and Sick-of-it-all? How *does* one live a life without ignoring the letters? The Marxist in me notes that most of the letter-writers are ignorant and poor and that a more decent economic order might provide the crippled Mr. Doyle with a job that did not require him to drag his crippled leg around all day "with it all the time hurting fit to burst so that near quitting time I am crazy with pain" (p. 46). But it is hard to feel that political or social change would ease much of the pain experienced in the book. Or how it would improve either the body or character of Mrs. Doyle, to say nothing of the misery of no-nose.

In some respects the experience of reading the book is comparable to Miss Lonelyhearts' when he keeps reading and rereading the letters: "for the same reason that an animal tears at a wounded foot: to hurt the pain" (p. 39). But finally, I think, I feel injured by the book in another way, as though I were the victim of some violence, a controlled violence, more like that of Shrike, perhaps, than of Miss Lonelyhearts. And though it would not be accurate to say that Shrike is the narrator of the book, I think its ultimate tone and meaning more nearly resembles the furious despair of a Shrike than the incompetent thrashing about of Miss Lonelyhearts.

It is true that West presents Shrike in his full ugliness. His face is "a dead, gray triangle" (p. 6). His method of seducing a woman is to alternate between raising his fist at her and caressing her, and finally he buries "his triangular face like the blade of a hatchet in her neck" (p. 8). Like the reporters who imitate him, he is a machine for making jokes, jokes that are frequently sophomoric or hysterical. On one occasion Miss Lonelyhearts regards him as "a gull trying to lay an egg in the smooth flank of a rock, a screaming, clumsy gull"; and sometimes we must see him so, as well as in the more predatory form his name suggests (that hawklike shape which seems so drawn toward this book). And yet West is clearly fascinated by his cynicism and destructive wit. One hears his assent as Shrike mocks, one after the other, the various escapes of writers and artists that Miss Lonelyhearts might try: return to the soil, the South Sea islands, hedonism, art, suicide, and drugs. Here is the beginning of his fun with the South Seas: "You live in a thatch hut with the daughter of the king, a slim young maiden in whose eyes is an ancient wisdom. Her breasts are golden speckled pears, her belly a melon, and her odor is like nothing so much as a jungle fern. In the evening, on the blue lagoon, under the silvery moon, to your love you croon in the soft sylabelew and vocabelew of the labgorour tangorour" (p. 33). And here is the way he takes on Wordsworth, Lawrence, Thoreau, and perhaps some others I do not recognize:

> "You are fed up with the city and its teeming millions. The ways and means of men, as getting and lending and spending you lay waste your inner world, are too much with you. The bus takes too long, while the subway is always crowded. So what do you do? So you buy a farm and walk behind your horse's moist behind, no collar or tie, plowing your broad swift acres. As you turn up the rich black soil, the wind carries the smell of pine and dung across the fields and the rhythm of an old, old work enters your soul. To this rhythm, you sow and weep and chivy your kine, not kin or kind, between the pregnant rows of corn and taters. Your step becomes the heavy sexual step of a dance-drunk

> Indian and you tread the seed down into the female earth. You plant, not dragon's teeth, but beans and greens. . . . " (P. 33; author's ellipsis)

In the chapter "Miss Lonelyhearts in the Country," West's own examination of the rural scene is perhaps a bit more complex but, finally, equally if not more cynical and cruel.

But the alignment is deeper and scarier than this because the book in its entirety is Shrike-like in its insistent emphasis on the absurdities of Miss Lonelyhearts at the same time that it demolishes all alternatives; Shrike-like in the icy chapter titles such as "Miss Lonelyhearts and the Clean Old Man," and "Miss Lonelyhearts Has a Religious Experience"; and Shrike-like in its cruelty, for there is cruelty as well as humor in West's treatment of nearly all the characters. It is the cruelty of bitter disappointment, perhaps, but cruelty nevertheless. I still have not satisfactorily explained, though, what I mean by saying that I feel injured by the book, as though I had received an insufficiently earned blow. It is partly the sense of encountering the Shrike-like part of West, the broken-backed idealist biting all and sundry and himself with his tongue. But there is something more, which I can only get at indirectly. Early in the book, after being sent away by Betty, feeling as if "his heart were a bomb, a complicated bomb that would result in a simple explosion, wrecking the world without rocking it" (p. 13), Miss Lonelyhearts goes to Delehanty's speakeasy and drinks until he feels "warm and sure." It is the first time since we have met him that Miss Lonelyhearts seems out of pain, and we are glad about that. What follows is this:

> He forgot that his heart was a bomb to remember an incident of his childhood. One winter evening, he had been waiting with his little sister for their father to come home from church. She was eight years old then, and he was twelve. Made sad by the pause between playing and eating, he had gone to the piano and had begun a piece by Mozart. It was the first time he had ever voluntarily gone to the piano. His sister left her picture book to dance to his music. She had never danced before. She danced gravely and carefully, a simple dance yet formal. . . . As Miss Lonelyhearts stood at the bar, swaying slightly to the remembered music, he thought of children dancing. Square replacing oblong and being replaced by circle. Every child, everywhere; in the world there

> was not one child who was not gravely, sweetly dancing.
> He stepped away from the bar and accidently collided with a man holding a glass of beer. When he turned to beg the man's pardon, he received a punch in the mouth. (P. 15)

Apparently knocked out by the blow, Miss Lonelyhearts comes to in another room with a loose tooth and a lump on the back of his head, at which point "his anger swung in large drunken circles" and he thinks: "What in Christ's name was this Christ business? And children gravely dancing? He would ask Shrike to be transferred to the sports department" (p. 16). It is immediately after this that he goes out and finds the Clean Old Man whose arm he so painfully twists.

That punch in the mouth is a piece of gratuitous brutality to inflict on Miss Lonelyhearts and on the reader as well. The iamge of the children gravely dancing is without question the loveliest in the book, and it is the only pleasant image that West does not undercut in the very act of creating it. The language in which the scene is developed is like the sister's dancing, grave and careful, simple yet formal. Then the punch in the mouth. That punch in the mouth feels like it comes from West, and even if it also feels like self-laceration, a blow he is inflicting on himself, it hurts this reader. In a way the whole book is like that. The style and organization are exquisitely controlled, grave and careful, simple yet formal, but the content comes through with all the rage that accompanies a punch in the mouth.

In some respects the book works similarly to *The Secret Agent.* Just as he is by that book, the reader is mercilessly exposed to a world in which suffering is one of the chief occupations. He is made to feel that something ought to be done to alleviate the pain, made to feel so not only by the depiction of the suffering itself but by the fact that the most sympathetically drawn figure in each book is obsessed with that very same feeling. He is made to view the failures of that figure with an odd mixture of sympathy and amusement and to stand at some distance from him. Neither author makes any suggestions as to what might be alternative actions or reactions, and neither leaves the reader with a sense of guilt (unless he goes out of his way to supply it himself). And yet I do not feel with West that sense of being unduly protected and immunized that I experienced with Conrad, that sense of being forced into a distance I did not want to occupy. I am not entirely sure why. I think it has to do with that punch in the mouth and with the precise degree of pain immanent in West's pity and scorn. Conrad seems more comfortable with his, though even he is by no means rubbing his innocent behind against a tree.

In saying this I am aware that I am back with Ivan Ivanovich again, distrustful of comfort, wanting everyone—characters, authors, readers, myself—to suffer because others suffer. And yet I do not really think we should all wear hair shirts. But neither do I want to settle yet for one more happy medium—in this case a cotton shirt and only a slight tap from Ivan's man with a hammer.

The books are alike in another respect. Both authors are unhappy about how easily their thin-skinned characters move from "immoderate compassion" to rage, a rage that in Miss Lonelyhearts' case can lead him to injure the very objects of his compassion. But neither author seems aware that he himself is a victim of a similar affliction. Both, I believe, would have assented eagerly to the notions expressed by Agee when he writes to Father Flye that "irony and savage anger and even certain planes of cynicism are, used right, nearly as good instruments and weapons as love, and not by any means incompatible with it; good lens-wipers and good auxiliaries. In plenty of ways I care most for those who lack the easing and comfort of direct love, Swift above any; and a lot for smaller, sharp intelligent soreheads like Bierce."[6] I do not think either West or Conrad would have troubled himself sufficiently over the conjunction of "weapons" and "love" or wondered at all whether his own rage had anything to do with the killings off of Stevie and Miss Lonelyhearts. Nor do I think either would have worried how close his scorn toward the majority of humankind had taken him toward a Robinson Jeffers–like condition of wishing not so much for man's redemption as for his extermination. None of this would be so troublesome if most of us, writers and nonwriters alike, did not have such a remarkable aptitude for moving from righteous indignation to self-righteous indignation, a condition we obviously find easier than "direct love," just as we have usually found it easier to punish victimizers than to care for victims.

Both books compel me toward some further atrocious questions: To what extent can Stevie and Miss Lonelyhearts be viewed as incomplete or failed saints? Insofar as they are such, to what extent is their failure to attain a fuller stature the result of their own inadequacies and to what extent of their creators' inability to conceive of sainthood in the modern world? It is so easy to mock impulses toward sainthood. West is critical of such facility when he has the cynical newsmen who imitate Shrike call Miss Lonelyhearts "a leper licker" and say that even if he were to have a genuine religious experience, it would be personal and so meaningless, except to a psychologist" (p. 15). And yet West himself cannot quite bring himself to view Miss Lonelyhearts' conversion at the end as other than a personal and meaningless event.

In weighing the characters' own inadequacies, it may be helpful to notice that while Miss Lonelyhearts *has* tried to live up to one ideal—to become his brother's keeper—he has not followed another: to do unto others as he would have done unto himself. Despite his sincerity and despite his exercises in humility, he sees himself as a savior, not one of those needing to be saved. Stevie is more humble. Although he lacks the language to conceptualize either, he tries to realize both ideals, the second of them with precise fidelity when his "tenderness to all pain and to all misery" and his "desire to make the horse happy and the cabman happy, had reached the point of a bizarre longing to take them in bed with him" just as he had been taken into his sister's bed when as a young child he was most miserable.

A final observation about these two books: although Stevie and Miss Lonelyhearts suffer from their immoderate compassion and are immobilized by it, it is not that which destroys them. What does destroy them is a concentration of people with peculiarly deafened hearts.

IV ❖ A Terrible Promiscuous Compassion

ANOTHER THINLY-WADDED SPECTER WHO MUST BE BROUGHT into witness as a possible observer of the fall of Icarus is the police officer Major Henry Scobie, who suffers through the pages of Graham Greene's *The Heart of the Matter.* For those who have not read the book, no summary can capture the complexities of the man himself or of the tone the author takes toward him. But I must try, for Scobie is for me one of those fictional characters without whom the world would be a much emptier place. If only there were a way to have told him that.

Scobie is a fifty-year-old assistant commissioner of police in a West African coastal town. An Englishman, he has been stationed in the town for fifteen years and has just been passed over for promotion to commissioner, probably because he has been too honest and honorable to play the political games required for advancement. For fourteen years he has been married to Louise, a melancholy and discontented woman whose unhappiness and sense of humiliation have been so increased over his failure to become commissioner that she begs him somehow to find the money to send her to live in South Africa until it is time for him to retire. We know almost nothing about their earlier lives apart from the fact that their only child, a nine-year-old girl, has died three years before while at school in England, and that Scobie feels responsible for having made his wife the unhappy and insecure creature she has become. "No man could guarantee love forever," he thinks at one point, "but he had sworn fourteen years ago, at Ealing, silently, during the horrible little elegant ceremony among the lace and candles, that he would at least always see to it that she was happy."[1] This noble and presumptuous oath he is determined to keep.

Neither Scobie himself nor the reader can tell how much his bond to his wife remains composed of love and how much of the pity and sense of responsibility that have come to dominate his feelings toward her. To some degree this sense of responsibility for her happiness has been heightened by his lessening need for her and his increasing wish for a kind of simplicity and peace offered by his barely furnished office—"a table, two kitchen chairs, a cupboard, some rusty handcuffs hanging on a nail like an old hat, a filing cabinet" (p. 8), and by the bathroom with "the bath of scratched enamel with a single tap which always ceased to work before the end of the dry season: the tin bucket under the lavatory seat emptied once a day: the fixed basin with another useless tap: bare floorboards: drab green black-out curtains" (p. 37). He had come to dread the thought of retirement, cooped up with Louise in a prettified comfortable home with artistic curtains and a tiled bath, "no office anywhere" (p. 41). But the yearning is even more profound than this, and in the midst of a rare moment of anger and honesty toward his wife, he cries out angrily: "'You haven't any conception . . . of what peace means.' It was as though she had spoken lightly of a woman he loved." Peace seems to him "the most beautiful word in the language: My peace I give to you, my peace I leave with you: O Lamb of God, who takest away the sins of the world, grant us thy peace. In the Mass he pressed his fingers against his eyes to keep the tears of longing in." (p. 61)

But his sense of responsibility arises most powerfully from the kind of appeal it is his peculiar affliction not to be able to resist—the appeal that ugliness and failure make to his pity. On the day she learns of his failure to be promoted, he comes home from work to find Louise in bed, and he watches her through the muslin net. "Her face had the yellow-ivory tinge of atabrine: her hair, which had once been the colour of bottled honey, was dark and stringy with sweat. These were the times of ugliness when he loved her, when pity and responsibility reached the intensity of a passion" (p. 16). And later that evening when he watches "her fist open and close, the damp inefficient powder lying like snow in the ridges of the knuckles" and listens to her pathetic "'O Ticki, Ticki . . . you won't leave me ever, will you? I haven't got any friends," he "lifted the moist hand and kissed the palm: he was bound by the pathos of her unattractiveness" (p. 23).

It is this same appeal that leads Scobie to dent his integrity a little by not reporting a minor wartime infraction of a fat, ugly Portuguese sea captain who when he was caught "kept on wiping his eyes with the back of his hand like a child—an unattractive child, the fat boy of the school" (p. 49). His affection for the corrupt and ugly town has a similar basis:

> Why, he wondered, swerving his car to avoid a dead pye-dog, do I love this place so much? Is it because here human nature hasn't had time to disguise itself? Nobody here could even talk about a heaven on earth. Heaven remained rigidly in its proper place on the other side of death, and on this side flourished the injustices, the cruelties, the meannesses, that elsewhere people so cleverly hushed up. Here you could love human beings nearly as God loved them, knowing the worst. (P. 32)

And, as we shall see, it is in great part his inability to resist the unattractiveness of another woman ("the ugliness was like handcuffs on his wrists" [p. 172]) that eventually leads to his destruction.

At the same time, however, unlike some who enjoy the pathos of failure and unattractiveness, he cannot bear to see suffering:

> And now, Scobie thought, I must return home. . . . I shall read in her face the story of what she has been thinking all day. She will have been hoping that everything is fixed, that I shall say, "I've put your name down at the agents for South Africa," but she'll be afraid that nothing so good as that will ever happen to us. She'll wait for me to speak, and I shall try to talk about anything under the sun to avoid seeing her misery. . . . I shall go in and I'll say, "Good evening, sweetheart," and she'll say, "Good evening, darling. What kind of a day?" and I'll talk and talk, but all the time I shall know I'm coming nearer to the moment when I shall say, "What about you, darling?" and let the misery in. (Pp. 56–57)

At one point, in a rare moment of losing control, late in the book, he cries out "'I can't bear to see suffering, and I cause it all the time'" (p. 259).

It would be possible to argue that Scobie is most deeply

motivated by this inability to stand others' suffering and by his yearning for peace, and a severely hostile view might accuse Scobie of hating suffering only because it keeps him from finding peace. (In another of Greene's novels, *The Quiet American,* it *is* suggested that one of the characters cannot stand suffering because of a selfish desire for peace of mind, but the suggestion is made by the character himself, Fowler, who is shown to be far more worthy and complex than this, and undeserving of his harsh self-judgment.) If I had to reduce Scobie to those two dimensions, I would say that the reason he wants peace so much is that he suffers so acutely the suffering of others, a relation that we shall observe again and one that surely holds for many good people. At one point Scobie puts the two in this conjunction: "When we say to someone, 'I can't live without you,' what we really mean is, 'I can't live feeling you may be in pain, unhappy, in want.' That's all it is. When they are dead our responsibility ends. There's nothing more we can do about it. We can rest in peace" (p. 167). It is possible Greene wants us to bridle at the shift in the final sentence from "they" to "we," but I think he only wants us to notice it with interest.

This all seems too simple, though. I do not suppose it is possible to prove or demonstrate that Scobie's wish for other's happiness has an existence independent of his inability to stand their suffering, and perhaps it is pointless even to try to distinguish between the two. He would no doubt accuse himself of the conjunction. But I think it does have an existence of its own and want to believe it does. I believe he is thinking essentially of the other and not himself when he prays, even though "vaguely and ramblingly," that Louise "might be happy now at this moment and so remain, that no evil should ever come to her through him" (p. 163). And I believe the same is true when he prays, "O God, give me death before I give them unhappiness" even though, or perhaps because, "the words sounded melodramatically in his own ears" (p. 206) and even though the line is preceded by a complex interplay between the two. I believe it, above all, when he begs on his knees: "'Oh God . . . if, instead, I should abandon you, punish me, but let the others get some happiness'" (p. 244).

Greene makes certain that we wonder fairly early in the book about both the possibility of making others happy and the presumption of trying to do so. At one point, when Scobie thinks, "If I could just arrange for her happiness," the narrator goes on to comment "and in the confusing night he forgot for the while what experience had taught him—that no human being can really understand another, and no one can arrange another's happiness" (p. 84). And a little later, Scobie himself has a momentary realization of greater significance than he gives it: "It occurred to him as it hadn't occurred to him, for years, that she loved him: poor dear, she loved him: she was someone of human stature with her own sense of responsibility, not simply the object of his care and kindness" (p. 97). Although I do not think it would be fair to place too much weight on the word *object* and to accuse him of treating people like things, it is true that he rarely listens when his wife talks, except for "notes of distress" (p. 21); and it is true that he does not allow others the full human stature he assigns to himself—that stature which includes the obligation to take responsibility for others and the right to exercise pity while refusing it for oneself. He gives himself the privilege as well as the burden of lying to others if he believes it will lessen their pain, and he will do so even when he cannot believe he could "fall so far as this and survive" (pp. 228–29). He feels there is "only one person in the world who was unpitiable—himself" (p. 192). Though there is certainly pride in this, he does not usually feel prideful—it is more as though his own pity for others is so strong that it closes him off from the sense that he, himself, needs or deserves it. Only on one occasion does he exhibit the ugliest facet of this self-exemption, when he says to the untrustworthy Syrian trader Yusef, "'I don't think the time's ever like to come, Yusef, when I shall need *your* pity'" (p. 95). (Such a time, of course, does come, as it must to any fictional character who would voice such a sentiment.) Only on rare occasions does he lapse into self-pity.

What ultimately and most deeply seems to rule Scobie is an "automatic terrible pity that goes out to any human need" (p. 227). For him it is a "terrible promiscuous passion" (p. 172), one that I believe falls somewhere in between the two states of mind defined so well in Bernano's *The Diary of a Country Priest* when the priest writes "and it's a long while now since I gave up trying to identify with true pity—the strong gentle pity of the saints—my childish shrinking from other people's pain."[2] It is a pity of such an order that he can ask whether if "we knew . . . the facts, would one have to feel pity even for the planets? if one reaches what they call the heart of the matter?" (p. 128). Unlike many whom pity seems to place at a contemplative or scornful distance, Scobie's is accompanied by an equally automatic feeling of responsibility. When his wife has made him promise to find a way to pay her fare to South Africa, she falls quickly asleep "like a tired carrier who has slipped his load. . . . The load lay beside him now, and he prepared to lift it" (p. 41). Listening to the labored breathing of a dying child, "as if she were carrying a weight with great effort up a long hill," he feels "it was an inhuman situation not to be able to carry it for her" (p. 130). On one occasion Greene puts it this way: "He couldn't shut his eyes or ears to any human need of him: he was not the centurian, but a man in the ranks who had to do the bidding of a hundred centurians, and when the door opened, he could tell the command was going to be given again—the command to stay, to love, to accept responsibility, to lie" (p. 203).

Unlike most forms of pity, his is so intimately involved with an ability to see the other's point of view, even the point of view of those he dislikes ("inexorably the other's point of view rose on the path like a murdered innocent" [p. 196], that one almost wants to quarrel with Greene over his insistence on using the word *pity* rather than *sympathy* or even *compassion*. But Greene is right. There is just enough condescension in his absolute insistence that he be the one to take the responsibility, that the other's need is greater than his, to make Greene's word the right one. Like Miss Lonelyhearts he sees himself as a savior, not one of those needing to be saved.

I have expanded as much as I have on Scobie's character before going on to tell his story partly because I get lost in my fascination with him and partly because the story makes little sense, is scarcely believable, until one is more than a little acquainted with these dimensions of Scobie. Perhaps it will not make much sense to some even so. At any rate, Scobie's determination to make his wife happy is such that he compromises his integrity by borrowing money for her fare to South Africa from Yusef, someone too shady for a policeman to become involved with, even though the arrangement is strictly a business one.

Shortly after his wife leaves, his official duties require him to travel to an outlying village to witness the arrival of a group of survivors from a torpedoed ship, survivors who had just spent forty days in an open lifeboat. Among them two make special demands on his pity as they are carried past him on their stretchers. The first is a small girl, no more than six, whose parents were both lost and who is on the verge of death herself. "She was deeply and unhealthily asleep; her fair hair was tangled and wet with sweat; her open mouth was dry and cracked, and she shuddered regularly and spasmodically" (p. 124). Scobie can accept that the child will die, "but that the child should have been allowed to survive forty days and nights in the open boat—that was the mystery, to reconcile that with the love of God. And yet he could believe in no God who was not human enough to love what he had created" (pp. 124–25).[3] The other is introduced so:

> The face was ugly with exhaustion: the skin looked as though it were about to crack over the cheekbones: only the absence of lines showed that it was a young face. The French officer said, "She was just married—before she sailed. Her husband was lost. Her passport says she is nineteen. She may live. You see, she still has some strength." Her arms as thin as a child's lay outside the blanket, and her fingers clasped a book firmly. Scobie could see the wedding-ring loose on her dried up finger.
>
> "What is it?"
>
> *"Timbres,"* the French officer said. He added bitterly, "When this damned war started, she must have been still at school."
>
> Scobie always remembered how she was carried into his life on a stretcher, grasping a stamp-album, with her eyes fast shut. (P. 125)

That evening he is haunted by the sense of the misery behind the peaceful-looking lights of the rest-house, which has been converted into a temporary hospital. "It was as if he had shed one responsibility only to take on another. This was a responsibility he shared with all human beings, but there was no comfort in that, for it sometimes seemed to him that he was the only one who recognized it. In the Cities of the Plain a single soul might have changed the mind of God" (p. 126). As one is reading along, I do not think we take much note of the pride Scobie reveals here or even of the fact that some others like the French officer and the missionary's wife have taken on considerable responsibility; for he is juxtaposed against others who do not seem much affected, and he does reveal a greater degree of anguish than any of the others. And shortly after that prideful note, we witness a scene in which we are compelled to view Scobie with sympathy and respect.

Wandering restlessly outside the temporary hospital, he is asked by the missionary's wife, who is serving as nurse, to stay in the little cubicle with the dying six-year-old and the still unconscious girl with the stamp album while she goes off to get some medicine. Reluctantly he sits down and silently prays that nothing will happen before she gets back. This prayer is not answered, for a moment later, the child's heavy uneven breathing (a burden that it was already "an inhuman situation" not to be able to carry for her) "broke, choked, began again with terrible effort" and "her six-year-old face convulsed like a navvy's with labour" (p. 130). At this point he utters an incredible prayer, one that is, in a sense granted, something we must remember when at the end of the book we and others are making final earthly judgments on Scobie. "'Father,' he prayed, 'give her peace. Take away my peace forever, but give her peace.' The sweat broke out on his hands. 'Father . . . '" (p. 130; author's ellipsis). Hearing this, the child who has not been told of her parents' deaths and who has from time to time been asking for her father, in "a small scraping voice" repeats the word "Father,"

> and looking up he saw the blue and bloodshot eyes watching him. He thought with horror: this is what I thought I'd missed. He would have called Mrs. Bowles, only he hadn't the voice to call with. He could see the breast of the child struggling for breath to repeat the heavy word; he came over to the bed and said, "Yes, dear. Don't speak, I'm here." The nightlight cast the shadow of his clenched fist on the sheet and it caught the child's eye. An effort to laugh convulsed her, and he moved his hand away. "Sleep, dear," he said, "you are sleepy. Sleep." A memory that he had carefully buried returned, and taking out his handkerchief he made the shadow of a rabbit's head fall on the pillow beside her. "There's your rabbit," he said, "to go to sleep with. It will stay until you sleep. Sleep." The sweat poured down his face and tasted in his mouth as salt as tears. "Sleep." He moved the rabbit's ears up and down, up and down. Then he heard Mrs. Bowles' voice, speaking low just behind him. "Stop that," she said harshly, "the child's dead." (P. 130)

Although the scene sometimes strikes me as heavy-handed, just too, too poignant, it has enormous impact and must help complicate any easy judgment one would make about the relation that develops between Scobie and the other still unconscious occupant of the room.

I must take a moment, though, to comment here on a passage in this scene that I have so far left out. Just before his terrible prayer, as Scobie is watching the child struggling to breathe, he thinks: "This is what parents feel year in and year out, and I am shrinking from a few minutes of it. They see their children dying slowly every hour they live" (p. 130). Even in the heavy context of the scene, that perception seems a kind of willful morbidity on Scobie's part, the invention of a weight that, in fact, most parents do not carry. Although it is true that all living things, our children included, can be said to start dying at the moment of their birth, it is perverse to view them in such a light, as perverse as if we were to look at puppies or young birds and young flowers and to notice chiefly their drift toward death. Such morbidity is not so much an attentiveness to that roar on the other side of silence as a ventriloquism that produces it.[4]

Scobie's relation with Helen Rolt, the young girl with the album, develops innocently and accidently, although as we have seen, he has been haunted from the first by the image of her clutching the stamp album. The next day while he is back in the hospital reading to a young boy, she wakes for long enough to listen, "the eyes large as a child's in the starved face" (p. 135), to say "Thank you" when he has finished, and when Scobie turns "reluctantly to take in the young devastated face" (p. 137), to exchange a word or two with him.

About a month later, back at home, Scobie notices a blackout violation in one of the Nissen huts where the minor officials live, a hut that had been unoccupied the day before. When he knocks on the door, it is opened by the girl, who has been released from the hospital. She still bears the ugly marks of her ordeal: "The young worn-out face, with the hair gone dead . . . the pyjamas she was wearing were too large for her: the body was lost in them. They fell in ugly folds. He looked to see whether the ring was still loose upon her finger, but it had gone altogether" (pp. 142–43; author's ellipsis). Scared by the air raid sirens and obviously starved for a sympathetic ear, she asks him to stay for a drink and talks to him about her family and her days at school; and by the time they part, she feels more relaxed and peaceful than she has for some time.

A week later he brings her some stamps that he has collected from various people around the town, and they talk at length. She speaks frankly about her responses to the death of her husband and he about his to the death of his daughter. As she tells him of her recent discomfort on the beach where everyone pretended to be happy and Flight-Lieutenant Bagster stroked her leg, and about her utter lack of any talents or skills to give her a livelihood ("I'm not really good at anything," she says), his sense of responsibility grows; and as he sees her bend to pick up one of the stamps and takes in "the straight hair falling in rats' tails over the nape as though the Atlantic had taken the strength out of it forever, the hollowed face," it seems to him that "he had not felt so much at ease with another human being for years—not since Louise was young" (p. 171). Still feeling "safe" because of his age and his feeling that "his body in this climate had lost the sense of lust"

(p. 171), he watches her with "sadness and affection and enormous pity because a time would come when he couldn't show her around in a world where she was at sea. When she turned and the light fell on her face she looked ugly, with the temporary ugliness of a child. The ugliness was like handcuffs on his wrists" (p. 172). He is even more trapped when, after again telling him how safe she feels with him and how good she feels he is, she says, "I have a feeling that you'd never let me down," words that come to him "like a command he would have to obey, however difficult" (p. 172).

At this point a somewhat drunken Freddie Bagster knocks on the door and begs her to let him in. She whispers to Scobie not to answer and putting her arm in his, standing pressed against him, watches the door with "her mouth a little open as though she were out of breath. He had the sense of an animal which had been chased to its hole." When Bagster leaves, "she raised her mouth and they kissed. What they had both thought was safety proved to be the camouflage of an enemy who works in terms of friendship, trust, and pity" (p. 173).

They make love that night, and on his way home before dawn Scobie knows a few moments of jubilation; but that is all. Once back home he begins to think about the future and to envy the butterfly that died in the act of love: "But human beings were condemned to consequences. The responsibility as well as the guilt were his—he was not a Bagster: he knew what he was about. He had sworn to preserve Louise's happiness, and now he had accepted another and contradictory responsibility. He felt tired by all the lies he would sometime have to tell: he felt the wounds of those victims who had not yet bled" (p. 175).

Before long Helen becomes irritated by the caution that he takes to hide their relation and grows increasingly jealous of his wife. And one night there is an ugly scene in which she rejects his statement that he cannot marry her because he is a Catholic, with an angry, "'It's a wonderful excuse. . . . It doesn't stop you from sleeping with me—it only stops you marrying me' " (p. 193).

Scobie, of course, takes on the responsibility, says, "'Yes,' . . . heavily as though he were accepting a penance," and thinks, "How much older she is than she was a month ago. She hadn't been capable of a scene then, but she had been educated by love and secrecy: he was beginning to form her. He wondered whether, if this went on long enough, she would be indistinguishable from Louise. In my school, he thought wearily, they learn bitterness and frustration and how to grow old." His patient apologies and efforts to comfort her only infuriate her more, and she finally bursts into tears and screams at him: "'Go to hell. Clear out . . . and don't come back'" (p. 195).

He leaves thinking how much easier life would be for him if he took her at her word, but then he thinks of her alone in the hut wondering if her words are irrevocable and her future would consist only of Mrs. Carter and Bagster until she went home to England "with nothing to remember but her misery." And he thinks: "I would never go back there, to the Nissen hut, if it meant that she were happy and I suffered. But if I were happy and she suffered . . . that was what he could not face" (pp. 195–96; author's ellipsis). A moment later he decides, "She's right . . . who could bear my caution?"

Here, I think, Greene finds him more foolish and pathetic than I do, for he introduces Scobie's next act with an odd shift from Scobie's to the narrator's point of view. As he opens the door to his own house, he sees a rat and thinks, "This was what Louise had hated and feared: he had at least made her happy." But there is a comma after "happy" and the sentence continues "and now ponderously, and with planned and careful recklessness, he set about trying to make things right for Helen" (p. 196).

He does this by taking a sheet of his official stationery (in order to put himself entirely in her hands) and composing a letter to her in which he tells her that he loves her "more than myself, more than my wife, more than God I think" (p. 196) and that he wants more than anything else in the world to make her happy. He goes out in the rain to deliver the letter wondering why he wrote "'more than God'" when she would have been satisfied with "'more than Louise.' Even if that's true, why did I write it?" (p. 197). And slipping the letter under the door, remembering "the childish figure carried past him on the stretcher, he was saddened to think how much had happened, how uselessly, to make him now say to himself with resentment: She will never again be able to accuse me of caution" (p. 197). For me the human frailty of that moment of resentment helps keep Scobie a mortal, although I must note that even as he experiences the resentment he is enough the observer of himself to be saddened by the pity of it all.

It turns out that the letter slips under the rug where it is retrieved by a servant who turns it over to Yusef who later uses it to blackmail Scobie into assisting in a smuggling operation, an event that adds to his growing self-loathing and despair. But he ends up binding himself even more tightly to Helen. For when he knocks on her door the next night, reluctantly, hoping that she will still be angry and will not want him, she is desperately thankful and he promises always to come if she wants him. Even more than this, she asks him to promise never to pay attention to her when she tells him to go away, and he does so "with a sense of despair, as though he were signing away the whole future" (p. 203). And still one further knot in the cord: "'If you hadn't come back . . . ' she said, and became lost in thought between the lamps. He could see her searching for herself, frowning in the effort to see where she could have been. . . . 'I don't know. Perhaps I'd have slutted with Bagster, or killed myself, or both. I think both" (pp. 203-4; author's ellipsis). To this he says, "'I'll always be here if you need me, as long as I'm alive,' which for him constituted an oath as ineffaceable as the vow [to his wife] at the Ealing altar" (p. 205).

When he gets home that night, there is a telegram from his wife: "*Have written am on my way home have been a fool stop love*—and then that name as formal as a seal" (p. 205). The timing is unfortunately melodramatic, but one must forgive Greene such things, as one does Dickens or Hardy, if one is to share in the riches he has to offer.

For a moment he lapses toward self-pity: "Why me . . . why do they need me—a dull, middle-aged police officer who has failed for promotion? I've got nothing to give them that they can't get elsewhere: why can't they leave me in peace?" (p. 206). Then he tries to pray, but the "Lord's Prayer lay as dead on his tongue as a legal document: it wasn't his daily bread that he wanted, but so much more. He wanted happiness for others and solitude and peace for himself" (p. 206). Suddenly he says aloud: "'I don't want to plan anymore. . . . They wouldn't need me if I were dead," and a few moments later lets a notion of suicide into his mind:

> The priests told you it was the unforgiveable sin, the final expression of an unrepentant despair, and of course one accepted the Church's teaching. But they taught also that God had sometimes broken his own laws, and was it more impossible for him to put out a hand of forgiveness into a suicidal darkness and chaos than to have woken himself in the tomb, behind the stone? Christ had not been murdered: you couldn't murder God: Christ had killed himself: he had hanged himself on the Cross. . . . (Pp. 206–7)

Upon first reading I think one notes in the commentary on Christ only the beginning of a rationalization that one fears might help clear the path toward self-destruction. Upon reflection, though, one may well be bothered by the pride involved in the analogy between himself and Christ, latent though it is.

When Louise returns, Scobie devotes himself to making her feel loved and wanted, and in this effort finally accedes to her request for him to go to mass and take Communion with her. This is a devastating step for him, for without real repentance about the adultery and an honest determination to stop it, such an act means damnation—taking his God in mortal sin. He sees this as much worse than the adultery itself, for as he tries to explain to an uncomprehending Helen: "There *is* a difference—a big difference. . . . *Now* I'm just putting our love above—well, my safety. But the other—the other's really evil. It's like the Black Mass, the man who steals the sacrament to desecrate it. It's striking God when he's down—in my power" (p. 232).

On the way to confession, he tries desperately to persuade himself, as he puts it, "to save my own soul and abandon her to Bagster and despair" or else to commit the "ordinary honest *wrong* answer: to leave Louise, forget that private vow, resign my job" (p. 234). Knowing he can do neither, he still enters the church, where he kneels and prays for a miracle: " 'O God, convince me, help me, convince me. Make me feel that I am more important than that child. . . . Make me put my own soul first. Give me trust in your mercy to the one I abandon' " (pp. 243-44). And just before entering the confessional he adds, " 'O God . . . if, instead, I should abandon you, punish me, but let the others get some happiness' " (p. 244).

There is no miracle. He confesses the adultery but cannot promise he will not see Helen alone again. He cannot even though upon his wife's return Helen had written him a note releasing him from his promise never to abandon her and ending, "My dear my dear leave me if you want to or have me as your hore [*sic*] if you want to." Even as the priest, Father Rank, is explaining as he already knows, that no one can forgive the uncontrite, he is capable of noticing the weariness of the priest and thinking, "What is the good of keeping him in this discomfort?" (p. 245). When he leaves the confessional, it seems to Scobie "that he had left for his exploration only the territory of despair" (pp. 245–46).

At mass the next morning, he feels immeasurably distant from the other celebrants and sees himself as worse than the priests at Black Mass who at least were performing the act of damnation with an emotion larger than human love—hate of God or devotion to Satan—whereas he "was desecrating God because he loved a woman—was it even love, or was it just a feeling of pity and responsibility?" (p. 248). Kneeling at the rail, he thinks again that only a miracle can save him, "but God would never work a miracle to save himself. I am the Cross, he thought: He will never speak the word to save Himself from the Cross, but if only wood were made so that it didn't feel, if only the nails were senseless as people believe" (p. 249). Just as Father Rank is approaching with the wafer, he makes one last attempt at prayer; " 'O God, I offer up my damnation to you. Take it. Use it for them,' and was aware of the pale papery taste of his eternal sentence on the tongue" (p. 250).

A few days later, Scobie is told he is to be promoted to commissioner, which, of course, makes his wife very happy. But Scobie feels only an increasing loneliness and despair and a sense that his whole personality has disintegrated from the deceptions in which he has become involved, a feeling that is heightened when he comes to be nearly certain that Ali, his servant of fifteen years whom he has loved and trusted, has begun to spy on him. His self-awareness and self-loathing are such that he tries to tell himself that he is "just trying to find a companion in this region of lies" (p. 255) and wonders whether the next stage for him will be the corruption of others. He comes to feel that he has "no shape left, nothing you could touch and say: This is Scobie" (p. 275). He feels that "even self-pity was denied him because he knew so exactly the extent of his guilt" (p. 262). He is deprived even of the satisfaction of feeling that his sacrifice has been good for Helen, for she remains bitter about his wife and his secrecy and refuses to accept that he too is suffering. He is human enough to shout angrily on one occasion, " 'The sacrifice isn't all on your side. . . . I've given up the future. I've damned myself' " (p. 258) and, when she continues to mock his belief in hell, to take her furiously by the wrists and say: " 'I believe. I tell you I believe I am damned for all eternity—unless a miracle happens. . . . What I've done is far worse than murder—that's an act, a blow, a stab, a shot: it's over and done, but I'm carrying my corruption around with me. It's the coating of my stomach. I can never void it. . . . Never pretend I haven't shown my love' " (p. 259). In a moment, though, his anger drains out and he says, " 'I can't bear to see suffering, and I cause it all the time.' "

In what some will find an admirable extension of compassion and some an absurd extension of pride, he continues to worry about the pain he is inflicting on God as well. Upon thinking of the repeated Communion services he will have to attend with his wife, he has a "sudden picture before his eyes of a bleeding face, of eyes closed by the continuous shower of blows: the punch-drunk head of God reeling sideways" (p. 264). And he sees himself striking God under the eye and watching "the bruised skin break," "watching God bleed" (p. 265). And throughout this period, without letting his motives rise to full consciousness, he sows some seeds for pretending he has angina, which he has learned from a doctor would lead to the possibility of a suicide that would fool the doctors and insurance companies.

His increasing weariness and despair allow him to say things to Yusef about his distrust of Ali, which leads to the murder of that once beloved servant, for which he then, and with some justice, feels responsible. The shock of this fills him with determination "to clean up whatever the cost. Life is going to start again: the nightmare of love is finished" (p. 278). And he sets off for Helen's hut with the full intention of saying a final good-bye. En route he encounters her walking down the road, so distracted that she has not seen the car. He runs after her, and when she turns "it was the face he had seen at Pende carried past him [on the stretcher]—defeated, broken, as ageless as a smashed glass" (p. 278). She tells him she has been looking for him, and then, insisting he not speak, she tells him sincerely and gallantly, yet unconsciously making clear in every sentence how devastating it will be for her, that she cannot go on ruining him anymore and that she is going away immediately. Had she been able to manage more stoically and briefly, it seems possible he for once would have allowed another to make the sacrifice, have shown himself capable of the humility that allows another to sometimes carry the burden, of being the saved and not the savior. But she is so pathetic in her childish bravery and goes on about it so long that it is hard to imagine anyone, much less Scobie, abandoning her.

At one point, as she is explaining why she is going on so long (" 'Don't speak, dear, I'm really being quite good, but I can't say these things to another living soul. In books there's always a confidant. But I haven't got a confidant. I must say them all at once' " [p. 281]), he thinks directly, "If I were dead, she would be free of me" (p. 281). And after her childish " 'Now, dear, I'm going to do it. Shut your eyes. Count three hundred slowly, and I won't be in sight. Turn the car quickly dear, and drive like hell. I don't want to hear you go. And I'll stop my ears. . . . ,' " he prays: "Oh God . . . kill me now, now. My God, you'll never have more complete contrition. What a mess I am. I carry suffering with me like a bloody smell. Kill me. Put an end to me. Vermin don't have to exterminate themselves. Kill me. Now. Now. Now. Before I hurt you again" (p. 281). Finally, neither of them can go through with the parting; but by the end of the scene, he has decided to kill himself.

That evening, as his wife is talking happily about giving a party on Christmas Eve and then going on to midnight mass, he looks "up at her with momentary hatred as she sat so cheerfully there, so smugly it seemed to him, arranging his further damnation. He was going to be Commissioner. She had what she wanted—her sort of success, everything was all right with her now" (p. 283). And he thinks:

> It was the hysterical woman who felt the world laughing behind her back that I loved. I love failure: I can't love success. And how successful she looks, sitting there: one of the saved—and he saw laid across that wide face like a news-screen the body of Ali . . . , the exhausted eyes of Helen, and all the faces of the lost, his companions in exile, the unrepentant thief, the soldier with the sponge. Thinking of what he had done and was going to do, he thought, with love, even God is a failure. (P. 284)

The hatred passes a moment later, however, when after pretending an angina attack he touches her to tell her not to worry about him and thinks "she wasn't so successful as all that: she would never be married to the Commissioner of Police" (p. 284). After she has gone to bed, he begins very carefully to doctor up his diary in such a way that the coroner and insurance inspectors will be convinced he died of angina. He is careful not only for his life insurance but because "the happiness of others had to be protected. It was not so easy to forget a suicide as a middle aged man's death from angina" (p. 288).

The most poignant and revealing moments toward the end of the book are his dialogues with God. After getting the doctor to give him the package of evipan he will use to kill himself, he goes to the church, where he sits far in the back. Knowing that no prayer was effective in a state of mortal sin, he watches two devout old women with "sad envy," and thinks this "was what human love had done to him—it had robbed him of love for eternity" (p. 288). And he goes on to the terrible thought that it "was no use pretending as a young man might that the price was worth while" (p. 288). But if "he couldn't pray he could at least talk," and here I must quote at length, for the passage is so rich in all the awarenesses and impulses that make Scobie the rich and perplexing character he is:

> O God, I am the only guilty one because I've known the answers all the time. I've preferred to give you pain rather than give pain to Helen or my wife because I can't observe your suffering. . . . I can only imagine it. But there are limits to what I can do to you—or them. I can't desert either of them while I'm alive, but I can die and remove myself from their blood-stream. . . . And you too, God—you are ill with me. . . . You'll be better off if you lose me once and for all. I know what I'm doing. I'm not pleading for mercy. I'm going to damn myself, whatever that means. I've longed for peace and I'm never going to know peace again. But you'll be at peace when I am out of your reach. . . .
>
> No one can speak a monologue for long alone: another voice will always make itself heard: . . . it spoke from the cave of his body: . . . You say you love me, and yet you'll do this to me—rob me of you forever. I made you with love. I've wept your tears. I've saved you from more than you will ever know. I planted in you this longing for peace only so that one day I could satisfy your longing and watch your happiness. And now you push me away, you put me out of your reach. Can't you trust me as you'd trust a faithful dog? I have been faithful to you for two thousand years. All you have to do now is ring a bell, go into a box, confess . . . the repentance is already there, straining at your heart. It's not repentance you lack, just a few simple actions: to go up to the Nissen hut and say good-bye. Or if you must, continue rejecting me but without lies anymore. Go to your house and say good-bye to your wife and live with your mistress. If you live you will come back to me sooner or later. One of them will suffer, but can't you trust me to see that the suffering isn't too great?
>
> The voice was silent in the cave and his own voice replied

> hopelessly: No. I don't trust you. I love you but I've never trusted you. If you made me, you made this feeling of responsibility that I've always carried about like a sack of bricks. . . . I can't shift my responsibility to you. . . . I can't make one of them suffer so as to save myself. I'm responsible and I'll see it through the only way I can. (Pp. 289-90)

Despite all this, there is a part of Scobie that very much does not want to die, an important perspective to consider when it comes to gauging the extent of his sacrifice and possible saintliness. Despite all his pain and unhappiness, the thought that he will never see or touch Helen again gives him "a constriction in his breast worse than any pain he had ever invented to [Doctor] Travis" (p. 294); and on the night he has determined to kill himself, when bedtime came "he felt a terrible unwillingness to let his wife go [to bed]. There was nothing to do when she had once gone but die" (p. 295). A voice within him cries out: "Nothing, nobody, can force me to die"; and he prays, "Oh God . . . help me to leave you" (p. 296). To delay the moment, he asks his wife to read to him and watches her with a "hungry absorption of what he was never going to see again," the "graying hair, the line of nerves upon the face, the thickening body" holding him "as her beauty never had" (p. 296). When he has forced himself to say his final goodnight without any demonstrations that would arouse her suspicion and she has gone upstairs he sits with the fatal dose of evipan "like seeds in the palm of his hand" as a voice says to him:

> Throw away the tablets. You'll never be able to collect enough again. You'll be saved. Give up play-acting. Mount the stairs to bed and have a good night's sleep. In the morning you'll be woken by your boy, and you'll drive down to the police station for a day's ordinary work. The voice dwelt on the word "ordinary" as it might have dwelt on the word "happy" or "peaceful". (Pp. 297–98)

He answers himself aloud, "No," and downs the tablets six at a time. He starts an entry in his diary and breaks it off abruptly as though he had been stopped by a heart attack and sits bolt upright waiting for death. He tries to pray, "but the

Hail Mary evaded his memory." Then he tries an Act of Contrition, "but when he reached, 'I am sorry and beg pardon,' a cloud formed over the door and drifted down over the whole room and he couldn't remember what it was that he had to be sorry for" (p. 298). The cloud grows into what seems a storm to him, and he is taken from us thus:

> It seemed to him as though someone outside the room were seeking him, calling him, and he made a last great effort to indicate that he was here. He got on his feet and heard the hammer of his heart beating out a reply. He had a message to convey, but the darkness and the storm drove it back within the case of his breast, and all the time outside the house, outside the world that drummed like hammer blows within his ear, someone wandered, seeking to get in, someone appealing for help, someone in need of him. And automatically at the call of need, at the cry of a victim, Scobie strung himself to act. He dredged his consciousness up from an infinite distance in order to make some reply. He said aloud, "Dear God, I love . . . " but the effort was too great and he did not feel his body when it struck the floor or hear the small tinkle of the medal as it span like a coin under the ice-box—the saint whose name nobody could remember. (Pp. 298–99; author's ellipsis)

That saint in the final sentence, strictly speaking, is the one on the holy medal given him by the Portuguese sea captain he had taken pity on, "a very obscure saint" whose name the captain does not remember. But set off as it is at the end of the sentence and chapter, one must also, if one does not already, wonder about the extent to which that strange label belongs to Scobie.

Let me be careful to follow the book though, for Greene leaves that issue dangling and hurries to the questions that we, and Scobie too, would most like answered. Was the suicide discovered? Did his death accomplish what he hoped it would? Officially the death is classified as due to *angina pectoris* and one presumes will remain so. But a young man who had become infatuated with Louise discovers discrepancies in the colors of the ink and tells her that Scobie had doctored up his diary. Before learning this, Louise had said, " 'It's odd how easily I can talk about him . . . now that he's gone. Yet I did love him, Wilson. I did love him, but he seems so very very gone' " (p. 301). And she also tells Wilson that she had known about Helen all along: " 'It's why I came home. Mrs. Carter wrote to me. She said everybody was talking. Of course he never realized that. He thought he'd been so clever. And he nearly convinced me—that it was finished. Going to Communion the way he did' " (p. 301). Greene is very hard on Louise here, for he has her go on to answer Wilson's query about how he squared that with his conscience with a glib: " 'Some Catholics do, I suppose. Go to Confession and start over again. I thought he was more honest, though. When a man's dead, one begins to find out' " (p. 301). And when Wilson tells her that he took money from Yusef (for *her* passage, we remember), she says, " 'I can believe that now' " (p. 301). A moment later—it is three days after the funeral—Wilson, who is in fact a secret agent, says, " 'I'm straight, Louise. I love you' " (p. 301) and the two "didn't kiss: it was too soon for that, but they sat in the hollow room, holding hands, listening to the vultures clambering on the iron roof" (p. 302). The ironies are heavy and ugly, and perhaps overdone, but I think Scobie would feel that he had accomplished one of his ends insofar as his wife's suffering is hardly very acute. When Wilson discovers the altered diary and begins to speculate, she interrupts him with horror: " 'Oh no, he couldn't have done that. After all, in spite of everything, he *was* a Catholic' " (p. 302). At this Greene breaks off and turns to Helen, who is returning from the beach with Bagster where they have already had four drinks.

When he begs to come in, she says, " 'All right,' " for there "seemed to be no reason so far as she could see to deny anyone anything anymore for ever" (p. 303). And when he moves her toward the bed for what he calls a "prang," she thinks: " 'Why not . . . if he wants it. Bagster is as good as anyone else. There's nobody in the world I love, and out of it doesn't count' " (p. 303; author's ellipsis). She lies back "mutely" on the bed and shuts her eyes: "I'm alone, she thought, without self-pity, stating it as an explorer might after his companions have died from exposure" (p. 303).

When he notes her lack of enthusiasm and asks if she does not love him a little, she answers that she does not love anyone; and upon his accusation that she loved Scobie, for which he apologizes quickly, she repeats that she does not love anyone. " 'You can't love the dead, can you? They don't exist, do they? It would be like loving the dodo, wouldn't it?' questioning him as if she expected an answer, even from Bagster. She kept her eyes shut because in the dark she felt nearer to death, the death which had absorbed him" (p. 304).

Bagster is decent enough not to persist, for which she feels relieved, though she agrees to see him tomorrow. As he is leaving, she asks him whether he believes in a god. To his " 'Oh, well, I suppose so,' " she responds " 'I wish I did. . . . I wish I did.' " When he has gone we are given this final view of her:

> She was alone again in the darkness behind her lids, and the wish struggled in her body like a child: her lips moved, but all she could think of to say was, "For ever and ever, Amen. . . . " The rest she had forgotten. She put her hand out beside her and touched the other pillow, as though perhaps after all there was one chance in a thousand that she was not alone, and if she were not alone now she would never be alone again. (P. 304; author's ellipsis)

It is difficult to decide from this the extent to which we and Scobie should be content to find her in no greater pain than this, especially in view of the ambiguities in that final paragraph. I take some hope from that wish to believe which is struggling in her body like a child, and I think that "one chance in a thousand" of never being alone again refers as much to the possibility of her finding a god as finding Scobie still beside her.

The book ends with a short conversation between Louise and Father Rank, to whom Greene has earlier given the sort of credentials that should make us seriously attentive to what he has to say. When she asks him drearily whether he hasn't any comfort to give her, he answers: " 'You've been given an awful lot of comfort in your life, Mrs. Scobie. If what Wilson thinks is true, it's he [Scobie] who needs our comfort' " (p.

305). And in answer to her question whether he knows all that she knows about him, he responds: " 'Of course I don't. . . . A priest only knows the unimportant things,' " and to her puzzlement adds impatiently, " 'Oh, I mean the sins. . . . A man doesn't come to us and confess his virtues' " (p. 305). When she asks if he knew about Mrs. Rolt [Helen], he responds, " 'Poor woman.' " The conversation goes on as follows until the end of the book:

> "I don't see why."
> "I'm sorry for anyone happy and ignorant who gets mixed up in that way with one of us."
> "He was a bad Catholic."
> "That's the silliest phrase in common use," Father Rank said.
> "And at the end, this—horror. He must have known that he was damning himself."
> "Yes, he knew that all right. He never had any trust in mercy—except for other people."
> It's no good even praying . . . "
> Father Rank clapped the cover of the diary to and said, furiously, "For goodness' sake, Mrs. Scobie, don't imagine you—or I—know a thing about God's mercy."
> "The church says . . . "
> "I know the church says. The Church knows all the rules. But it doesn't know what goes on in a single human heart."
> "You think there's some hope then?" she wearily asked.
> "Are you so bitter against him?"
> "I haven't any bitterness left."
> "And do you think God's likely to be more bitter than a woman?" he said with harsh insistence, but she winced away from the arguments of hope.
> "Oh why, why, did he have to make such a mess of things?"
> Father Rank said, "It may seem an odd thing to say—when a man's as wrong as he was—but I think, from what I saw of him, that he really loved God."
> She had denied just now that she felt any bitterness, but a little more of it drained out now like tears from exhausted ducts. "He certainly loved no one else," she said.
> "And you may be in the right of it there, too," Father Rank replied. (Pp. 305-6; author's ellipses)

As respectful readers, we must, of course, accept Father Rank's remark as the last word and give it appropriate weight. But I am unwilling to take it as the final and ultimate word about so complex a consciousness and heart as Scobie's, if indeed any human, no matter how simple, does not deserve more than one such word. Perhaps because he judged himself so continuously and harshly I have a peculiarly strong aversion to judging him at all. I hope his God will feel the same way. I wish sometimes the book had ended with his death—with that last automatic dredging up of his consciousness "at the call of need, at the cry of a victim" (p. 299). Then it would be easier, for a while at least, simply to admire and pity and be moved by him, to rest for a while in the awe of contemplating someone who deliberately chooses what he believes is eternal damnation in an effort to reduce the suffering of others. For whatever his other motives, however great his self-deception, it is only that motive which permits him to take his life.

But by ending as he has with the issue of Scobie's relative love for God and man, Greene has thrown so deliberate a gauntlet, one cannot ignore it entirely, even though it could with equal justice be termed a curved ball one is entitled to duck and even though a merely moderate pursuit of the challenge leads to moral and religious conundrums whose subtleties could nourish whole armies of Scholastic philosophers. Setting aside for a moment the relation between love of God and love of man, I would be willing to accept the notion that he loved no one but God provided it was understood that the no one else included himself and that the definition of "love" implied is not the only one possible. I would agree that his degree of condescension, his inability except at rare moments to see the other in terms apart from those defined by his pity and sense of responsibility, his unwillingness to let them make sacrifices and choices or to carry the burdens, his willingness to pretend and to lie to them, in short, his essential failure to respect them, to say nothing of his own frequent acknowledgement that he feels pity rather than love, are not compatible with any relation we should easily or usefully call "love." I know I do not want to be loved that way. But I believe also, as Scobie sometimes does and Greene perhaps does, that the quality of his response to ugliness and failure is of an order that can hold the word "love." At least I do not resist when I read about him watching Louise sleeping, her face with "the yellow-ivory tinge of atabrine," her hair "dark and stringy with sweat," and am told these "were the times of ugliness when he loved her, when pity and responsibility reached the intensity of a passion" (p. 16). Nor when he thinks that

> people said you couldn't love two women, but what was this emotion if it were not love? This hungry absorption of what he was never going to see again? The greying hair, the line of nerves upon the face, the thickening body, held him as her beauty never had. She hadn't put on her mosquito boots, and her slippers were badly in need of mending. It isn't beauty that we love, he thought, it's failure—the failure to stay young forever, the failure of nerves, the failure of the body. Beauty is like success: we can't love it for long. He felt a terrible desire to protect—but that's what I'm going to do, I am going to protect her from myself forever. (P. 296)

Suppose one had an ugly and sickly child. It might be better to behave in such a way as to help the child learn independence and self-respect. But would it not be love if one wished desperately to protect it from realities, about both itself and oneself. Apart from considering the *quality* of his response to failure, I would want to ask whether there is not a degree of caring, regardless of how destructive or wrongheaded, that is entitled to be called "love," and to suggest that Scobie's caring may be of that order.

With respect to the relation between Scobie's love for God and love for man, or anyone's, or with respect to the meaning of such terms, it is hard to imagine saying anything that is not pompous, silly, or embarrassing, which is no doubt why Greene gave that commentary entirely over to his characters. And it is no doubt why I want to begin by letting another speak the most simpleminded reconciliation of the two. It is not a formulation that Father Rank or Scobie or Greene would accept. Nor can I really accept it, though neither can I reject it. The formulation is Leigh Hunt's, and my mother used to recite it to me as she gave me my bath when I was a very little child.

Abou Ben Adhem (may his tribe increase!)
Awoke one night from a deep dream of peace,
And saw, within the moonlight of his room,
Making it rich, and like a lily in bloom,
An angel writing in a book of gold:—
Exceeding peace had made Ben Adhem bold,
And to the presence in the room he said,
"What writest thou?"—The vision rais'd its head,
And with a look made all of sweet accord,
Answer'd, "The names of those who love the Lord."
"And is mine one?" said Abou. "Nay, not so,"
Replied the angel. Abou spoke more low,
But cheerly still; and said, "I pray thee, then,
Write me as one that loves his fellow men."
The angel wrote, and vanish'd. The next night
It came again with a great wakening light,
And show'd the names whom love of God had blest,
And lo! Ben Adhem's name led all the rest.

I do not think I ever asked my mother exactly what was meant by love of fellow men or how Abou Ben Adhem showed his, and I do not think she ever told me; nor had either of us yet been taught to distrust anyone who could speak of himself without ironic self-awareness as possessing such a love. That warm bath of water and sentiment washed easily together.

Scobie views himself most often as one who has chosen love of man (or women) over love of God ("This is what human love had done to him—it had robbed him of love for eternity" [p. 288]); or, to be more accurate, he believes that what he is obligated to do from love of humans is opposed to what he believes are his obligations to God. "He was desecrating God because he loved a woman—was it even love, or was it just a feeling of pity and responsibility" (p. 248). He thinks, "O God, I can't leave her. Or Louise. You don't need me as they need me. You have your good people, your Saints, and all the company of the blessed" (pp. 259–60).

Father Rank, of course, is suggesting somewhat the reverse of this; and though he does not go quite so far as to suggest that Scobie's love of God approaches that of a saint, the book as a whole forces us to look at him in such a light. I am not thinking only of the explicit connection made as he dies with the saint whose name no one remembered, but of the fervor with which he believes in his own unworthiness and sinfulness in God's eyes and his absolute acquiescence in what he believes will be his just punishment. He is saintlike in the frequency and degree of his self-laceration and in his renunciation of many of the usual claims of self. And in the degree of his compassion for the unattractive and unfit. Helen and Louise are not quite lepers, but they are among the outcasts: "It was the face for which nobody would go out of the way . . . the face which would soon be used to rebuffs and indifference, that demanded his allegiance" (p. 172). He loves the town in which he works because all the sores of injustice, cruelty, and meanness are exposed. He is saintlike in his sense of life as a spiritual test and the extent to which he yearns for peace. At one point, quite early in the book, even before he is much trapped by complications, it seems to him "that life was immeasurably long. Couldn't the test of man have been carried out in fewer years? Couldn't we have committed our first major sin at seven, have ruined ourselves for love or hate at ten, have clutched at redemption on a fifteen-year-old deathbed" (p. 52). And finally, he seems saintlike, to me at least, in that strange combination of pride which makes him feel he must be much better than other people, and humility, which makes him quite certain he is worse. It is paradoxical, of course, to speak so of one who could not even be buried in consecrated ground, much less be canonized, were the truth known about either his life or death. But these are paradoxes that Greene clearly delights in and are the kinds of paradoxes that have been welcomed by many with a deep devotion to the spirit rather than the letter of Christian faith.

I do not want to add paradox to paradox, but I cannot leave the question of Scobie's allegiance to God or man without turning to another formulation of the issue, one by which Scobie emerges in a different though not quite contradictory light. The formulation is the one George Orwell erects in his "Reflections on Gandhi." That essay begins with the provocative pronouncement that "Saints should always be judged guilty until they are proved innocent"[5] and goes on to develop a dichotomy between the human and the saintly in which saintliness is defined largely in Gandhi's terms as requiring a disciplined asceticism and a rejection of individual loyalties and loves, both sexual and spiritual, in favor of a love for God or humanity as a whole. Orwell grants that the saintly attitude is "perhaps a noble one," but also terms it "inhuman." "The essence of being human," he insists, "is that one does not seek perfection, that one *is* sometimes willing to commit sins for the sake of loyalty, that one does not push asceticism to the point where it makes friendly intercourse impossible, and that one is prepared in the end to be defeated and broken up by life, which is the inevitable price of fastening one's love upon other human individuals" (p. 182). Given such a division, Scobie would seem to fall onto the human side, for surely few have been more defeated and broken up by life as a result of individual human attachments. Scobie's special difficulty, and special quality, is that he also seeks perfection and measures himself with the kind of yardstick normally used by saints.

Orwell continues by arguing that we should not too readily assume that most people reject the ideals of saintliness because they are too difficult, "in other words, that the average human being is a failed saint" (p. 183). He believes that many people "genuinely do not wish to be saints" and thinks it probable that "some who achieve or aspire to sainthood have never felt much temptation to be human beings." Finally he insists that the two ideals are "incompatible. One must choose between God and Man" (p. 183). Poor Scobie's plight can perhaps most sympathetically be understood if we see him as one who is seriously beset by both temptations, and despite his own belief in the incompatibility of the two ideals, and his certainty that he has made a choice between God and Man, one who has chosen both.

But Scobie has already suffered too much for me to want to go on stretching him out on the rack of these divisions. Let me give him one last bruise and then try to bandage him a little. In a recent introduction to the novel, Greene asserts that it has not successfully conveyed his real intentions. He says that he "had meant the story of Scobie to enlarge a theme I had touched on in *The Ministry of Fear*, the disastrous effect on human beings of pity as distinct from compassion," that the "character of Scobie was intended to show that pity can be the expression of an almost monstrous pride," and that "the particular motive of his suicide, to save even God from himself, was the final twist of his inordinate pride. Perhaps Scobie should have been a subject for cruel comedy rather than for tragedy."[6] I think we must acknowledge that Scobie does exhibit a quite monstrous pride: in his certainty that he must be the responsible, pitying, and self-sacrificial one, in the extent of his concern with his own worthiness, and above all, in his sense of himself as a kind of moral and rhetorical adversary of God and sometimes even as a pitier of God. And I think it is almost fair to characterize his concern for others as pity rather than compassion. But I would note immediately that there is almost never any scorn in his pity, that his concern with his own worthiness is nearly always related to the plight of others, that his distance from the suffering is rarely such as to permit only what Greene elsewhere calls "a formal compassion,"[7] and that the God who governs the world Scobie inhabits seems to manage things and psyches in such a way as to demand an adversary. One need not go so far as to share Bertrand Russell's vision of all mankind adrift on the seas of an indifferent universe to share with Scobie some difficulty in trusting to the mercy of the God who has presumably watched over that lifeboat in which the widowed Helen and orphaned child drifted for forty days. And though I do not think it excuses the pride, we should be aware that Scobie is not full of pride, not puffed up with it. He is not a proud man. Even after we have finished the book and seen the full extent of his presumption, I think we can still see in him the same man that Greene presents as he goes to sleep at Pende on the night before the lifeboat survivors arrive. He is described as praying out of habit:

> He said the Our Father, the Hail Mary, and then, as sleep began to clog his lids, he added an Act of Contrition. It was a formality

> not because he felt himself free from serious sin but because it had never occurred to him that his life was important enough one way or the other. He didn't drink, he didn't fornicate, he didn't even lie, but he never regarded this absence of sin as virtue. When he thought about it at all, he regarded himself as a man in the ranks, the member of an awkward squad, who had no opportunity to break the more serious military rules. "I missed Mass yesterday for insufficient reason. I neglected my evening prayers." This was no more than admitting what every soldier did—that he had avoided a fatigue when the occasion offered. "O God, bless—" but before he could mention names he was asleep. (Pp. 118–19)

Is it too paradoxical to say that Scobie is afflicted with a self-deflating pride?

On Scobie's behalf I would also note how little pleasure he takes in his feelings of guilt and self-loathing, how little sense of self-exaltation as he prepares his self-sacrifice. It is true that after he secures the evipan we are told that the "solemnity of the crime lay over his mind almost like happiness"; but that is momentary and occurs chiefly because "it was action at last—he had fumbled and muddled too long" (p. 288). And there is some self-indulgence and love of his own failure as well as pride in his extended dialogues with God. But it is minimal—only a touch now and again of that condition which Baudelaire describes as produced by hashish but which is easily achieved without it, in which "remorse, that odd ingredient of pleasure, is soon drowned in the delicious contemplation of remorse, in a sort of voluptuous self-analysis" and in which the moral drunkard "admires his remorse" and "glories in himself."[8] And none at all of the passionate longing for suffering of the sort reported about the founder of the Sacred Heart order whose "love of pain and suffering was insatiable."

> "She said that she could cheerfully live till the day of judgment, provided she might always have matter for suffering for God; but that to live for a single day without suffering would be intolerable. She said again that she was devoured by two unassuageable fevers, one for the holy communion, the other for suffering, humiliation, and annihilation. 'Nothing but pain,' she continually said in her letters, "makes my life supportable.' "[9]

Mostly what Scobie experiences toward the end is only pain, loneliness, and a sense of loss.

In his behalf also, I would note that he is almost never self-righteous and has none of that anger at injustice which compels a Swift, Conrad, or Nathanael West toward cruelties of his own. And though he cannot stand to watch suffering, his pity never turns to rage as does Miss Lonelyhearts' when he beats to death the frog he has accidently stepped on or when he twists the arm of the old homosexual, "twisting the arm of all the sick and miserable, broken and betrayed, inarticulate and impotent" (p. 18) His immoderate compassion is not, as Conrad says of Stevie Verloc, "succeeded by the pain of an innocent but pitiless rage" (*SA,* p. 144).

He does resemble Stevie though, in the extent to which his pity is automatic and irresistible. And at the risk of generating a snicker, I want even to suggest that we can view Scobie's initial sexual relation with Helen as arising not so much from lust as from the same "tenderness to all pain and all misery" that leads Stevie in his "desire to make the horse happy and the cabman happy" to the "point of a bizarre longing to take them in bed with him" (*SA*, p. 143) to be comforted as he had been comforted as a child.

Finally, I want to return to my earlier wish to rest in the awesomeness of his sacrifice. For no matter what the balance of pride and humility, no matter what the mix of adjunct motives, regardless of the effectiveness of the sacrifice, when all else has been said, it is awesome to contemplate someone who has chosen eternal damnation in the effort to reduce the suffering of others. That Scobie does not believe in flames and torment does not reduce the awesomeness; for what he does believe he is giving up forever is peace, and it is peace for which he has most longed throughout his life.

It is odd that Scobie remains for me such a haunting figure because the book is in some ways such an obviously manipulative one. The scenes and characters seem shaped toward their ends with nearly the tidiness and clarity of the novels that Greene calls his "entertainments." At moments (though only at moments for me), one feels that Scobie behaves as he does not so much from the necessities of his character as from Greene's determination to organize his destruction. The reason Scobie and the book transcend all this for me, I suspect, is that the truth of Scobie is validated by Greene's own pity, which like Scobie's is a terrible automatic and promiscuous passion that infects as well as ennobles him and his writing. It is what allows Greene to begin a chapter "The sirens were wailing for a total blackout, wailing through the rain which fell in interminable tears" (p. 141) or to drench us in the pathos of Scobie's continuing to wiggle the ears of his handkerchief rabbit for the orphaned child after the child is dead. But it is also what allows him to produce Scobie's consciousness with a fervor that attests to its truth. In retrospect, or in conscious intention, Greene may have thought he was writing a story about the ugliness of pride. In fact, he not only shares Scobie's compassion for all those whom Scobie pities, but pities Scobie as well. And despite his momentary pleasure at the end in a ventriloquism that distances us into an intellectual consideration of Scobie's relative love for man and God, the book forces—not urges, *forces*—us too to read with a similar compassion.

How we finally evaluate such compassion—by Scobie, by Greene, by us—relates to how much we believe in the possibility, value, and efficacy of the kind of perception Scobie rarely retained with respect to either his wife or Helen, the perception that "she was someone of human stature with her own sense of responsibility, not simply the object of his care and kindness" (p. 97). This, God help us, belongs to some larger mysteries of self and other, to which we shall be turning later.

I am unable to resist, however, a final note—a note whose ugliness warns how difficult it should be to settle upon a fitting view of those like Scobie who too easily make us the objects of their compassion, far more difficult than is comprehended by most current psycho-moral pieties. The note is a remark made by an uncle of the young boy in Agee's *The Morning Watch*. He mouths thus of the Christ whose agony Richard is trying so desperately to apprehend: " 'Well who *asked* him to die for me? *I* didn't. He needn't try and collect on the debt . . . because there's no debt, far's I'm concerned' " (p. 113).

V ❖ Heights and Depths of Distance

In juxtaposition to these individual people and vantage points, I wish now to place some larger visions, some distances, mostly heights, from which some have sought to view the scenes that so torment the Stevies, Miss Lonelyhearts, and Major Scobies of the world and of one's own heart. I choose them not because they provide a just or adequate sampling of such possibilities (if such a thing can be imagined) but because they are the ones that have most figured in my own debate. I will not even pretend to be fair to some of them.

The first vantage point is the one within whose wadding Friedrich Nietzsche sought to nurture his vision of superman and his dream of a nobler race. Here are some of his thoughts about pity, that "promiscuous passion" which governed Scobie's life:

> Christianity is called the religion of *pity*. Pity stands opposed to the tonic emotions which heighten our vitality; it has a depressing effect. We are deprived of strength when we feel pity. That loss of strength which suffering as such inflicts on life is further increased and multiplied by pity. Pity makes suffering contagious. . . .
>
> It preserves what is ripe for destruction; it defends those who have been disinherited and condemned by life; and by the abundance of the failures of all kinds which it keeps alive, it gives life itself a gloomy and questionable aspect.

And he goes on to argue that "this depressive and contagious instinct" is finally "nihilistic," a "hostility against life." "In our whole unhealthy modernity there is nothing more unhealthy than Christian pity."[1]

Health and "life" for Nietzsche involve an exercise of "the will to power," over self and others, and a joy in the struggle for such mastery and even in the suffering it may entail. They require not only the suppression of pity but a deliberate preservation and enforcement of distance.

> Every heightening of the type "man" hitherto has been the work of an aristocratic society—and thus it will always be; a society which believes in a long ladder of rank order and value differences in men, which needs slavery in some sense. Without the *pathos of distance* as it grows out of deep-seated differences of caste, out of the constant view, the downward view, that the ruling caste gets out of its subordinates and tools, out of its equally constant exercise in obeying and commanding, in keeping apart and keeping a distance—without this pathos of distance there could not grow that other more mysterious pathos, that longing for ever greater distances within the soul itself, the evolving of ever higher, rarer, more spacious, more widely arched, more comprehensive states—in short: the heightening of the type "man," the continued "self mastery of man," to take a moral formula in a supra-moral sense.[2]

Occasionally Nietzsche permits himself a begrudging concession to conventional morality or even to charitable action; but almost as though he literally feared its contagion, he quickly retreats. Thus:

> To refrain from wounding, violating, and exploiting one another, to acknowledge another's will as equal to one's own: this can become proper behavior, in a certain coarse sense, between individuals when the conditions for making it possible obtain (namely the factual similarity of the individuals as to power and standards of value, and their existence in one greater body). But as soon as one wants to extend this principle, to make it the *basic principle of society,* it shows itself for what it is: the will to negate life, the principle of dissolution and decay. Here one must think radically to the very roots of things and ward off all weakness of sensibility.[3]

Or again:

> The distinguished man, too, helps the unhappy, but not—at least not mainly—from compassion, but more from an internal pressure that has been built up by an excess of power. The distinguished man honors himself in the mighty, including those who have power over themselves; those who know when to talk and when to keep silent; those who take delight in being rigorous and hard with themselves and who have respect for anything rigorous and hard. "Wotan placed a hard heart in my breast," says an old Scandinavian saga: this is the proper poetic expression for the soul of a proud Viking. Such a type of man is proud *not* to have been made for compassion; hence the hero of the saga adds a

> warning: "Whoever has not a hard heart when young will never get it at all." Distinguished and courageous men with such thoughts are at the opposite end from that morality which sees the characteristic function of morality in pity or in doing for others or désinteréssement. Belief in oneself, pride in oneself, basic hostility and irony against "selflessness" is as sure a part of distinguished morality as an easy disdain and cautious attitude toward the fellow-feelings and the "warm heart."[4]

To all those passages and to much of Nietzsche's writing, I have an immediate and compelling response that had better come out at once: I want to cry out, "Bullshit!" That is not an adequate response, but I think it comes directly from a part of me that is sometimes worth attending to and that I would be tempted to call my soul if I were not upset at the notion that my soul would use such language. That response also has the virtue of carrying with it some of the ugliness that goes with pride and mastery and easy disdain once they are removed from the rhetorical distance at which Nietzsche places them. For it is largely that rhetorical distance which allows Nietzsche to think and say such things and which gives them what power or plausibility they possess.

It is easy enough to refute Nietzsche's logic and his historical and scientific accuracy, and plenty of critics have done so. There is no need to add to that chorus. Nor does the ultimate validity or invalidity of his vision rest on such issues.

In some ways it is an attractive vision. There is surely something in nearly all of us that responds to the idea of nobility, strength, and self-mastery and to figures who possess those qualities in some marked degree. There cannot be many people who do not admire at least some figure who embodies the Nietzschean virtues whether it be Achilles, Antigone, Caesar, a de Medici, Joan of Arc, Frederick the Great, D'Artagnon, Napoleon, Thoreau, Goethe, Wyatt Earp, John F. Kennedy, Charles de Gaulle, Humphrey Bogart, John Wayne, or Joe Louis, though I suspect Nietzsche would be hesitant to admit all of those to his own category of distinguished men. The weak and unfit are not usually very attractive either in body or spirit, and those who make claims on our pity are, in fact, often quite pitiful.

Healthy young aristocrats look better than lepers, lions are more inspiring than mice, and eagles have more appeal than buzzards, although dolphins and deer have their gentle distinction. It is nice sometimes to imagine a world of brave Viking warriors sailing in their graceful ships on lonely seas or a world of strong and noble spirits questing for ever greater freedom through mastery of their own weaknesses. Despite some tone of scorn here that I cannot quite master, I do mean to say that the dream or wish that Nietzsche offers has a certain power and beauty and that nobility is a serious virtue. He is also right about some of the destructive aspects of pity, especially its tendency to nurture mediocrity and failure; and he is right about some kinship between softness, timidity, cowardice and corruption, and between Christianity and the negation of the life of this world. Christianity *has* often called for the suppression of vital natural instincts and looked toward death as the only door to salvation. Christianity *has* worshiped the broken Christ over the rebellious leader.

Whatever its truth or attractiveness, however, I must return to my original comment: "Bullshit!"; for Nietzsche's is a vision that turns to nonsense the moment one steps down from his cloud of rhetorical abstraction and looks either at the actualities of human history or at the world of living creatures around one. I am not thinking so much of the vain and pompous, often hysterical little men like Caligula, Napoleon, or Hitler—or even our own General Patton, Richard Nixon's favorite hero—for any ideals can be misrepresented or perverted. The difficulty is that I can find scarcely any significant embodiments for his words. Whether I look at the overall course of history or the contemporary world or my own world of friends and acquaintances I can find no natural correlation between the will to power and the nobility of spirit that he celebrates. For every instance where such a will is accompanied by an austere or graceful masterfulness and pride, there are dozens where it is accompanied by, and seems to breed, pettiness, pomposity, obesity, gluttony, smugness, garrulousness, sickliness, suspiciousness, petulance, or general niggardliness of spirit, either individually or in combination. If I think of Lindbergh, I must think of Howard Hughes even if I forget Charles Manson and Leopold and Loeb. For every Churchill and de Gaulle, how many Stalins, Battistas, Francos, King Farouks, Idi Amins, Arafats and Begins nursing their vanities or paranoias. Oddly, a number of the towering figures who come closest in some respects to a Nietzschean ideal seem driven largely by a totally un-Nietzschean concern for their more humble fellows. I am thinking of Lincoln, Mao Tse Tung, and Fidel Castro, though the latter can hardly be said to "know when to keep silent." In preference to most Nietzschean supermen, I will choose Scobie, perhaps even poor Stevie Verloc. (Poor unfit Stevie, who was blown to bits by explosives manufactured by an embittered and sickly little man who regards himself as a kind of superman and who nurses his pitiful ego by walking about wired to a bomb and spouting ideas that can easily descend from Nietzsche. The weak are "the source of all evil," he says, and should "be taken in hand for utter extermination. . . . They are our sinister masters—the weak, the flabby, the silly, the cowardly, the faint of heart, the slavish of mind. . . . Theirs is the kingdom of the earth. Exterminate; exterminate! That is the only way of progress" [p. 246].)

For better or worse, the human animal does not in actual life develop in accord with Nietzschean theory. The exercise of courage and self-mastery and the rejection of compassion do not necessarily breed continued nobility of spirit. It is not even true, as General MacArthur said, that "old soldiers never die, they merely fade away." They are as likely to rot or turn to stone. Poor Nietzsche himself became hopelessly insane. Even Hemingway, who tried so very well and long to be strong, never could win his battle against anger and self-pity and blew his head off with very little grace at the end. And though I would not want to minimize the achievement of Goethe or equate him entirely with the figure of Aschenbach in "Death in Venice," Mann's tracing of the dissolution of the latter is an accurate and instructive account of the kind of revenge the mind and heart are likely to take when their owners have tried to be eagles rather than men. The analogy is not quite fair to Goethe, of course, who often felt and advocated a totally un-Nietzschean humanitarianism and who celebrated a state of mind where one "feels the happiness or the woe of a neighboring people as though it were his own."[5] Yet earlier in the same passage, there is an oddly disturbing and revealing note:

> The poet will love as man and citizen his native land, but the country of his poetic powers and his poetic work is the good, the noble, and the beautiful, which is bound to no particular province and to no particular land, and which he seizes and works upon wherever he finds it. In this he is like the eagle, who flies with free glance over every land, and to whom it makes no difference whether the hare on which he descends, dwells in Prussia or in Saxony.

What a strange confusion of men and eagles in the distance of that rhetorical flight, to say nothing of the poor hare, carried off to be torn and eaten in that realm of "the good, the noble, and the beautiful." And poor eagle, too, perhaps a more endangered species in the world of rhetoric than the one of hunters, co-opted also into the Boy Scouts and both the iconography and dollar bills of the United States, whose Congress saw fit to elect it to the office of national bird.

I am not sure I would like to abolish all eagle emblems and metaphors or denounce entirely all human impulses toward eaglehood. I even believe with Melville's Ishmael that

> there is a Catskill eagle in some souls that can alike dive down into the blackest gorges, and soar out of them again and become invisible in the sunny spaces. And even if he forever flies within the gorge, that gorge is in the mountains; so that even in his lowest swoop the mountain eagle is still higher than other birds upon the plain, even though they soar.[6]

But I would like to weigh down all such flights with some elephantine propositions:

1. Men are not eagles. Eagles are not men.
2. Eagles do not think and write about their lonely grandeur or their "will to power."

3. Eagles do not seem to have to resist any impulses to pity when they seize their prey. They are not hardhearted. They never even thought of inventing Christianity.
4. Eagles do not eat more than they need to. Nor do eagles use other hungrier or less able eagles to gather and cook their dinners. They do not go in for slavery, serfdom, or sharecropping, and none are reported to have said either "eagles cannot live by bread alone" or "let them eat cake." Some species of eagles might hover over those exploded Ethiopians and their horses waiting for a bite to eat, but none of them would have likened the explosion to a rose or been amused.
5. When eagles fly too close to the sun, the wax does not melt from their wings and they do not fall into the sea like Icarus. If one did fall into the sea, the others would not put it in a painting or write a poem about it.
6. Men do not have wings.
7. When men actually do fly, they are usually encased in metal that armors them from both the earth and sky. Occasionally they fly for fun. Most often they fly to overcome distance without experiencing it. Often they fly in order to crush the life beneath them without having to see, hear, touch or eat it.

I do not suppose anything I have said would give Nietzsche much pause, for it cannot penetrate his drama, which is peopled not by men or women or eagles but only by the collisions of passionate phrases and the flights of emotional freight. It may not be fair to hold him responsible, as some have done, for the atrocities of his compatriots who developed "the final solution" to the problem of fitness; but the survival of the fittest inevitably entails some kind of extermination of the unfit, an event that espousers of fitness have always found it easy to overlook, and not terribly difficult to oversee.

❖

A more interesting form of distance and of what looks at first like wadding or deafness is the one adopted by Robinson Jeffers. Even more than Nietzsche, by whose writings he was much influenced and impressed, he finds humankind a contemptible species, a blot or stain on the natural order, especially in its collective behavior, and he often insists the only cure for it would be extermination. Here is one of his portraits of us, in a poem he calls "Original Sin."

> The man-brained and man-handed ground-ape, physically
> The most repulsive of all hot-blooded animals
> Up to that time of the world: they had dug a pitfall
> And caught a mammoth, but how could their sticks and stones
> Reach the life in that hide? They danced around the pit, shrieking
> With ape excitement, flinging sharp flints in vain, and the stench of their bodies
> Stained the white air of dawn; but presently one of them
> Remembered the yellow dancer, wood-eating fire
> That guards the cave-mouth: he ran and fetched him, and others
> Gathered sticks at the wood's edge; they made a blaze
> And pushed it into the pit, and they fed it high, around the mired sides
> Of their huge prey. They watched the long hairy trunk
> Waver over the stifle-trumpeting pain,
> And they were happy.
> Meanwhile the intense color and nobility of sunrise,
> Rose gold and amber, flowed up the sky. Wet rocks were shining, a little wind
> Stirred the leaves of the forest and the marsh flag-flowers; the soft valley between the low hills
> Became as beautiful as the sky; while in its midst, hour after hour, the happy hunters
> Roasted their living meat slowly to death.
> These are the people,
> This is the human dawn. As for me, I would rather
> Be a worm in a wild apple than a son of man.
> But we are what we are, and we might remember
> Not to hate any person, for all are vicious;

And not to be astonished at any evil, all are deserved;
And not fear death; it is the only way to be cleansed.[7]

It would not be entirely accurate to say that from that low beginning it was thereafter all downhill, for Jeffers occasionally suggests that there were moments in human history one could think of as heights. But essentially the story he tells runs from bad to worse. "In the gallop of the world . . . come peace or war, the progress of America and Europe / Becomes a long process of deterioration—starred with famous Byzantines and Alexandrias, / Surely—downward . . . Our own time . . . has acids for honey and for fine dreams / The immense vulgarities of misapplied science and decaying Christianity" ("Prescription of Painful Ends"). Such short quotes, however, flatten out his vision, which often has a grandeur and vitality that complicates his effect. Here is a somewhat more fullsome cry.

MAY–JUNE, 1940

Foreseen for so many years; these evils, this monstrous
violence, these massive agonies: no easier to bear.
We saw them with slow stone strides approach, everyone
saw them; we closed our eyes against them, we looked
And they had come nearer. We ate and drank and slept, they
came nearer. Sometimes we laughed, they were nearer.
Now
They are here. And now a blind man foresees what follows
them: degradation, famine, recovery and so forth, and the
Epidemic manias: but not enough death to serve us, not
enough death. It would be better for men
To be few and live apart, where none could infect another;
then slowly the sanity of field and mountain
And the cold ocean and glittering stars might enter their
minds.
Another dream, another dream.
We shall have to accept certain limitations
In future, and abandon some humane dreams; only hard-
minded, sleepless and realist, can ride this rock-slide
To new fields down the dark mountain; and we shall have
to perceive that these insanities are normal;

We shall have to perceive that battle is a burning flower or
like a huge music, and the dive-bombers screaming
orgasm
As beautiful as other passions; and that death and life are
not serious alternatives. One has known all these things
For many years: there is greater and darker to know
In the next hundred.
And why do you cry, my dear, why do
you cry?
It is all in the whirling circles of time
If millions are born millions must die,
If England goes down and Germany up
The stronger dog will still be on top,
All in the turning of time.
If civilization goes down, that
Would be an event to contemplate,
It will not be in our time, alas, my dear,
It will not be in our time.

In this poem and elsewhere, he suggests that the most appropriate response to this human nightmare is to try to withdraw from it as far as possible, both emotionally and physically. In "Shine, Perishing Republic," he puts it this way:

But for my children, I would have them keep their distance
from the thickening center; corruption
Never has been compulsory, when the cities lie at the
monster's feet there are left the mountains.

And boys, be in nothing so moderate as in love of man, a
clever servant, insufferable master.
There is the trap that catches noblest spirits, that
caught—they say—God, when he walked on earth.

Unlike many poets, Jeffers tried to follow his own advice. He lived most of his life in an isolated home, a tower of stone high in the Sierra mountains overlooking the Pacific Ocean. And in poem after poem, in ways similar to those we have just seen, he tried to write of the human spectacle as though he were observing it from the distance of a star. From these distances he can try to reduce the human creature to insect or even bacteria size, try to perceive (like Vittorio Mussolini) "that battle is a burning flower or like a huge music . . . and that life and death are not serious alternatives." He can celebrate again and again the unselfconscious beauty, power, and magnificence of mountains, oceans, stars, and storms, and of pelicans, hawks, and wild swans, "the beauty of things . . . born before eyes . . . the heartbreaking beauty [that] will remain when there is no heart to break for it" ("Credo"). And he can say that 'I'd sooner, except the penalties, kill a man than a hawk" ("Hurt Hawks") and warn his children "to be in nothing so moderate as in love of man." I do not want to deny the truth of his vision (partial though it is) or its power. Surely man has done much to earn the judgment Jeffers delivers. The obvious paradox, of course, is that Jeffers is also a man, and that it is his human brain that is making such judgments. Neither the hawk nor mountain nor glittering stars care enough to do so, although in one poem, "The Inquisitors," Jeffers personifies three hills as giants who peel and then split open the skulls of human "mites" in the effort to discover how they can be so "noxious" and destructive.

The further paradox in Jeffers's case, I think, is that he cares too much and that his quest for distance and his retreat to the armor of a stony house is a futile effort to diminish the intensities of his own heart. At times one can even catch him in the act, so to speak, of destroying the distance, for himself and us, in the very act of creating it:

> Below on a sea-cliff,
> A lonely clearing; a little field of corn by the streamside; a roof under spared trees.
> Then the ocean
> Like a great stone someone has cut to a knife edge and polished to shining.
> Beyond it, the fountain
> And furnace of incredible light flowing up from the sunk sun. In the little clearing a woman
> Was punishing a horse; she had tied the halter to a sapling at the edge of the wood; but when the great whip
> Clung to the flanks the creature kicked so hard she feared he would snap the halter! She called from the house

> The young man her son; who fetched a chain tie-rope, they
> working together
> Noosed the small rust links round the horse's tongue
> And tied him by the swollen tongue to the tree.
> Seen from this height they are shrunk to insect size.
> Out of all human relation. You cannot distinguish
> The blood dripping from where the chain is fastened,
> The beast shuddering; but the thrust neck and the legs
> Far apart. You can see the whip fall on the flanks. . . .
> The gesture of the arm. You cannot see the face of
> the woman.
>
> ("Apology for Bad Dreams")

It is not enough to say of this that he fails to keep his distance, for he is, in fact, rubbing his eyes and ours in that horse's swollen and bleeding tongue that is presumably too far away to "distinguish," just as he plunges himself and us into that far distant "human dawn" in which "hour after hour, the happy hunters / Roasted their living meat slowly to death." More than most, he is outraged and obsessed by such spectacles and by the larger "monstrous violence" and "massive agonies" that characterize human history and that he finds "no easier to bear" because they were to be expected. Only a desperate human dream of what ought to be could call forth the stream of epithets by which he characterizes human behavior: vicious, noxious, insufferable, vulgar, degraded, corrupt. Insects are not capable of such failures and violations, nor are they visible from the stars or even a mountaintop unless the observer is looking into something much closer at hand.

As with Jonathan Swift, it seems just to say that it is because he cares so much that he feels so much disgust and contempt. I do not want to make any firm or final judgments about the quality and value of such caring. I much prefer it to cynicism or complacency and think it has some distant kinship with love. But it is also a particularly dangerous kind of caring because a certain degree of indignation, disappointment, and disgust can swing over into hate and cruelty and, finally, into desire to punish or even crush the creatures that have so offended you. In the savagery of your indignation, you too may become a savage, even a gleeful one like those "happy hunters" in "Original Sin." Jeffers takes too much pleasure in lines like these from "The Inquisitors":

> . . . One of the hills moved a huge hand
> And poured its contents on a table-topped rock that stood in
> the fire-light; men and women fell out;
> Some crawled and some lay quiet; the hills leaned to eye
> them. One said: "It seems hardly possible"
> Such fragile creatures could be so noxious." Another
> answered,
> "True, but we've seen. But it is only recently they have the
> power." The third answered, "That bomb?"
> "Oh," he said,"—and the rest." He reached across and
> picked up one of the mites from the rock, and held it
> Close to his eyes, and very carefully with finger and
> thumbnail peeled it: by chance a young female
> With long black hair: it was too helpless even to scream. He
> held it by one white leg and stared at it:
> "I can see nothing strange: only so fragile." The third hill
> answered, "We suppose it is something
> Inside the head." Then the other split the skull with his
> thumbnail, squinting his eyes and peering, and said,
> "A drop of marrow. How could that spoil the earth?"
> "Nevertheless," he answered,
> "They have that bomb. The blasts and the fires are nothing:
> freckles on the earth: the emanations
> Might set the whole planet into a tricky fever
> And destroy much." "Themselves," he answered. "Let
> them. Why not?" "No," he answered, "life."
> Azevedo
> Still watched in horror, and all three of the hills
> Picked little animals from the rock, peeled them and
> cracked them, or toasted them
> On the red coals, or split their bodies from the crotch
> upward to stare inside. . . .

Azevedo, the human observer of the event, may watch "in horror," but Jeffers does not. It may well be that the human mites have done more to deserve their suffering than the horse in "Apology for Bad Dreams" or the mammoth in "Original Sin," but I am troubled by the enormity of the difference between Jeffers's compassion for the latter and his near delight at the treatment of the former. I would be less troubled if moral indignation had not in literal human history led to so much actual peeling, cracking, and roasting of living human meat.

At a moment like this when I am, myself, indignant at Jeffers, I want to accuse him of the further selective compassion involved in self-pity and to offer as evidence the many poems in which he speaks of life as being nearly unendurable and seems to yearn for the peacefulness of old age or death. "One always went envying the quietness of stones," he writes in "Ante Mortem," and begins another poem, "Age in Prospect": "Praise youth's hot blood if you will, I think that happiness / Rather consists in having lived clear through / Youth and hot blood, on to the wintrier hemispheres / Where one has time to wait and to remember." But my own indignation is no wiser a guide than his, and it is fairer to say that though he does, in fact, again and again suggest that life as he experienced it was terribly painful, he usually avoids the tone of self-pity and does not seem to be requesting our pity. I doubt he would be pleased even to be viewed as I must finally view him, as one who sought to distance and armor himself because he suffered too much—both from the ways in which mankind violated his vision of a sane and wholesome world and from the evidence he found in his own violent desires that he belonged to that noxious species. There is some real as well as artful self-contempt in his poem "Love the Wild Swan," which begins, "I hate my verses, every line, every word," and in this commentary about some of his own ideas: "This is far from humanism; but it is in fact the Christian attitude:—to love God with all one's heart and soul, and one's neighbor as one's self: as much as that, but as *little* as that."[8] And there is, I believe, a real desire for self-obliteration in his many expressions of a wish to belong to the nonhuman world, to become a part of the peaceful earth or stones, or even, as in his poem "Vulture," "to be eaten by that beak and become part of him, to share those wings and those eyes— / What a sublime end of one's body, what an enskyment; what a life after death."

Of the many succinct commentaries that might be made about this and the numerous other instances we have seen of man's infatuation with high-soaring, inhuman birds, I would like to choose only two; and although both have been the subject of enormous explication, let them speak essentially for themselves. With respect to the first, Hopkins's "The Windhover," I will point out only that the windhover is a small falcon or hawk and that, however one interprets the word "Buckle," the poem clearly affirms that there is a fire born of human suffering and sacrifice that is a billion times lovelier and more dangerous than the masterful glide and brute beauty of the bird.

THE WINDHOVER
To Christ Our Lord

I caught this morning morning's minion, kingdom of
daylight's dauphin, dapple-dawn-drawn Falcon, in
his riding
Of the rolling level underneath him steady air, and
striding
High there, how he rung upon the rein of a wimpling wing
In his ecstacy! then off, off forth on swing,
As a skate's heel sweeps smooth on a bow-bend: the hurl
and gliding
Rebuffed the big wind. My heart in hiding
Stirred for a bird,—the achieve of, the mastery of the thing!

Brute beauty and valour and act, oh, air, pride, plume, here
Buckle! AND the fire that breaks from thee then, a billion
Times told lovelier, more dangerous, O my chevalier!

No wonder of it: shéer plód makes plough down sillion
Shine, and blue-beak embers, ah my dear,
Fall, gall themselves, and gash gold-vermillion.[9]

With respect to the second, Yeats's "Leda and the Swan," some readers may need to be reminded that the rapist from the sky is Zeus in the guise of a swan, and that the offspring of that union are Castor and Pollux and Helen of Troy, whose arrival on the human scene led to a quite remarkable amount of human suffering, as well as to some very great poems.

A sudden blow: the great wings beating still
Above the staggering girl, her thighs caressed
By the dark webs, her nape caught in his bill,
He holds her helpless breast upon his breast.

How can those terrified vague fingers push
The feathered glory from her loosening thighs?
And how can body, laid in that white rush,
But feel the strange heart beating where it lies?

A shudder in the loins engenders there
The broken wall, the burning roof and tower
And Agamemnon dead.
Being so caught up,
So mastered by the brute blood of the air,
Did she put on his knowledge with his power
Before the indifferent beak could let her drop?[10]

There are no firsthand reports of Leda's feelings about that encounter any more than there are of Mary's about her more immaculate impregnation from above, and Yeats himself seems here to draw back from them. I suspect, however, that both ladies would have more second thoughts than we have yet encountered here about human traffic with the skies.

But I had better stop this trafficking of my own with birds before I start talking about the harpies or the vulture who fed on the liver of Prometheus or what sometimes seems to me the most curious human attempt to escape his native habitat, the invention of the angel. As though one really could drown out the roar which lies on the other side of silence with the plinking of the harp and the music of the spheres.

For many years I thought that the single wisest and most moving answer to the Nietzschean and kindred points of view, and the best expression of my own deepest sentiments about man's appropriate response both to the powers outside himself and to his own kind was that contained in Bertrand Russell's essay "A Free Man's Worship." And whenever I could, I urged it upon my students and my friends. Now I am made somewhat uncomfortable by the grandiloquence of both its rhetoric and conceptions. For like many of the voices we have just been hearing, it presumes to speak of all mankind in a tone that contains too little awareness of the pretensions of such an undertaking. Still, I find it an eloquent, powerful, and important testament and want to share something of its content and flavor here.

For Russell the world apart from man is utterly purposeless and void of meaning:

> That Man is the product of causes which had no prevision of the end they were achieving; that his origin, his growth, his hopes and fears, his loves and his beliefs, are but the outcome of accidental collocations of atoms; that no fire, no heroism, no intensity of thought and feeling, can preserve an individual life beyond the grave; that all the labors of the ages, all the devotion, all the inspiration, all the noonday brightness of human genius, are destined to extinction in the vast death of the solar system, and that the whole temple of Man's achievement must inevitably be buried beneath the debris of a universe in ruins—all these things, if not quite beyond dispute, are yet so nearly certain, that no philosophy which rejects them can hope to stand. Only within the scaffolding of these truths, only on the firm foundation of unyielding despair, can the soul's habitation henceforth be safely built.[11]

"Somehow," Russell writes, in its "blind hurryings through the abysses of space," Nature "brought forth at last a child, subject still to her power, but gifted with sight, with knowledge of good and evil, with the capacity of judging all the works of his unthinking Mother." Unlike Nietzsche and Jeffers, Russell cherishes these capacities in man that can give him a degree of freedom from, and even superiority to, "the resistless forces that control his outward life." Far from wishing to join up with those forces—to celebrate the survival of the fittest as Nietzsche does or to melt into the mountains, rocks or hawks as Jeffers does, he finds the indifference, thoughtlessness, and reliance on power of that nonhuman world profoundly repugnant to his best aspirations and urges us to free ourselves as much as possible from it. Freedom means not only refusing to worship power, whether the worship is like that of the savage or of Job or of Nietzsche, but resisting also the "position which we have become accustomed to regard as specially religious, maintaining that, in some hidden manner the world of fact is really harmonious with the world of ideals." It means also passing beyond a Promethean "spirit of fiery revolt, of fierce hatred of the Gods" in which it appears one's duty to keep actively defying a hostile universe, for "indignation is still a bondage."[12] It means finally, for Russell, a renunciation of selfhood and of those eager personal wishes that make us subject to "the empire of Fate" and an imaginative refashioning of the relation between man and the nonhuman world; a new religion in which one "builds a temple for the worship of our own ideals" of goodness and beauty and learns to contemplate with awe and sympathy the spectacle of man's doomed but gallant adventure in a world that was not made for him, or as he puts it once, his existence on a "narrow raft" on "the dark ocean on whose rolling waves we toss for a brief hour."[13]

But to do justice to the quality of this religion, one must listen for a while to the music of his worship:

> In the spectacle of Death, in the endurance of intolerable pain, and in the irrevocableness of a vanished past, there is a sacredness, an overpowering awe, a feeling of the vastness, the depth, the inexhaustible mystery of existence, in which, as by some strange marriage of pain, the sufferer is bound to the world by bonds of sorrow. . . .
>
> United with his fellow-men by the strongest of all ties, the tie of a common doom, the free man finds that a new vision is with him always, shedding over every daily task the light of love. The life of Man is a long march through the night, surrounded by invisible foes, tortured by weariness and pain, towards a goal that few can hope to reach, and where none may tarry long. One by one, as they march, our comrades vanish from our sight, seized by the silent orders of omnipotent Death. Very brief is the time in which we can help them, in which their happiness or misery is decided. Be it ours to shed sunshine on their path, to lighten their sorrows by the balm of sympathy, to give them the pure joy of a never-tiring despair. Let us not weigh in grudging scales their merits and demerits, but let us think only of their need—of the sorrows, the difficulties, perhaps the blindnesses, that make the misery of their lives; let us remember that they are fellow-sufferers in the same darkness, actors in the same tragedy with ourselves. And so, when their day is over, when their good and their evil have become eternal by the immortality of the past, be it ours to feel

that, where they suffered, where they failed, no deed of ours was the cause; but wherever a spark of the divine fire kindled in their hearts, we were ready with encouragement, with sympathy, with brave words in which high courage glowed.[14]

Under the spell of such music, it is hard to know how to proceed—particularly hard when one believes that one of the least fortunate of man's talents is that which he has for walking out of temples, churches, and cathedrals and going on untroubled about his daily business; for transforming himself almost instantaneously from the sort of noble creature Russell worships into something more like the insect that Jeffers and Nietzsche suppose him to be. I would like to postpone that transformation of myself for a moment and remain under the spell.

Under such a spell, it is difficult to be cruel, petty, or even ironic. One can feel a sense of kinship with all those other human children who share one's brief journey from birth to death: with Nietzsche as well as Stevie and Scobie, perhaps even with Shrike. And one can do so without having to make up any religion, nation, sect, society, or club that defines brotherhood or sisterhood by excluding others from the family. With no motherly Nature or fatherly God, one knows that there is nothing for oneself or anyone else to turn to but human caring. One can, without the need to make up any deity, feel the necessity and wisdom of charity, and know the force of Donne's "any man's death diminishes me, because I am involved in Mankinde; and therefore never send to know for whom the bell tolls; It tolls for thee."

Under the spell here, I want to go on quoting passages that resound with similar music, like King Lear's:

Poor naked wretches, wheresoe'er you are
That bide the pelting of this pitiless storm,
How shall your houseless heads and unfed sides,
Your loop'd and window'd raggedness, defend you
From seasons such as these? O! I have ta'en
Too little care of this! Take physick, pomp;
Expose thyself to feel what wretches feel,
That thou may'st shake the superflux to them,
And show the heavens more just.

And certain passages from James Agee, who uses this passage from *King Lear* as an epigraph for his *Let Us Now Praise Famous Men* about which I shall want to say a great deal more later. Here he is writing in the home of an abysmally poor tenant farmer "in a room of a house set deep and solitary in the country" in which "all in this house save myself are sleeping," and he thinks thus of the immensity of space beyond that house:

> Above that shell and carapace, more frail against heaven than fragilest membrane of glass, nothing, straight to the terrific stars; whereof all heaven is chalky; and of whom the nearest is so wild a reach my substance wilts to think on: and we, this Arctic flower snow-rooted, last match flame guarded on a windy plain, are seated among these stars alone: none to turn to, none to make us known; a little country settlement so deep, so lost in the shelve and shade of dew, no one so much as laughs at us. Small wonder how pitiably we love our home, cling in her skirts at night, rejoice in her wide star-seducing smile, when every star strikes us sick with the fright: do we really exist at all? . . .
>
> And thus, too, these families, not otherwise than with every family in the earth, how each, apart, how inconceivably lonely, sorrowful, and remote![15]

From this he goes on to think of all individuals, each "a new and incommunicably tender life, wounded in every breath, and almost as hardly killed as easily wounded; sustaining, for a while, without defense, the enormous assaults of the universe."[16] And finally, going beyond Russell to include in his compassion all existences:

> So that how can it be that a stone, a plant, a star, can take on the burden of being; and how is it that a child can take on the burden of breathing; and how through so long a continuation and cumulation of the burden of each moment one on another, does any creature bear to exist, and not break utterly to fragments of nothing: these are matters too dreadful and fortitudes too gigantic to meditate long and not forever to worship.[17]

As is evident here, Agee often reaches toward a mystical vision in which man is more a part of a cosmic unity than Russell would allow; but I think his sympathy, like Russell's and Lear's, comes mainly from his sense of man as a frail and transient being, powerless against "the enormous assaults of the universe." As he is. As we are.

Probably it is time to break the spell though, at least for a while. It could be done violently by introducing suddenly any one of many single real human "actors in the same tragedy with ourselves," a particularly self-pitying beggar or politician, say, or one of the idle rich lamenting his lot. I would rather slip from it more gradually though. First by remembering how Russell's vision can sound in another tone, the tone provided by Virginia Woolf as she has Peter Walsh muse about the way Clarissa Dalloway may be thinking to herself about life:

> As we are a doomed race, chained to a sinking ship (her favorite reading as a girl was Huxley and Tyndall, and they were fond of these nautical metaphors), as the whole thing is a bad joke, let us at any rate, do our part, mitigate the sufferings of our fellow-prisoners (Huxley again); decorate the dungeon with flowers and air cushions; be as decent as we possibly can. Those ruffians, the Gods, shan't have it all their own way. . . . [18]

Then by thinking for a moment of what the young Stephen Dedalus in Joyce's *A Portrait of the Artist as a Young Man* wrote on the flyleaf of his geography book:

> Stephen Dedalus
> Class of Elements
> Clongowes Wood College
> Sallins
> County Kildare
> Ireland
> Europe
> The World
> The Universe[19]

We may not be at home in the universe, but we do have more local addresses. And if we do not presume to be on speaking terms with it, we may not even have to hear its reply, as does the man in this little poem by Stephen Crane:

A man said to the universe:
"Sir, I exist!"
"However," replied the universe,
"The fact has not created in me
A sense of obligation."[20]

Once the spell is broken, a great many thoughts come rushing in. The first, since I am writing this on a lovely day in June, is that the universe we see, and especially in its manifestations as Nature, does not seem so unremittingly alien, indifferent, and hostile as Russell makes it. It will kill us finally, to be sure; but it also houses and feeds some of us quite gently and deliciously, at least some of the time. It does provide some year-round literal Tahitis as well as various more temporary figurative ones. Even Captain Ahab—that most determined of all challengers of the universe, who chose for his home that most indifferent of all habitats, the ocean—is for a moment moved and softened by the gentleness of a mild and lovely day, and so is Melville:

> But the lovely aromas in that enchanted air did at last seem to dispel, for a moment the cankerous thing in his soul. That glad, happy air, that winsome sky, did at last stroke and caress him; the step-mother world, so long cruel-forbidding—now threw affectionate arms around his stubborn neck, and did seem to joyously sob over him, as if over one, that however wilful and erring, she could yet find it in her heart to save and to bless. From beneath his slouched hat Ahab dropped a tear into the sea.[21]

Our sun, though from one point of view only one of those cold, indifferent stars, helps keep us warm, and warms the plants and other animals (which, I cannot help observing, help nourish the stomachs on which our high idealism depends); and perhaps within their local spheres, those other stars we see provide a similar warm benevolence. If one might say of Nietzsche and Jeffers that they are asking us to lick the hand that kills us, one might say that Russell would have us bite at the hand that feeds us.

Out from under the spell, the two apparently opposed visions may be seen as two sides of the same romantic coin. On one side Nature romanticized and man judged with undue harshness; on the other, Nature totally condemned while men are idealized and we are told not to "weigh in grudging scales their merits and demerits" but "to think only of their need—of the sorrows, the difficulties, perhaps the blindnesses, that make the misery of their lives." In both instances the hugely complex relation between man and his surrounding world is transformed into a simple conflict with only two sides, to one of which one must give allegiance. In some respects this is more disappointing in Russell's case because the vision appeals to one of man's particularly unpleasant qualities, his ever-ready chauvinism—his eagerness to form bonds against what he is told is a common enemy. It is true that by turning the entire nonhuman universe into an "empire of Fate," a "wanton tyranny," a "trampling march of unconscious power," and by painting man's ethical quest as a battle against these forces, Russell has enlarged the chauvinism to embrace all mankind and provided an intellectual and emotional basis for universal sympathy. Still, by framing the appeal in such a way, he is stirring up and relying upon forces in man that can easily redefine the enemy and narrow the ranks of those whom one perceives as sharing a common doom—as Russell has already narrowed it by excluding all creatures but man.

Russell's appeal also touches another of man's not entirely fortunate qualities—his capacity for self-pity. (My phrasing "not entirely fortunate" is not ironic, for I suspect that quality is deeply involved with his capacity to sympathize with others and may, in fact, never be entirely absent in sympathy.) Russell does not, in this essay or anywhere to my knowledge, himself wallow in self-pity, and he asks us to help, encourage, and sympathize with others; but we are to do so because they are "fellow-sufferers in the same darkness, actors in the same tragedy with ourselves." And though he counsels a brave and generous stoicism as the proper response to the tragic human predicament, he defines that predicament in terms that could be invented only by a creature capable of self-pity and that surely entitle mankind to feel sorry for itself.

One further uncomfortable thought is that, despite the

concern expressed for his fellow creatures, the voice and vision of the piece also involve a gigantic distance, a vantage point in some ways beyond the soaring eagle, farther even than the nearer skies. By his frequent use of the words "we" and "our," Russell acknowledges his part in the drama; but he is also watching it, has become an audience for our "common doom" and even for "the vast death of the solar system." To make such a theater of one's imagination is a remarkable undertaking, and it is, of course, precisely what Russell is encouraging us to do; but it also has made of the whole human struggle a kind of spectator sport. It is not fair to say that Russell enjoys the sport (or to follow the other metaphor, the tragic drama), but neither does he watch it without some sense of satisfaction and even vicarious excitement.

In his actual life, whether due to his vision or more to a naturally hopeful and energetic temperament, Russell went on striving until the age of ninety-eight to fashion a world that would be more in accord with his human ideals of justice and decency. Since, despite the unpleasant questions I have just been raising about the Russell view, I still respond to its generous sympathies, and since I ultimately detest the Nietzschean view, I wish I could attribute Russell's long-lived health to his vision and Nietzsche's early madness to his, especially since Nietzsche had to rely finally on the pity for the weak and unfit he so despised. But obviously that is only one more kind of human wish (and not a very creditable one) that Nature, perhaps wisely, ignores.

Apart from such musings, however, it does seem astonishing that, both in his rhetoric and life, Russell found that tragic vision as invigorating as he did and that his sympathy, which seems sincere, apparently incapacitated him so little. One wonders what immunizes him so completely to George Eliot's sense that it would be unbearable to have "a keen vision and feeling" of the tragedy of all ordinary human life or to the susceptibilities that lead Virginia Woolf to write, as E. M. Forster "half fancifully, but wholly seriously" puts it, "But sympathy we cannot have. Wisest Fate says no. If her children, weighted as they already are with sorrow, were to take on that burden too, adding in imagination other pains to their own, buildings would cease to rise; roads would peter out into grassy tracks; there would be an end to music and painting; one great sigh alone would rise to Heaven, and the only attitudes for men and women would be those of horror and despair."[22] It is too easy to say that Russell is well wadded or deafened by his distance or that he has the "vision" of human suffering without the "feeling," and Russell could easily argue that those other views smack of self-indulgence and are more attuned to the sensibilities of the compassionate ones than to the needs of the fellow sufferers. Still, there is a certain comfortableness in Russell's vision, and I cannot help wishing I heard a bit more anguish in his tone. Only a little more, however, because it is quite wonderful to find a compassionate man who seems utterly without the urge for self-crucifixion.

To appreciate the remarkable quality of Russell's sympathy and vigor, one need only listen a little to Schopenhauer and observe how easy it is to slide, both intellectually and emotionally, from a vision like Russell's to a state in which one's energies are directed not at all toward the needs of others but only toward the mortification of one's own will. Judging from his treatment of Schopenhauer in his *A History of Western Philosophy*, the older Russell would not like to think he shared anything with that pessimistic philosopher (and it is true that the Russell of 1945 saw the universe in less gloomy terms than he did in 1902). But in "A Free Man's Worship," his gloomy image of man's existence against a backdrop of indifferent chance and fate is very much like the one Schopenhauer envisions as becoming visible when a man moves beyond egoism and comprehends the essential nature of existence. Such a man "finds that it consists in a constant passing away, vain striving, inward conflict, and continual suffering. He sees wherever he looks suffering humanity, the suffering brute creation, and a world that passes away."[23]

As Russell does, Schopenhauer also cherishes such a state of selfless awareness as a ground for the expression of man's noblest qualities and aspirations, as rendering possible and explaining "perfect goodness of disposition, extending to disinterested love and the most generous self-sacrifice for others."

Very quickly, however—too quickly, I think—Schopenhauer makes his way beyond benevolence:

> If that veil of Mâyâ, the principle of individuation, is lifted from the eyes of a man to such an extent that he no longer makes the egotistical distinction between his person and that of others, but takes as much interest in the sufferings of other individuals as in his own, and therefore is not only benevolent in the highest degree, but even ready to sacrifice his own individuality whenever such a sacrifice will save number of persons, then it clearly follows that such a man, who recognizes in all beings his own inmost and true self, must also regard the infinite suffering of all suffering beings as his own, and take on himself the pain of the whole world.[24]

Almost as quickly as he moves through the "then it clearly follows," he asks why such a man, "with such a knowledge of the world," should "assert this very life through constant acts of will, and thereby bind himself more closely to it, press it ever more firmly to himself?" And he answers that such a man will try, and should try, to subdue his will and strive as much as possible to remain in a state of "voluntary renunciation, resignation, true indifference, and perfect will-lessness." He will move, and should move, from "virtue to asceticism. That is to say, it no longer suffices for such a man to love others as himself, and to do as much for them as for himself; but there arises within him a horror of the nature of which his own phenomenal existence is an expression, the will to live, the kernel and inner nature of that world which is recognized as full of misery. He therefore disowns this nature which appears in him . . . and seeks to confirm in himself the greatest indifference to everything."[25]

Since the will keeps asserting itself, the ascetic must continually do battle with it and also with its visible form, the body. "So he practices fasting, and even resorts to self-inflicted torture, in order that by constant privation and suffering, he may more and more break down and destroy the will, which he recognizes and abhors as the source of his own suffering existence and that of the world." Only death, of course, can fully suppress all manifestation of will, so "it is most welcome, and is gladly received as a longed-for deliverance."[26]

It may be that "to take on . . . the pain of the whole world" leads always to an undue preoccupation with the state of one's own psyche; and it may even be, as Auden has suggested, that almost any sorrowing for others is likely to be a form of self-indulgence; it may also be that ascetics are often motivated in part by a mere wish for the comfort of will-lessness (and these are all matters that will receive attention later). But there is a peculiar and instructive ugliness in the ease with which Schopenhauer gives up the burden of others' pain and returns to the egoism he thinks he has transcended, and there is a peculiar emptiness in his vision of asceticism. By contrast, Russell's perhaps too comfortable shouldering of the burden and his perhaps too easy urgings of practical benevolence are good to contemplate.

As one might expect, his benevolence does not extend to Schopenhauer. He calls it an "insult" for Schopenhauer to claim that real Christian mystics behave in accord with his "mythology" and goes on to say:

> Nor is the doctrine sincere, if we may judge by Schopenhauer's life. He habitually dined well, at a good restaurant; he had many trivial love-affairs, which were sensual but not passionate; he was exceedingly quarrelsome and unusually avaricious. On one occasion he was annoyed by an elderly seamstress who was talking to a friend outside the door of his apartment. He threw her downstairs, causing her permanent injury. She obtained a court order compelling him to pay her a certain sum (15 thalers) every quarter so long as she lived. When at last she dies, after twenty years, he noted in his account book: "Obit anus, abit onus" ["The old woman dies, the burden departs"]. It is hard to find in his life evidences of any virtue except kindness to animals, which he carried to the point of objecting to vivisection in the interests of science. In all other respects he was completely selfish. It is difficult to believe that a man who was profoundly convinced of the virtue of asceticism and resignation would never have made any attempt to embody his convictions in his practice.[27]

But then Russell has, in effect, pushed poor Schopenhauer down the stairs, and that poor man, so long gone, cannot sue Russell for philosophical malpractice, just as neither gentleman, thank goodness, can sue me for the way I have converted him into a path for my own meanderings.

As is plainly evident here, a preoccupation with the suffering of all mankind does not necessarily lead anyone, including myself, to a wise and judicious, or even kindly, state of mind. And much of the consciousness and self-consciousness we have witnessed so far, including my own, could be viewed as evidence in favor of Jeffers's view of man as an insufferable little beast, infatuated with his own cleverness.

I would prefer for now, however, to take a more Russell-like view and to notice that all the people and other living creatures I have been concerned with have within their fictional or real worlds already shared our common doom. They are all dead: Icarus with his "white legs disappearing into the green water"; the children, ploughmen, dogs, and torturer's horse who went about their business as he fell; Bruegel, who painted the picture, and Auden, who wrote about it; George Eliot, who heard so well that roar which lies on the other side of silence, and Vittorio Mussolini, who could not hear it at all; the Ethiopian horsemen and their horses, who exploded into his rosy bomb-blast; a few billion real roses; young Nick Adams and his father, Ivan Velikopolsky, who was once only twenty-two, and the widows he used; Richard, who tried so hard to keep a proper vigil; Stevie, Miss Lonelyhearts, and Scobie and all those they wished to rescue; Nietzsche and all his heroes; Goethe and his eagle who eats hares in the realm of "the good, the noble, and the beautiful"; Robinson Jeffers; his happy hunters and the mammoth they roasted alive, the hawks and vultures and wild swans he preferred to man; the Windhover that Hopkins's heart buckled for; Leda and swanish Zeus, who raped her (unless old gods like Zeus and Christ go on living somewhere in their separate heavens); King Lear; James Agee and most of the tenant farmers he so valued (though some of their children are still living); Schopenhauer, who argued for taking on oneself the pain of the whole world and lived quite comfortably; Virginia Woolf, who said we should not and could not bear such pain and drowned herself, perhaps as much to end the pain of others as her own; and Russell, who could see the world as a "dark ocean on whose rolling waves we toss for a brief hour" and lived for ninety-eight years without incapacitating despair.

In such a cemetery, we can pause for a while simply to be awed.

Part Two

VI ❖ The Engulfing of Others and Delicious Unions with Death

HAVING SO RUTHLESSLY APPROPRIATED THAT CANVAS AND text which once belonged to Bruegel and Auden, I think it only fair to bring them back intact for a moment, especially since I am about to exploit them once again.

MUSEE DES BEAUX ARTS

About suffering they were never wrong,
The Old Masters: how well they understood
Its human position; how it takes place
While someone else is eating or opening a window or just
walking dully along;
How when the aged are reverently, passionately waiting
For the miraculous birth, there always must be
Children who did not specially want it to happen, skating
On a pond at the edge of the wood:
They never forgot
That even the dreadful martyrdom must run its course
Anyhow in a corner, some untidy spot
Where the dogs go on with their doggy life and the torturer's
horse
Scratches its innocent behind on a tree.

In Breughel's *Icarus*, for instance: how everything turns
away
Quite leisurely from the disaster; the ploughman may
Have heard the splash, the forsaken cry,
But for him it was not an important failure; the sun shone
As it had to on the white legs disappearing into the green
Water; and the expensive delicate ship that must have seen
Something amazing, a boy falling out of the sky,
Had somewhere to get to and sailed calmly on.

I am about to open the picture to some new and rather different sorts of witnesses, but I want to gaze just a little longer upon those already present who have not turned away quite leisurely from the disaster. Along with the children skating on the pond at the edge of the wood, there are those other children: Nick Adams, who is still young enough to believe in his own immortality and to wish for it, but who has not turned away from the sympathies and questions engendered by the childbirth and suicide he has witnessed; Ivan Velikopolsky, somewhat deaf to the pain of the widows and the torment of Jesus, and padded enough to blot up all his knowledge of suffering into an enchanted sense of his own intelligence and vitality, but still much penetrated for a while with his understanding of Peter's bitter weeping; Richard, desperately seeking to appreciate Christ's agony through acute discomfort of his own without tripping into fantasies of his own saintliness; and poor Stevie, unable to witness anyone's suffering without a desperate wish to ease it. If only he could have been taken to skate on a pond at the edge of a wood instead of to Greenwich as a tool to blow up the Observatory. The grown men are harder to think about. There is enough of Shrike in me to envision Miss Lonelyhearts leaping into the water to save Icarus and drowning both Icarus and himself in the process. But I still prefer his Christ-complex to Shrike's amusement and to the Shrike in myself. If I were Icarus, I would rather drown in Miss Lonelyhearts' embrace than to the sound of Shrike's laughter. And if somehow my battered Icarus self had been pulled out of the water by that lifeboat in which Helen lay clutching her stamp album, I would be glad if Scobie were waiting on shore. Among other things, he would understand that after so momentous a failure I might not wish to be saved. I suppose, though, that I would wish to be attended as well by a skilled nurse even if she were one of those "literal examples of practical charity" with "the brisk, decided, undisturbed, and slightly brutal air of a busy surgeon" and a face devoid of compassion. After a few days, I might welcome a visit from Bertrand Russell.

I do not know how one saves the victims of "that dreadful martyrdom." But were I one such nameless victim about to be tortured, I would rather have as witnesses any of the foolish rescuers, whether Stevie, Scobie, or Miss Lonelyhearts, or such "idiots" as Don Quixote or Prince Myshkin, than any of the sensible men and women who sentenced me, or any of the thirty-eight sensible residents of Kew Gardens in Queens, New York, who watched and listened behind their windows for thirty-five minutes while I was being stabbed to death and would not become involved enough even to call the police,[1] to say nothing of those who sensibly did their duty at Dachau or Gulag 17. I would rather have nearly any of those who are now about to be pulled into the picture, even though most of them would have a hard time giving my predicament as much attention as they would their own responses to it and their sense of their own relationship to me. In my own person, I sometimes want to resist them quite vigorously, although I cannot imagine the full picture or even my own life without them and their lonely embraces. I will look first at some who wish to eliminate distance entirely and then at a larger number who are driven by the more usual human wish both to preserve and overcome it.

The new witness I remain most mixed up about is the one who seeks most persistently to obliterate distances and who, far from turning leisurely away, again and again responds to other's misfortunes with sentiments like these:

> I am the man, I was there.
> The disdain and calmness of martyrs,
> The mother of old, condemn'd for a witch, burnt with dry
> wood, her children gazing on,
> The hounded slave that flags in the race, leans by the fence,
> blowing cover'd with sweat,
> The twinges that sting like needles his legs and neck, the
> murderous buckshot and the bullets,
> All these I feel or am.
>
> I am the hounded slave. I wince at the bite of the dogs,
> Hell and despair are upon me, crack and again crack the
> marksmen,
> I clutch the rails of the fence, my gore dribs, thinn'd with the
> ooze of my skin,

I fall on the weeds and stones,
The riders spur their unwilling horses, haul close,
Taunt my dizzy ears and beat me violently over the head
with whipstocks.

Agonies are one of my changes of garments.
I do not ask the wounded person how he feels, I myself
become the wounded person.
My hurts turn livid upon me as I lean on a cane and
observe.[2]

There is no way to be fair to Whitman without quoting pages and pages of him because his effect depends so much upon the sweep of his tone and the hypnotic repetition of the idea that he is both Walt Whitman and the spirit of us all: his effort to flesh out the opening lines of *Leaves of Grass* ("One's-self I sing, a simple separate person, / Yet utter the word Democratic, the word En-Masse") and these that open the most powerful poem within those leaves, "Song of Myself" ("I celebrate myself, and sing myself. / And what I shall assume you shall assume / For every atom belonging to me as good belongs to you"). And the persuasiveness of a passage like the one I have begun with depends especially upon the incantatory effect of what has gone before. But even in its context, there is something abstract and unconvincing about the passage and glib about the "all those I feel or am" that encourages me to make the kind of observation Auden might have made about it—that Whitman does not, in fact, become the wounded person but remains the poet writing about himself becoming the wounded person; he is experiencing not the full ache of the wound but the exaltation of writing. Yet even as I write this, I must insist that it is better for him to say what he does as he does than to say, "It's no skin off my ass," or "It serves him right," or even an official "I'm sorry, but there's nothing I can do."

More moving and convincing to me is a similar passage that suggests that an armored part of himself guards against the identifications and that he finds them really painful, as they should be.

You laggards there on guard! look to your arms!
In at the conquer'd doors they crowd! I am possess'd!
Embody all presences outlaw'd or suffering,
See myself in prison shaped like another man,
And feel the dull unintermitted pain.

For me the keepers of convicts shoulder their carbines and
keep watch,
It is I let out in the morning and barr'd at night.

Not a mutineer walks handcuff'd to jail but I am handcuff'd
to him and walk by his side,
(I am less the jolly one there, and more the silent one with
sweat on my twitching lips.)

Not a youngster is taken for larceny but I go up too, and am
tried and sentenced.
Not a cholera patient lies at last gasp but I also lie at the last
gasp,
My face is ash-color'd, my sinews gnarl, away from me
people retreat.
Askers embody themselves in me and I am embodied in
them,
I project my hat, sit shame faced, and beg.

(Pp. 55–56)

Despite the power and necessity of these embodiments, however, I respond most to Whitman when he is most aware of the spaces as well as the connections between self and other and of the paradoxes in his attempt to be both. As he is when he writes:

Apart from the pulling and hauling stands what I am,
Stands amused, complacent, compassionating, idle,
unitary,
Looks down, is erect, or bends an arm on an impalpable
certain rest,
Looking with side-curved head curious what will come
next,
Both in and out of the game and watching and wondering at it.

(P. 27)

As he is when he remembers to intersperse injunctions like "You shall not look through my eyes either, nor take things from me, / You shall listen to all sides and filter them from yourself" (p. 26), "You are also asking me questions and I hear you, / I answer that I cannot answer, you must find out for yourself" (p. 64), and "He most honors my style who learns under it to destroy the teacher" (p. 65). And as he is in this wonderful duet between "I" and "you" at the end of "Song of Myself," even though it begins with too much traffic with those sorts of hawks and eagles I worried so much about earlier:

> The spotted hawk swoops by and accuses me, he complains
> of my gab and my loitering.
>
> I too am not a bit tamed, I too am untranslateable,
> I sound my barbaric yawp over the roofs of the world.
>
> The last scud of day holds back for me.
> It flings my likeness after the rest and true as any on the
> shadow'd wilds,
> It coaxes me to the vapor and the dusk.
>
> I depart as air, I shake my white locks at the runaway sun,
> I effuse my flesh in eddies, and drift it in lacy jags.
>
> I bequeath myself to the dirt to grow from the grass I love,
> If you want me again look for me under your boot-soles.
>
> You will hardly know who I am or what I mean,
> But I shall be good health to you nevertheless,
> And filter and fiber your blood.
>
> Failing to fetch me at first keep encouraged,
> Missing me one place search another,
> I stop somewhere waiting for you.
>
> (P. 68)

(I think more than a footnote is owed to a similar duet to be found in a book by a far less confident espouser of the American Dream, the black writer Ralph Ellison. His *Invisible Man* begins: "I am an invisible man," goes on to illustrate many of the ways in which the black man has been made invisible to himself and others, and ends, "Who knows but that, on the lower frequencies, I speak for you.")

But however much I would like to see this duet or dialectic as the heart of Whitman's vision, I think his deepest yearning is toward a mystical unity of time and space and past and present in which all distance will be dissolved, not only between man and man but between man and nature; a unity in which there will even be "the marriage of continents, climates and oceans!" Here is a moment of such yearning from "Passage to India," perhaps his loveliest and farthest-reaching expression of that dream:

> After the seas are all crossed, (as they seem already cross'd)
> After the great captains and engineers have accomplish'd
> their work,
> After the noble inventors, after the scientists, the chemist,
> the geologist, ethnologist,
> Finally shall come the poet worthy that name,
> The true son of God shall come singing his songs.
>
> Then not your deeds only O voyagers, O scientists and
> inventors, shall be justified,
> All these hearts as of fretted children, shall be sooth'd,
> All affection shall be fully responded to, the secret shall
> be told,
> All these separations and gaps shall be taken up and
> hook'd and link'd together,
> The whole earth, this cold, impassive, voiceless earth,
> shall be completely justified,
> Trinitas divine shall be gloriously accomplish'd and
> compacted by the true son of God, the poet,
> (He shall indeed pass the straits and conquer the
> mountains,
> He shall double the Cape of Good Hope to some purpose,)
> Nature and Man shall be disjoin'd and diffused no more,
> The true son of God shall absolutely fuse them.
> (Pp. 290–91)

I cannot help wondering what Richard, Miss Lonelyhearts, or Scobie would make of such a son of God. Yet each of them, and Icarus too, would find interest, and perhaps solace also, in the lines with which the poem ends.

Reckless O soul, exploring, I with thee, and thou with me,
For we are bound where mariner has not yet dared to go,
And we will risk the ship, ourselves and all.
O my brave soul!
O farther farther sail.
O daring joy, but safe! Are they not the seas of God?
O farther, farther, farther sail!

(P. 294)

Despite a faint stirring of youthful yearning at such sentiments, I shall have to give way soon to my middle-aged inclination to shrink from Whitman and nearly all such vociferous expansionists and engulfers. But first I should remember the service he performs for many young Romantics. Like James Agee, for instance, who at the age of eighteen wrote to Father Flye: "I've been reading *Leaves of Grass* since I came back. You know, since last winter or so I've been feeling something—a sort of universal—oh, I don't know, feeling the beauty of everything, not excluding slop jars and foetuses—and a feeling of love for everything—and now I've run into Walt Whitman—and it seems as if I'd dived into a sort of infinitude of beautiful stuff—all the better (for me) because it was just what has been knocking at me unawares."[3] And like a student of mine who ended an essay on Whitman by saying: "Before Whitman if something dropped into the toilet bowl, like the soap, or toothbrush, whatever, I'd fish for it with a hanger. Now I'd roll up my sleeve and reach in."[4] And I should remember how much all such huge affirmations of human unity truly require substantial time and space to achieve their resonance. As is true of all great choral Masses and Messiahs and of Beethoven's Ninth, to whose sounds and final sentiments Auden and his poem should also be exposed and which he might find more difficult to dismiss than those of Whitman.

A somewhat older Agee, five years so, also writes to Father Flye about this music, and in a context that provides it with a sobering counterpoint that I shall wish to develop further later on.

> Are you fond of Swift? I never read him till last winter, and am rereading *Gulliver's Travels* now. I can't *say* the love and dumb reverence for him I feel. I don't think many people have ever lived with as little compromise to the cruelties in human nature, with such acute pain at the sight of them, and such profound love for what the human race *could* or *might* be. People who call him a Hater of Humanity make me writhe—they are likely to be the very hardest of human sorts to show true humanity to—because the *are* by intention kind and easy-living, and *resigned* to the expedient corruption of living quietly and happily in the world.
>
> When you get down here again I'll have my phonograph working—not here but in my office, to play at night. An empty skyscraper is just about an ideal place for it—with the volume it has. Something attracts me very much about playing Beethoven's Ninth Symphony there—with all New York about 600 feet below you, and with that *swell* ode, taking in the whole earth, and with everyone on earth supposedly singing it; all that estranged them and all except joy and the whole common world-love and brotherhood idea forgotten. With Joy speaking over them: O ye millions, I embrace you . . . I kiss all the world . . . and all mankind shall be as brothers beneath thy tender and wide wings.
>
> In all this depression over the world, and the whole Communist thing, I get two such feelings as strongly as I have the capacity for them: one the feeling of that music—of a love and pity and joy that nearly floors you, and the other of Swift's sort, when you see the people you love—any mob of them in this block I live in—with a tincture of sickness and cruelty and selfishness in the faces of most of them, sometimes an apparent total and universal *blindness* to kindliness and good and beauty. You have a feeling that they could never be cured and that all effort is misspent—and then you also know the generations of training in pain that have made the evil in them, and know it would be more than worth dying for.[5]

Let me hold off the darker side a while longer though by sounding for Auden and Icarus a somewhat less pretentious note on human unity than Beethoven's Ninth, one struck by another young traveler who plunges into the sea, Ishmael of Melville's *Moby-Dick.* The scene occurs before everything has been swallowed up in the wild chase of Moby Dick and while the crew is still engaged in the normal tasks associated with whaling. One of these is the squeezing of lumps of sperm back into liquid form, and Ishmael and other members of the crew are sitting around a huge tub of such lumps engaged in what he calls that "sweet and unctuous duty." It is a lovely, peaceful day in which the ship sails serenely along, and as Ishmael bathes his hands in that rich aromatic substance, he forgets about his horrible oath to follow Ahab's mad pursuit of Moby Dick and feels "divinely free from all ill-will, or petulance or malice, of any sort whatsoever." And he goes on with this wonderful ejaculation:

> Squeeze! squeeze! squeeze! all the morning long; I squeezed that sperm till I myself almost melted into it; I squeezed that sperm till a strange sort of insanity came over me; and I found myself unwittingly squeezing my co-laborers' hands in it, mistaking their hands for the gentle globules. Such an abounding, affectionate, friendly, loving feeling did this avocation beget, that at last I was continually squeezing their hands and looking up into their eyes sentimentally; as much as to say,—Oh! my dear fellow beings, why should we any longer cherish any social acerbities, or know the slightest ill-humor or envy! Come; let us squeeze hands all round; nay, let us all squeeze ourselves into each other; let us squeeze ourselves universally into the very milk and sperm of kindness.
>
> Would that I could keep squeezing that sperm for ever! For now, since by many prolonged, repeated experiences, I have perceived that in all such cases man must eventually lower, or at least shift, his conceit of attainable felicity; not placing it anywhere in the intellect or the fancy; but in the wife, the heart, the bed, the table, the saddle, the fire-side, the country; now that I have perceived all this, I am ready to squeeze case eternally. In thoughts of the visions of the night, I saw long rows of angels in paradise, each with his hands in a jar of spermaceti.[6]

The passage may be jocular and reflect only one of Melville's moods, and Ahab is also able to call upon those same impulses toward unity for his ugly and unattainable ends; but it is an aspect of Melville's vision worth more attention than it gets, especially in conjunction with the fact that Ishmael is the only survivor in the book, saved by the loyal and loving Queequeg's coffin and by the compassionate quest of the Rachel "that in her retracing search after her missing children, found only another orphan."[7] While Ahab, that eagle, that man who would strike the sun if it offended him, joins Icarus in his watery grave.

In a mood such as this, I want to think about some of

William James's more hopeful thoughts and observations about impulses toward unity, as when he is describing how well charitableness and humility harmonize with all the states of mind and feeling he regards as more or less religious.

> . . . We must, I think consider them (i.e., charity and humility) not subordinate but coordinate parts of that great complex excitement in the study of which we are engaged. Religious rapture, moral enthusiasm, ontological wonder, cosmic emotion, are all unifying states of mind, in which the sand and grit of selfhood tend to disappear, and tenderness to rule. The best thing is to describe the condition integrally as a characteristic affection to which our nature is liable, a region in which we find ourselves at home, a sea in which we swim; but not to pretend to explain its parts by deriving them too cleverly from one another. Like love or fear, the faith state is a natural psychic complex, and carries charity with it by organic consequence. Jubilation is an expansive affection and all expansive affections are self-forgetful, and kindly so long as they endure.[8]

Still immersed in the spermaceti, I like it also when James tells me that although he has never had a truly mystical experience, the keynote of all his partial or artificial mystical experiences is "a reconciliation. . . . as if the opposites of the world, whose contradictoriness and conflict make all our difficulties, were melted into unity."[9] So immersed, I am not anxious to observe that opposites also make for much of the pleasure and interest in our world. And I remember only the less sodden and pugnacious conditions I have witnessed when he notes the affinity of alcoholic states and mystical ones, and goes on to say that

> the sway of alcohol over mankind is unquestionably due to its power to stimulate the mystical faculties of human nature, usually crushed to earth by the cold facts and dry criticisms of the sober hour. Sobriety diminishes, discriminates and says no; drunkenness expands, unites, and says yes. It is in fact the great exciter of the *Yes* function in man. It brings its votary from the chill periphery of things to the radiant core. It makes him for the moment one with truth. . . . The drunken consciousness is one bit of mystical consciousness, and our total opinion of it must find its place in our opinion of that larger whole.[10]

Giddy from such spirits I cannot resist saying yes to a poem that ordinarily strikes me as too cute. It shows how far metaphorical alcoholism can take even one normally so self-contained as Emily Dickinson.

> I taste a liquor never brewed—
> From Tankards scooped in Pearl—
> Not all the Vats upon the Rhine
> Yield such an Alcohol!
>
> Inebriate of Air—am I—
> And Debauchee of Dew—
> Reeling—thro endless summer days—
> From inns of Molten Blue—
>
> When "Landlords" turn the drunken Bee
> Out of the Foxglove's door—
> When Butterflies—renounce their "drams"—
> I shall but drink the more!
>
> Till Seraphs swing their snowy Hats—
> And Saints—to windows run—
> To see the little Tippler
> Leaning against the—sun—

No doubt Icarus would have something to say worth listening to about those final lines—not only about the heat of the sun but about the probabilities of such an inebriate noticing his or any other human predicament. But even if we are unwilling to fly quite so high as James or Dickinson, we can take some comfort in recognizing that the enormous human appetite for alcohol is not just a measure of how much people wish to escape the pain or poverty of their lives and not just a measure of their loneliness, but a measure also of their yearning for oneness and connection. For alcohol can penetrate armors and loosen intellectual catatonias, and can allow warmth and intimacy that are not adequately defined as loss of inhibition. And it can also provide a finer as well as coarser tuning to what is going on around one.

But this is really a willed cheerfulness because, at bottom, I fear, distrust, and usually dislike drunkards. And do so whether their intoxication comes from alcohol, religion, patriotism, a cause, an idea, love, or even an excess of good will. The same impulse toward unity that immerses Ishmael and other crew members into a vast bath of benevolence as they squeeze the spermaceti earlier helped them become one with Ahab when he demanded their allegiance in his vengeful quest, a union into which even Ishmael is carried away. And if it can sweep up people into reassuring white-robed choirs singing "Halleluja" or "We Shall Overcome," or as in Beethoven's Ninth "Be embraced all ye Millions! / With a Kiss for all the world!" it can whip them into rows of brown- and black-shirted drunkards heiling Hitler and singing "Deutschland über Alles," believing so much in unity that they provided it even for their victims—in mass graves.

The same intoxication that impels Shelley and Whitman to obliterate themselves and me into a seasonal circle that always returns to springtime also entices them, and would me, toward a less fertile annihilation. Thus Shelley coaxes in "Adonais":

> . . . . From the world's bitter wind
> Seek shelter in the shadow of the tomb
> What Adonais is, why fear we to become?
>
> The One remains, the many change and pass;
> Heaven's light forever shines, Earth's shadows fly;
> Life, like a dome of many-colored glass,
> Stains the white radiance of Eternity,
> Until Death tramples it to fragments.—Die,
> If thou wouldst be with that which thou dost seek!
> Follow where all is fled!—Rome's azure sky,
> Flowers, ruins, statues, music, words, are weak
> The glory they transfuse with fitting truth to speak.
>
> Why linger, why turn back, why shrink, my Heart?
> Thy hopes are gone before; from all things here
> They have departed; thou shouldst now depart!
> A light is past from the revolving year,
> And man, and woman; and what still is dear
> Attracts to crush, repels to make thee wither.
> The soft sky smiles,—the low wind whispers near:
> 'Tis Adonais calls! oh hasten thither,
> No more let life divide what Death can join together.[12]

And Whitman, seeking in "Out of the Cradle Endlessly Rocking" a final word that will answer his "cries of unsatisfied love . . . the sweet hell within, / the unknown want, the destiny of me", happily accepts the answer of the sea, which

> Lisp'd to me the low and delicious word death
> And again death, death, death, death,
> Hissing melodious, neither like the bird nor like my arous'd child's heart,
> But edging near as privately for me rustling at my feet,
> Creeping thence steadily up to my ears and laving me softly all over
> Death, death, death, death, death, death.
>
> (P. 184)

In passing I must observe that it is a bird, a mockingbird who has lost its mate, that stimulates Whitman's painful yearnings in this poem, helps him give voice to them, and forms part of the constellation that makes him seek that delicious oceanic extinction. Worth noticing too is how much the boy and the bird are governed by loneliness: "Oh you singer solitary, singing by yourself, projecting me, / O solitary listening, never more shall I cease perpetuating you" (p. 184).

I am moved when Jonathan Edwards tells me that as he approached his conversion experience there came into his mind "so sweet a sense of the glorious *majesty* and *grace* of God, that I know not how to express. I seemed to see them both in a sweet conjunction; mystery and meekness joined together; it was a gentle, an holy majesty; and also a majestic meekness; a high, great, and holy gentleness." But I am chilled when he keeps repeating and repeating that he wishes to be "swallowed up" in God and says he yearns desperately to be "emptied and annihilated; to lie in the dust."[13] And I am mostly chilled by the mystics whose acquaintance I have made in William James's *The Varieties of Religious Experience*. When I read this passage from Jacob Behman, I cannot block out the sound of the old waiter's voice in Hemingway's "A Clean Well Lighted Place." Behman says, "Love" is nothing, for

> when thou art gone forth wholly from the Creature and from that which is visible, and art become Nothing to all that is Nature and Creature, then thou art in that Eternal One, which is God himself, and then thou shalt feel within thee the highest virtue of Love. . . . The treasure of treasures for the soul is where she goeth out of the Somewhat into that Nothing out of which all things may be made. The soul here saith, *I have nothing,* for I am utterly stripped and naked; *I can do nothing*, for I have no manner of power, but am as water poured out; *I am nothing*, for all that I am is no more than an image of Being, and only God is to me I AM; and so, sitting down in my own Nothingness, I give glory to the eternal Being, and *will nothing* of myself, that so God may will all in me, being unto me my God and all things.[14]

The old waiter insists on the need for clean, pleasant, well-lighted cafes to be open late at night to protect the lonely ones from the kind of nothingness he knows and talks about in lonely conversation with himself, for "he knew it was all nada y pues nada y nada y pues nada. Our nada who are in nada, nada be thy name thy kingdom nada thy will be nada in nada as it is in nada / Give us this nada our daily nada and nada us our nada as we nada our nadas and nada us not into nada but deliver us from nada; pues nada. Hail nothing full of nothing, nothing is with thee."[15]

I am chilled even when I read of an experience like this one of Malwida von Meysenbug, where again, as for Whitman (and Icarus too) the ocean is the entrance to eternity:

> . . . I was impelled to kneel down, this time before the illimitable ocean, symbol of the Infinite. I felt that I prayed as I had never prayed before, and knew now what prayer really is: to return from the solitude of individuation into the consciousness of unity with all that is, to kneel down as one that passes away, and to rise up as one imperishable. Earth, heaven, and sea resounded as in one vast world-encircling harmony. It was as if the chorus of all the great who had ever lived were about me. I felt myself one with them, and it appeared as if I heard their greeting: "Thou too belongest to the company of those who overcome."[16]

I should think the final sentence might read "who have been overcome." But here, as with many mystics, there is a curious ambiguity that goes beyond the usual Christian paradox of gaining the self through losing it, an ambiguity as to whether the soul has been absorbed by, become part of, the larger unity or whether it has expanded to such a degree that it has incorporated everything else.

I *know* the self has taken over when I read:

> He who would hear the voice of Nada, "the Soundless Sound," and comprehend it, he has to learn the nature of Dhanana. . . . When to himself his form appears unreal, as do on waking all the forms he sees in dreams; when he has ceased to hear the many, he may discern the ONE—the inner sound which kills the outer. . . . For then the soul will hear and will remember. And then to the inner ear will speak THE VOICE OF SILENCE. . . . And now the *Self* is lost in SELF, *thyself* into THYSELF, merged in that SELF from which thou first did radiate. . . . Behold! thou hast become the Light, thou has become the Sound, thou art thy Master and thy God. Thou art THYSELF the object of thy search: the VOICE unbroken, that resounds through eternities, exempt from change, from sin exempt, the seven sounds in one, the VOICE OF THE SILENCE. *Om tat Sat.*[17]

Probably I should feel more sympathy here than I do, for surely the strength of these desires for unity and even death reflects an equally strong sense of unwholeness, incompleteness, and loneliness, or, as with some of the more Christian mystics, profound unworthiness. The extent to which this is true is suggested by the number of people like Tolstoi and Bunyan whose conversions or mystical experiences followed upon serious periods of depression. It is worth noting that even Agee's celebration of Beethoven's Ninth Symphony that I quoted earlier follows and remains intimately connected with despair and that the symphony itself was perhaps in part the creation of Beethoven's own despair as his deafness progressively increased his distance from the rest of mankind. Similar conjunctions occur with Jonathan Edwards, Emerson, Melville, Dickinson, John Stuart Mill, Dostoevsky, Virginia Woolf, and William James himself, and no doubt numerous other authors I am less acquainted with. One need not reduce all mysticism to pathology to understand that for many the religious sense itself might adequately be defined as "the feeling of unwholeness, of moral imperfection, of sin, to use the technical word [as Scobie might] accompanied by the yearning after the peace of unity,"[18] or to accept James's phrase "sick soul" to describe the condition of many who are particularly susceptible to the deliverance of all-engulfing religions.[19] I should try to remember Rollo May's sympathetic observation that extremely isolated and lonely people often feel in danger of losing their boundaries and their ability to discriminate " 'between wakefulness and sleep—between the subjective self and the objective world around them.' "[20] Though I do not wish to "explain" Whitman in such a way, his Calamus poems suggest he was hardly the comfortable "comarado" he often made himself out to be. One can even go so far as to view most of these self-annihilations as a form of metaphorical suicide that saves such anguished people from literal self-destruction.

Having said all this, however, I still am frightened of all those who want to unify me or themselves into one kind of stuff—whether they are messiahs, mystics, monists, or mere moneymakers, and whether that stuff is death, pure spirit (either Western or Eastern style), Leibnitz's monads, Bergson's *elan vitale,* Blake's "Universal Man," a totalitarian organism (either right or left), or one of those blobs that science fiction writers love to scare us with. But even much gentler intoxications, expansivenesses, and impulses toward unity leave me with a fear of being gobbled up. There are so many ways of swallowing things. I am uneasy when Emerson writes: "From within or behind, a light shines through us upon things, and makes us aware that we are nothing, but the light is all. A man is the facade of a temple wherein all wisdom and all good abide. What we commonly call man, the eating, drinking, planting, counting man, does not, as we know him represent himself, but misrepresents himself. Him we do not respect, but the soul, whose organ he is, would he let it appear through his action, would make our knees bend."[21] It seems to me dangerous, perhaps even suicidal or murderous, to remove respect from that part of us which plants and eats. I am even more frightened by the ending of the celebrated passage in which he says: "Standing on the bare ground [in the woods]—my head bathed by the blithe air, and uplifted into infinite space,—all mean egotism vanishes. I become a transparent eyeball; I am nothing; I see all; the currents of the Universal Being circulate through me; I am part or parcel of God. The name of the nearest friend sounds then foreign and accidental: to be brothers, to be acquaintances,—master or servant, is then a trifle and a disturbance."[22] How dare he say that so blithely! Such a bath makes it necessary to repeat that observation of Orwell that "the essence of being human is that one does not seek perfection, that one *is* sometimes willing to commit sins for the sake of loyalty, that one does not push asceticism to the point where it makes friendly intercourse impossible, and that one is prepared in the end to be defeated and broken up by life, which is the inevitable price of fastening one's love upon other human individuals."[23] Somewhere, though quite distant at the moment, is a voice that mocks: "Swallowed up or broken up. Some choice!"

Although I will later have some kind things to say about voyeurism, I think Jonathan Bishop gives a necessary warning when he writes in his book on Emerson that "the eye is the megalomaniac among the senses; it takes possession of the universe from a distance and seems itself to be the center from which all existence radiates."[24] With all his awareness of the dangers of appropriating the tenant farmers in *Let Us Now Praise Famous Men,* James Agee, as Dan McCall observes, is in danger of "summon[ing] the world into an imperious eye."[25] And here is probably as good a place as any to present McCall's brilliant observation in connection with Agee's visual possessiveness, that the "deepest feeling of guilt is incurred when the eye of the artist is affronted by the opposing eye of his subject—where the urge to locate the world's suffering in a visual moment is suddenly brought up short by one of the world's sufferers looking back."[26] How slippery that line is between observing and ingesting is evident in even so seemingly innocent a comment as this one in another of Agee's letters to Father Flye:

> At night I'm starting to draw, heads of Alma and copies of postcard American streets. I would never have known how much even a little of it sharpens your eye and gives you more understanding

> and affection for even some small part of a human or architectural feature. Also back with the whole primitive bases of art, when people made effigies that they might have power over the animals they needed for food. I now "possess" and "know" Alma's face and a Brooklyn street in 1938 as if they were a part of me, as much as my hand, the same with one of the tenant houses from memory.[27]

In this very mild intoxication, how smooth the transition from "understanding and affection" to "power over" to "possess[ion]" to translation into a part of his own body. The more I look at such a passage, the less distant it seems from that frightening equation of Goethe's in which the artist is likened to "the eagle, who flies with free glance over every land" and carries off his prey into the realm of "the good, the noble and the beautiful." The less distant from the frightening image in this passage from Kierkegaard, of eaglehood, suffering, loneliness, artistic possession, and self-annihilating self-inflation (or self-inflating self-annihilation).

> My grief is my castle, which like an eagle's nest is built high up in the mountain peaks among the clouds; nothing can storm it. From it I fly down into reality to seize my prey; but I do not remain down there. I bring it home with me, and this prey is a picture I weave into the tapestries of my palace. There I live as one dead. I immerse everything I have experienced in a baptism of forgetfulness unto an eternal remembrance. Everything finite and accidental is erased.[28]

In the face of such obliteration—of acquaintances, friends, and brothers, of everything finite and accidental—there is little to be said or done, for life itself, and even love, are extinguished. It does, of course, solve all the problems of suffering and distance, end all internal division and debate. And there can be few of us who have not at some time been tempted by one or another of the delicious unions with death proposed above. It *is* more comfortable to be rocked in the cradle of the ocean than to worry about Icarus or that nameless martyr. It may be that there is in every one of us, as the psychiatrist Edith Weigert says is present in every "patient," "a repressed nostalgia for the oceanic feeling of trusting harmony, for the original symbiotic unity of mother and infant."[29] It may even be, though I doubt it, that we all are afflicted with some degree of death wish or natural entropy, but most of us have more interesting pursuits in mind.

If nothing else, we wish to do as Janie does in my favorite myth about a part of the mystery we have just been exploring, a myth, we may note, in which the unity is the point of departure and not the goal. It is the myth that Zora Neale Hurston uses to describe her heroine's efforts to exhibit to others her personal worth, "a jewel down inside herself," to walk "where people could see her and gleam it around." But the context is oddly ambiguous with respect to whether her fulfillment will lie more in connection with others or separation from them.

> When God made the Man, he made him out of stuff that sung all the time and glittered all over. Then after that some angels got jealous and chopped him into millions of pieces, but still he glittered and hummed. So they beat him down to nothing but sparks but each little spark had a shine and a song. So they covered each one over with mud. And the lonesomeness in the sparks made them hunt for one another, but the mud is deaf and dumb. Like all the other tumbling mud-balls, Janie had tried to show her shine.[30]

I like the myth in part because it counters a little George Eliot's and my own too gloomy sense that dominates what I have so far written, that what lies on the other side of silence is chiefly a roar, the sort of roar we would hear if we were not so well wadded with stupidity, and never a shine and a song.

I like the myth also because of the way it captures at once the loneliness of the separate sparks, their yearning for one another, and the muddy composition of their self-encasement. How much more simple it would be if we were made like billiard balls and could simply bump or kiss and bounce away, or else, like paramecia, had entirely permeable membranes and could ingest and absorb one another completely. But how dull. How we love the private space beneath our muddy skins, the silence in which to shine out our aloneness, the separateness with which to contemplate the idea of unity, the chance to select a few other mudballs to tumble against.

A final note:

The move here toward mysticism began with Whitman's "I was the man, I suffer'd, I was there," and went on into all sorts of extinctions, another commentary on the fruit of fusion. But we must not forget that Scobie's way too ended in self-annihilation. And I must be fair enough to allow William James a further word here about the mystical regions of consciousness: that although "they cannot furnish formulas," they "open a region though they fail to give a map. At any rate, they forbid a premature closing of our accounts with reality."[31]

VII ❖ Coming Together and Apart

I WISH NOW TO EXPLORE SOME PARTS OF THAT MORE FAMILIAR realm where the one and the many retain their more usual distances and where our chief preoccupation is not our relation to the ONE or ALL but coming together and apart with other individuals of our own species, a realm that is perhaps best entered by another myth, the one offered by Aristophanes in Plato's *Symposium* to explain the origin of human love. It is worth relating with something of the fullness with which it appears in the original. "In the beginning," Aristophanes explains, "we were nothing like we are now." For one thing, there were three sexes—male, female, and a third, an actual "hermaphrodite," a creature that was half male and half female. And secondly, each of these beings

> was globular in shape, with rounded back and sides, four arms and four legs, and two faces, both the same on a cylindrical neck; and one head, with one face one side and one the other, and four ears, and two lots of privates, and all the other parts to match. They walked erect, as we do ourselves, backwards or forwards, whichever they pleased; but when they broke into a run they simply stuck their legs straight out and went whirling around them like a clown turning cartwheels. And since they had eight legs, if you count their arms as well, you can imagine that they went bowling along at a pretty good speed.

Such was the strength, energy, and arrogance of these creatures that they actually tried (as Icarus probably did not) to scale the heights of heaven and set upon the gods. Zeus, who does not wish to destroy them completely, which would mean giving up all their offerings and devotions, decides to weaken them by cutting them in half, "thus killing two birds with one stone; for each one will be only half as strong, and there'll be twice as many of them, which will suit us very nicely. They can walk about, upright, on their two legs, and if . . . I have any more trouble with them, I shall split them up again, and they'll have to hop about on one." After cutting each in half, he tells Apollo to turn each of the faces toward the side that was cut away—"thinking that the sight of such a gash might frighten them into keeping quiet—and then to heal the whole thing up." Apollo does this by pulling the skin tight "like those bags you pull together with a string and tied up the one remaining opening so as to form what we call the navel."

When all this is done, each half creature is left with a desperate yearning for its other half, and they all run about flinging their arms around each other's necks, wishing somehow to be rolled back into one. Pretty soon they begin "to die of hunger and general inertia because neither would do anything without the other. And when one half was left alone by the death of its mate, it wandered about questing and clasping in the hope of finding a spare half-woman—or a whole woman, as we should call her nowadays—or half a man." Before long the race begins to die out because the sexual organs had "originally been on the outside—which was now the back" and they had conceived not upon each other but, like the grasshoppers, upon the earth.

Zeus takes pity on them and moves their sex organs around to the front and has the male beget upon the female—"the idea being that if, in all these clippings and claspings, a man should chance upon a woman, conception would take place and the race could be continued, while if a man should congregate with man, he might at least obtain such satisfaction as would allow him to turn his attention to the everyday affairs of life. So you see, gentlemen, how far back we can trace our innate love for one another; and how this love is always trying to reintegrate our former nature, to make two into one, and to bridge the gulf between one human being and another."

Aristophanes goes on to draw the obvious corollaries that heterosexual and homosexual proclivities depend upon the sex of the original slices and to develop the expected Greek emphasis upon the love of men for men, but also argues that the sexual pleasures can "hardly account for the huge delight lovers take in one another's company. The fact is that both their souls are longing for . . . that original state of ours . . . that primeval wholeness." He concludes that "the happiness of the whole human race, women no less than men, is to be found in the consummation of our love, and in the healing of our dissevered nature by finding each his proper mate. And if this be a counsel of perfection, then we must do what, in our present circumstances, is next best, and bestow our love upon the natures most congenial to our own." If we show sufficient reverence for the gods, love "will one day heal us and restore us to our old estate, and establish us in joy and blessedness."[1]

Despite its comic aspects, such a myth perhaps explains as well as any other the strength with which most of us feel the urge to unite with particular other members of our species, sexually and otherwise, the enormous amount of time, energy, and money we devote to that endeavor, and the curious extent to which we have chosen to describe, and to want to describe, such connections as achievements of oneness. At least until recently. The urge still seems to be there, of course, though now many of the lovers apparently prefer to be partners in a "relationship," sometimes with explicitly defined duties and privileges, rather than to be united in holy matrimony with a "better half." The injunction "What God hath joined let no man cut asunder" seems for some to have been replaced by something like "Don't get hitched too tightly," as though marriage were only a set of harnesses. And I have attended a marriage ceremony recently in which the dominant note was not the bonds between the two but Kahlil Gibran's warning to be sure to keep spaces between them. I understand there are those who prefer engaging in sexual congress to making love.

But this is the easy, though irresistible, grumbling of my middle age. I should remember the long, long line of marriages of the past not made in heaven, including the one in which the knot was tied with bride and groom and parson all falling through the sky harnessed to parachutes. And though there may have been some recent real damage to love and language, I believe it is local and that the condition described by the myth will continue to prevail. The couple, in fact, who were married with Gibran's spaces, appear to be closely and happily welded.

Popular lyrics will no doubt continue to say such things as

> Lovers are very special people,
> They're the luckiest people in the world.
> With one person
> One very special person
> A feeling deep in your soul
> Says. You were half, now you're whole.[2]

We will, I believe, go on responding to Romeo and Juliet and understanding the feeling that generates exchanges like the one between Maria and Robert Jordan in Hemingway's *For Whom the Bell Tolls* in which she says: "I am thee and thou art me and all of one is the other. And I love thee, oh, I love thee so. Are we not truly one?" and he answers, "Yes. . . . It is true."[3] I think we will go on having lovers, friends, comrades, pals, buddies, chums, mates, and sidekicks as well as "relationships," and will continue to understand when Saint Augustine writes this passage, which Auden did not choose to quote, about his response to the death of his friend: "I wondered yet more that myself, who was to him a second self, could live, he being dead. Well said one of his friends, 'Thou half of my soul:' for I felt that my soul and his soul were 'one soul in two bodies:' and therefore was my life a horror to me, because I would not live halved."[4] And I trust we will go on delighting in lines like John Donne's

> Call us what you will, we're made such by love;
> Call her one, me another fly,
> We're tapers too, and at our own cost die.
> And we in us find the eagle and the dove.
> The phoenix riddle hath more wit
> By us: we two being one, are it.
> So, to one neutral thing both sexes fit.
> We die and rise the same, and prove
> Mysterious by this love
>
> ("The Canonization")[5]

and the numerous other poems that might be anthologized under a title like *Two Becoming One*.[6]

Surely we will continue to understand the curious shifts in a passage like this one from Virginia Woolf's *To the Lighthouse* as Lily Briscoe wonders what it is that makes Mrs. Ramsay so remarkable. I quote at some length here in part as a way of introducing Lily, who will be an important presence later in this chapter.

> . . . Sitting on the floor with her arms around Mrs. Ramsay's knees, close as she could get, smiling to think that Mrs. Ramsay would never know the reason of that pressure, she imagined how in the chambers of the mind and heart of the woman who was, physically, touching her, were stood, like the treasures in the tombs of kings, tablets bearing sacred inscriptions, which if one could spell them out, would teach one everything, but they would never be offered openly, never made public. What art was there, known to love or cunning, by which one pressed through to those secret chambers? What device for becoming, like waters poured into one jar, inextricably the same, one with the object one adored? Could the body achieve, or the mind, subtly mingling in the intricate passages of the brain? or the heart? Could loving, as people called it, make her and Mrs. Ramsay one? for it was not knowledge but unity she desired, not inscriptions on tablets, nothing that could be written in any language known to men, but intimacy itself, which is knowledge, she had thought, leaning her head on Mrs. Ramsay's knee.
>
> Nothing happened. Nothing! Nothing! as she leant her head against Mrs. Ramsay's knee. And yet, she knew knowledge and wisdom were stored up in Mrs. Ramsay's heart. How then, she had asked herself, did one know one thing or another thing about people, sealed as they were? Only like a bee, drawn by some sweetness or sharpness in the air intangible to touch or taste, one haunted the dome-shaped hive, ranged the wastes of air over the countries of the world alone, and then haunted the hives with their murmurs and their stirrings; the hives, which were people. Mrs. Ramsay rose. Lily rose. Mrs. Ramsay went. For days there hung about her, as after a dream some subtle change is felt in the person one has dreamt of, more vividly than anything she said, the sound of murmuring and, as she sat in the wicker arm-chair in the drawing-room window she wore, to Lily's eyes, an august shape; the shape of a dome.[7]

Even Freud, who confesses he has never experienced oceanic feelings and who is inclined to see most blurrings of the self and the outer world as pathological, is willing to say: "There is only one state—admittedly an unusual state, but not one that can be stigmatized as pathological—" in which the ego does not maintain clear and sharp lines of demarcation between itself and the outside. "At the height of being in love the boundary between ego and object threatens to melt away. Against all the evidence of his senses a man who is in love declares that 'I' and 'you' are one, and is prepared to behave as if it were a fact."[8]

Even Auden, for a while at least, must have been overcome by a yearning enough like those defined in both myths to have written a stanza that ends as this one does:

> There is no such thing as the State
> And no one exists alone;
> Hunger allows no choice
> To the citizen or the police;
> We must love one another or die.
>
> ("September 1, 1939")[9]

There is enough truth in those myths that I felt a strong sense of loss and sorrow when I first learned that Auden changed the final line to read: "we must love one another and die," then deleted the whole stanza, and finally dropped the poem in its entirety from his collected works. And there is enough truth in both myths so that I feel a similar sense of loss and sorrow as I now follow, as I must, some turnings of mind and heart that neither myth takes proper account of. The androgyny myth itself provides as good a bridge as any.

Near the end of his speech, as he is celebrating the joy of lovers who find their other halves, Aristophanes asks what would happen if Hephaestus were to come and stand over such lovers with his tool bag as they lay together, and to offer to roll them into one, "so that you could always be together, day and night, and never be parted again? Because if that's what you want I can easily weld you together; and then you can live your two lives in one, and when the time comes, you can die a common death and still be two-in-one in the lower world. Now what do you say? Is that what you'd like me to do? And would you be happy if I did?" Without a moment's pause or hint of irony, Aristophanes goes on: "We may be sure gentlemen, that no lover on earth would dream of refusing such an offer, for not one of them could imagine a happier fate. Indeed, they would be convinced that this was just what they'd been waiting for—to be merged, that is, into an utter one-ness with the beloved."

I cannot resist suggesting immediately, and not just facetiously, that the lovers' response might depend a good deal upon whether Hephaestus had approached them just before or after their sexual climax. Yet even in the heat of sexual union, I suspect, most lovers might hesitate to accept Hephaestus's offer. At any other time, nearly all of us, I believe, would make the choice to remain incomplete and apart, within our separate skins.[10]

No doubt there are many reasons why this would be true, including some profound chemical or biological ones of the sort that cause us to reject transplanted organs even from our own kin unless the rejection is inhibited by drugs, that make us want to cut apart Siamese twins or else hide them away in freak shows where we can exercise a little ambivalence but not much, and that lead most of us, despite a wish to be close to our beloveds when we die, to choose to lie in separate graves.

But I think the deepest reason is that remaining incomplete allows us to be lonely and to devote much of our lives to that most fascinating of occupations—the effort at once to preserve and overcome our aloneness, even to perform the impossible feat of simultaneously merging and remaining separate. I do not mean to sound clever, for this contradiction more than any other, I believe, shapes our lives. It is hard to see how it could be otherwise given our elemental biological and psychological histories. For beneath all the subtleties and complexities spelled out by Freud, Jung, and the legions of developmental theorists who followed them, this much is clear. Each of us did at one time live within the body of another, sharing its food and blood (and if the New Puritans are right, nicotine and alcohol). Each of us came into being from the entrance of one body into another and from the profound mingling of the cells from two other bodies that, in turn and on and on back in time, came into being from a union of other bodies. Even if we are not all great-great-grandchildren of Adam and Eve or of a father who art in heaven, or of those eight-footed heaven-scaling creatures proposed by Aristophanes, or of the latest fossilized anthropoid announced by the anthropologists, we all must have some common great-grandparents somewhere in the past. All of us knew some kind of warm embrace or touch, at least in infancy, and reached out a small arm and hand to touch another. We all lived for a while in a state of helplessness in which we depended entirely on others to remain alive (and still do depend on others to help feed and clothe us). All of us very early watched others go away from us into separateness and distance, sometimes when we needed them or desired them. Nearly all of us, I would guess, began to try to tame this mystery, sometimes by crying, sometimes by little games of hide-and-seek in which, for a while at least, the other always reappeared, sometimes by pretending we did not care. All of us very early had encounters that gave us pain, and as we grew had to have the experience of others as intruding (with commands, demands, questions, touches, blows) upon our growing sense of selfhood and private space. We also had to have the experience again and again of discovering that others did not know what was going on inside us and of realizing that we were in some sense alone within our own skins and short of death could not fully merge again with any other. These things alone, even without any of the further experiences of weaning, adolescence, sex, and death, suggest how much our lives must come to be defined by motions toward and away from one another and how exquisitely complex our feelings and thoughts will come to be about such motions, or even about the possibilities of them.

These things alone go far toward explaining the special claim put on our attention by nearly anything that strikes the chords of separateness and oneness, distance and closeness, or loneliness and connectedness. And they *are* chords in that the poles are indissoluble, can be defined only in relation to each other. One could not conceive of the meaning of separateness were there not the possibility of union and vice versa. The same is true for loneliness and connectedness. The very word *loneliness* implies a yearning for connection. It is this indissolubility that probably accounts for much of our fascination with solitary or lonely figures—not only with romantic or heroic ones like Leatherstocking, Heathcliff, Ahab, and the Count of Monte Cristo but with hermits, recluses, and solitary voyagers of all kinds, both real and fictional; and it is tempting to dwell upon such figures, to stare at the space that surrounds one or another Bartleby, Prufrock, Sister Carrie, or Eben Flood. I sometimes think American literature is defined more by such spaces than by any of the geographical ones it populates. But it is the chords in which the antithetic states vibrate with more noticeable dissonance, the human connections in which the poles are in greater tension, that I wish most to sound, and which seem to me to resound most tellingly (tell most resoundingly?) of our human plight.

I am thinking of titles like *The Lonely Crowd* or *The Heart Is a Lonely Hunter*; phrases like "hardhearted," "parting is such sweet sorrow," "absence makes the heart grow fonder," "good fences make good neighbors," "keep your distance," "don't touch me," "nothing can touch me," "ships that pass in the night," and "each man kills the thing he loves"; the numberless lyrics that beg beloveds to come closer or lament how far off they have gone; the cowboy's plea to "bury me not on the lone prairie." I think of all those scenes in movies (which have made my tears spurt against my will) where the lovers are physically dragged apart by parents, policemen, soldiers, or things from outer space, or where they embrace across barbed wire, or one in a train and one on the platform, they hold together as long as they can as the train is pulling out and we must both watch and hear the growing distance and sometimes watch them wave. And all those train scenes in Thomas Wolfe's novels that once struck my adolescent heart, as they did his, as the most poignant representations of human loneliness and yearning for connection. And probably still would if not for the overwriting. Here is the culmination of an accidental race between two trains that had jolted the passengers out of their lonely isolation and caused them to crowd at the windows, "grinning like children for delight and jubilation" as first one train and then the other took the lead:

> And they looked at one another for a moment, they passed and vanished and were gone forever, yet it seemed to him that he had known these people, that he knew them better than the people in his own train, and that, having met them for an instant under immense and timeless skies, as they were hurled across the continent to a thousand destinations, they had met, passed, vanished, yet would remember this forever. And he thought the people in the two trains felt this, also: slowly they passed each other now, and their mouths smiled and their eyes grew friendly, but he thought there was some sorrow and regret in what they felt. For, having lived together as strangers in the immense and swarming city, they now had met upon the everlasting earth, hurled past each other for a moment between two points in time upon the shining rails, never to meet, to speak, to know each other any more, and the briefness of their days, the destiny of man, was in that instant greeting and farewell.[11]

(In airplanes we cannot have such experiences—one more price we pay for thinking we should be high-soaring birds.)

When I think of Wolfe, I think of Sherwood Anderson and all those lonely figures in *Winesburg, Ohio* who, as Irving Howe has so well put it, are alienated from each other partly because "the very extremity of their need for love [has] itself become a barrier to its realization"[12]; Louise Bentley, who feels "that between herself and all the other people in the world, a wall had been built up and that she was living just on the edge of some warm inner circle of life that must be quite open and understandable to others"[13]; the stranger in "Tandy," who, as Maxwell Geismar rightly observes, expresses the underlying obscurely felt emotion of the town when he says, "I am a lover and have not found my thing to love. . . . It makes my destruction inevitable, you see."[14] I think especially of Anderson's wonderfully explicit commentary when George Willard, after paroxysms of loneliness, takes a walk with Helen White: "The feeling of loneliness and isolation that had come to the young man in the crowded streets of his town was both broken and intensified by the presence of Helen."[15] I think more soberly of statements like Rilke's that "between even the closest human beings infinite distances continue to exist"[16]; of passages like the one by Olive Schreiner that Patrick White uses as an epigraph in his *The Aunt's Story*, a story about a woman who inhabits an exceptionally wonderful and terrible aloneness: "She thought of the narrowness of the limits within which a human soul may speak and be understood by its nearest of mental kin, of how soon it reaches the solitary land of the individual experience, in which no fellow footfall is ever heard"[17]; of the lines that end Emily Dickinson's "I Cannot Live with You":

> So we must keep apart,
> You there, I here,
> With just the door ajar
> That Oceans are,
> And prayer,
> And that pale sustenance,
> Despair.[18]

and of the terrifying passage that ends E.M. Forster's *A Passage to India*, that book which so powerfully mirrors the looks of certain distances between cultures, between individuals, and between man and his universe, and that also describes some quite remarkable efforts to look across those distances:

> Fielding mocked again.
> And Aziz in an awful rage danced this way and that, not knowing what to do and cried: "Down with the English anyhow. That's certain. Clear out, you fellows, double quick, I say. We may hate one another, but we hate you most. If I don't make you go, Ahmed will, Karim will, if it's fifty-five hundred years we shall get rid of you, yes, we shall drive every blasted Englishman into the sea, and then"—he rode against him furiously—"and then," he continued, half kissing him, "you and I shall be friends."
>
> "Why can't we be friends now?" said the other, holding him affectionately. "It's what I want. It's what you want."

> But the horses didn't want it—they swerved apart; the earth didn't want it; sending up rocks through which riders must pass single file; the temples, the tank, the jail, the palace, the birds, the carrion, the Guest House, that came into view as they issued from the gap and saw Mau beneath: they didn't want it, they said in their hundred voices, "No, not yet," and the sky said, "No, not there."[19]

It is the "not yet," I believe, with its possibility of future union that gives this distance its especially agonizing look.

I think of the passage in *Another Country* where James Baldwin says of Vivaldo, just after Ida has finished telling him about her whorishness with Ellis, that "his heart began to beat with a newer, stonier anguish, which destroyed the distance called pity and placed him, very nearly, in her body." A moment later he goes to her "resigned and tender and helpless, her sobs seeming to make his belly sore. And, nevertheless, for a moment, he could not touch her, he didn't know how."[20] During that night of their farthest penetration of one another, he does not physically enter her body; when they finally embrace, there "was nothing erotic in it; they were like two weary children" (p. 362). And though it hints at a large number of matters I am not ready to deal with yet, I must note also that immediately after this new oneness with Ida, Vivaldo is apparently able to close another distance, for he is able to work on his novel all that night, a novel that had been giving him great difficulty because his characters "did not seem to trust him. . . . He could move them about but they themselves did not move. He put words in their mouths which they uttered sullenly, unconvinced. With the same agony, or greater, with which he attempted to seduce a woman, he was trying to seduce his people: he begged them to surrender up to him their privacy. And they refused—without, for all their ugly intransigence, showing the faintest desire to leave him" (p. 111). Our final glimpse of the two figures draws much of its power from the space between them across which she calls his name and from the jostling in the spaces beyond them: "Much, much later, while he was still working and she slept, she turned in her sleep, and she called his name. He paused, waiting, staring at her, but she did not move again, or speak again. He rose, and walked to the window. The rain had ceased, in the black-blue sky a few stars were scattered, and the wind roughly jostled the clouds along" (p. 362). And I must mention one more phrase from that much undervalued book: Cass's saying that if her husband had been unfaithful to her she would not try to hold him, as he was trying to hold her, with threats or want to punish him because "after all—he doesn't belong to me, nobody belongs to anybody" (p. 339).[21]

Another lady (from the pen of a writer whose distance from James Baldwin seems at once astronomical and easily bridged), Virginia Woolf's Mrs. Dalloway, puts it this way: "And there is a dignity in people, a solitude; even between husband and wife a gulf; and that one must respect . . . for one would not part with it oneself, or take it, against his will, from one's husband, without losing one's independence, one's self-respect—something, after all, priceless."[22] Since it always seems a special distortion to offer only one perspective from a novel by Virginia Woolf, we should note that this same "priceless" "solitude" or "gulf" seems to make it impossible for her husband to say outright that he loves her even on a day when he has come home especially to do so and that he thinks on that occasion "it is a thousand pities never to say what one feels" (p. 175).[23] And note that Mrs. Dalloway on another occasion thinks of herself as one who "could not dispel a virginity preserved through childbirth which clung to her like a sheet," "a cold spirit" that often leads her to fail her husband. "She could see what she lacked . . . something central which permeated; something warm which broke up surfaces and rippled the cold contact of man and woman, or of women together" (p. 46). And she knows something of what it can mean to cross that gulf. For "she could not resist sometimes yielding to the charm of a woman . . . confessing, as to her they often did, some scrape, some folly. And whether it was pity, or their beauty, or that she was older, or some accident—like a faint scent, or a violin next door (so strange is the power of sounds at certain moments), she did undoubtedly then feel what men felt. Only for a moment; but it was enough" (p. 53).

Mrs. Dalloway is an especially fascinating mixture of desires to merge and to preserve herself intact. Even death she sees as something that permits both a preservation of self and a surrendering of it. Hearing about the suicide of a young man, she thinks how she and her old friends "would grow old. A thing there was that mattered; a thing, wreathed about with chatter, defaced, obscured in her own life, let drop every day in corruption, chatter. This he had preserved. Death was defiance. Death was an attempt to communicate; people feeling the impossibility of reaching the center which, mystically, evaded them; closeness drew apart; rapture faded, one was alone. There was an embrace in death" (pp. 280–81). She intuits correctly that the young man killed himself because of a certain kind of arrogant doctor's capability of committing "some indescribable outrage—forcing your soul, that was it . . . they make life intolerable, men like that" (p. 281). At one point while writing the book, Virginia Woolf had thought she might have Mrs. Dalloway kill herself. Instead she ends the book with a tribute to the power of her particular selfhood as Peter Walsh witnesses her return to the party:

> What is this terror? what is this ecstasy? he thought to himself. What is it that fills me with extraordinary excitement?
>
> It is Clarissa, he said.
>
> For there she was. (P. 296)

Tensions between self-preservation and self-annihilation and between separateness and connection are so central and fascinating a part of Virginia Woolf's vision (and life as well) that it is tempting to go on giving illustrations. And I shall return to her later to show ways by which some of her characters manage to cross distances between one another without surrendering their aloneness or private space. For now though, a brief look at one more pair of her characters, a Mr. Serle and Miss Anning, who have been introduced to one another by Mrs. Dalloway, though not in the novel bearing her name but in a short story with a title so blatantly in accord with my theme that I am embarrassed to exploit it—"Together and Apart." Two essentially lonely middle-aged people, Mr.

Serle and Miss Anning, chat with increasing warmth about Canterbury, which has been important to both of them, until they achieve a moment of real connection which is described so: "Their eyes met, collided rather, for each felt that behind the eyes the secluded being, who sits in darkness while his shallow agile companion does all the tumbling and beckoning, and keeps the show going, suddenly stood erect; flung off his cloak, confronted the other." For each of them this experience is both "alarming" and "terrific." Like "a white bolt in a mist . . . it had happened; the old ecstasy of life; its invincible assault; for it was unpleasant, at the same time that it rejoiced and rejuvenated the veins and nerves with threads of ice and fire; it was terrifying."[24] At this point Miss Anning says, " 'Canterbury twenty years ago,' . . . as one lays a shade over an intense light or covers some burning peach with a green leaf, for it is too strong, too ripe, too full." But she thinks about her occasional wish that she had married. "Sometimes the cool peace of middle life, with its automatic devices for shielding mind and body from bruises, seemed to her, compared with the thunder and the livid apple-blossom of Canterbury, base. She could imagine something different, more like lightening, more intense" (pp. 141–42). This moment is followed by another in which her nerves lie quiescent, "as if she and Mr. Serle knew each other so perfectly, were, in fact, so closely united that they had only to float side by side down the stream." As soon, however, as she notices herself thinking the word *love*, she rejects it and begins to orchestrate her retreat. As I read the closing passage, I am not sure whether to shudder more at their haste to disentangle or from fear that it will not happen quickly enough:

> That is what she felt now, the withdrawal of human affection, Serle's disappearance and the instant need they were both under to cover up what was so desolating and degrading to human nature that everyone tried to bury it decently from sight—this withdrawal, this violation of trust, and, seeking some decent acknowledged burial form, she said:
>
> "Of course, whatever they may do, they can't spoil Canterbury."

> He smiled; he accepted it; he crossed his knees the other way about. She did her part; he his. So things came to an end. And over them both came instantly that paralysing blankness of feeling, when nothing bursts from the mind, when its walls appear like slate; when vacancy almost hurts, and the eyes petrified and fixed see the same spot—a pattern, a coal scuttle—with an exactness which is terrifying, since no emotion, no idea, no impression of any kind comes to change it, to modify it, to embellish it, since the fountains of feeling seem sealed and as the mind turns rigid, so does the body; stark, statuesque, so that neither Mr. Serle nor Miss Anning could move or speak, and they felt as if an enchanter had freed them, and spring flushed every vein with streams of life, when Mira Cartwright, tapping Mr. Serle archly on the shoulder, said:
>
> "I saw you at *The Meistersinger*, and you cut me. Villain," said Miss Cartwright, "you don't deserve that I should ever speak to you again."
>
> And they could separate. (Pp. 142–43)

The tone of this story is deeply ambivalent and obviously reflects the author's pull in both directions. At times she encourages us to view the two characters almost as gamesters of a sort whose self-consciousness and fear of real intimacy has left them with empty lives, and yet she leads us also to participate in their drive to separate and to share their relief when they are finally released from one another.

Perhaps the most disturbing human relations are those in which the pulls together and apart are so strenuous, the self-enclosures so severe, the armor so thick that linkage can take place only through violence, sometimes limited to feelings, sometimes reaching a point where caresses may even become blows: like the relation between Joanna Burden and Joe Christmas in Faulkner's *Light in August.* Joanna, encased in a "spiritual privacy so long intact that its own instinct for preservation had immolated it, its physical phase the strength and fortitude of a man," whose sexual surrender Joe remembers as "hard, untearful and unselfpitying and almost manlike. . . . It was as if he struggled physically with another man for an object of no actual value to either, and for which they struggled on principle alone";[25] Joe himself, so terrified about the fragility of his armor that he must ward off all closeness and softness and whose relations with women are all marked by violence; and not incidentally, while still an adolescent, damaged by a ruthless stepfather into feeling "like an eagle: hard, sufficient, potent, remorseless, strong . . . though he did not then know that, like the eagle, his own flesh as well as all space was still a cage."[26]

But when considering such relations in Faulkner, whose works are full of them, mostly I think of Addie Bundren in *As I Lay Dying*, who as a teacher is tormented by having to look at her pupils "day after day, each with his and her secret and selfish thought, and blood strange to each other blood and strange to mine" and looks forward "to the times when they faulted, so I could whip them. When the switch fell I could feel it upon my flesh; when it welted and ridged it was my blood that ran, and I would think with each blow of the switch: Now you are aware of me! Now I am something in your secret and selfish life, who have marked your blood with my own forever and ever";[27] for whom sex and motherhood are defined by pain rather than words; who understands when her first child, Cash, is born, that the experience with her pupils "had been, not that my aloneness had to be violated over and over each day, but that it had never been violated until Cash came. Not even by Anse [her husband] in the nights. . . . and then made whole again by the violation" (p. 164); who thinks of her preacher lover as "dressed in sin" and "would think of him as thinking of me as dressed in sin, he the more beautiful since the garment which he had exchanged for sin was sanctified. I would think of the sin as garments which we would remove in order to shape and coerce the terrible blood to the forlorn echo of the dead word high in the air" (pp. 166–67). Out of this relation comes Jewel, who is the child she both whipped and petted most, and who becomes someone whose relation between himself and the thing he loves most, his horse, is marked by a terrible tension of union and repudiation. When Jewel whistles for him, the horse makes several rushes toward him and then when Jewel can almost touch him "stands on his hind legs and slashes down at Jewel." They struggle for a while until Jewel finds the horse's nostrils and then both "are rigid, motionless, terrific, the horse back-thrust on stiffened, quivering legs, with lowered head; Jewel with dug heels, shutting off the horse's wind with one hand, with the other patting the horse's neck in short strokes myriad and caressing, cursing the horse with obscene ferocity." When finally he has gotten the animal into his stall,

> the horse kicks at him, slamming a single hoof into the wall with a pistol-like report. Jewel kicks him in the stomach; the horse arches his neck back, crop-toothed; Jewel strikes him across the face with his fist and slides on to the trough and mounts upon it. Clinging to the hay-rack he lowers his head and peers out across the stall tops and through the doorway. . . . He reaches up and drags down hay in hurried armfuls and crams it into the rack.
>
> "Eat," he says. "get the godamn stuff out of sight while you got a chance, you pussel-gutted bastard. You sweet son of a bitch," he says. (Pp. 12–13)

Perhaps the most awful of such relations is the one between the officer and his orderly in D. H. Lawrence's "The Prussian Officer": the officer so long repressed, so unwilling to be touched into life by the "warm flame" of the orderly's soft unconscious grace that his passion for the youth takes the form of irritation accompanied by increasingly brutal kicks and blows: (to "see the soldier's young, brown, shapely peasant's hand grasp the loaf or the wine bottle" sends "a flash of hate or of anger through the elder man's blood"; when he has hit the servant in the face with a belt and watches "the youth start back, the pain-tears in his eyes and the blood on his mouth," he feels "a thrill of deep pleasure and of shame"); the orderly trying to keep himself "intact" and "impervious to the feelings of his master," but goaded into increasing consciousness by the flashes of heat that run through his heart until finally there are "only the two people in the world now—himself and the Captain," and he crosses the distance between them with this terrible embrace:

> The orderly, with serious, earnest young face, and underlip between his teeth, had got his knee in the officer's chest and was pressing the chin backward over the farther edge of the tree-stump, pressing, with all his heart behind in a passion of relief, the

tension of his wrists exquisite with relief. And with the base of his palms he shoved at the chin, with all his might. And it was pleasant, too, to have that chin, that hard jaw already slightly rough with beard, in his hands. He did not relax one hair's breadth, but, all the force of all his blood exulting in his thrust, he shoved back the head of the other man, till there was a little "cluck" and a crunching sensation. Then he felt as if his head went to vapour. Heavy convulsions shook the body of the officer, frightening and horrifying the young soldier. Yet it pleased him, too, to repress them. It pleased him to keep his hands pressing back the chin, to feel the chest of the other man yield in expiration to the weight of his strong, young knees, to feel the hard twitchings of the prostrate body jerking his own whole frame, which was pressed down on it.[28]

With this, of course, we have crossed into the realm of sadomasochism, in which I do not wish to remain very long. I must observe, though, how much such relations can be understood in terms of the intimate connections between the inviolateness of the self-enclosures and the violence required to break through or break out. The thicker the armor, the more powerful the blow needed to penetrate it.[29] The purpose of the blows is not so much to inflict pain as to make connection. It is as though the connection is defined or validated by pain, as though the other is not there unless there is pain. I must also observe the latent, and sometimes not so latent, violence nearly always involved in that most profound penetration and intermingling of personal space, sexual copulation, a violence most visibly confessed in the ease and universality with which such expressions as "fuck you" and "screw you" and "up yours" are used as verbal blows. I shall make no comment on the ingredients and tonal variations in distance of "fuck you, buddy," and "mother-fucker," or about the terrible conjunctions of distance and connection in hard-core pornography between the paid participants, and between them and the viewers.

Before retreating to what most will regard as more encouraging ways of seeking to preserve and overcome aloneness, we should view two further instances where the chord of separateness and connection (yes, cord, too) becomes a kind of quiet shriek. One, a not totally distant relative of "Ring around the Rosy" and "I Want to Hold Your Hand," is a poem with the inviting title "Let's All Join Sticky Hands."

> your politics and breath offend me
> and the mention of my name
> causes you to puke green bile
> but hold my hand tightly friend
> because there is nothing but you and me
> I boast of sleeping with your wife
> and denigrate her prowess
> you sell narcotics to my children
> and tickle my daughter's thighs
> but hug me to your bosom friend
> because there is nothing but you and me
> I murdered your grandmother
> and burned your family bible
> you crucified my brother
> and shot my old dog spot
> I have drawn your boarlike face
> on men's room walls across the land
> and you have denounced me
> to twenty three top secret federal agencies
> as a threat to the national security
> but I have forgotten all that went before
> and I can see nothing to follow
> no beginning no end and a damned poor middle
> with our palsied hands scratching at our rheumy eyes
> so take your foot off my neck friend
> because there is nothing but you and me.[30]

The other quiet shriek is that sounded by Parson Hooper of Hawthorne's "The Minister's Black Veil." Of all the ways we have found to figure forth our separateness—armor, walls, shells, curtains, spaces—his is perhaps the most awesome. This decent and well-liked young minister appears before his congregation one day wearing a black veil. It is a veil, we are told, that "seemed to consist of two folds of crape, which entirely concealed his features, except the mouth and chin, but probably did not intercept his sight, farther than to give a darkened aspect to all living and inanimate things."[31] Though the members of his congregation are perplexed and frightened by the veil, they are powerfully affected by his sermon, which "had reference to secret sin, and those sad mysteries which we hide from our nearest and dearest, and would fain conceal from our own consciousness, even forgetting that the Omniscient can detect them. . . . Each member of the congregation, the most innocent girl, and the man of hardened breast, felt as if the preacher had crept upon them, behind his awful veil, and discovered their hoarded iniquity of deed or thought" (p. 40). In public, however, they shrink from him and are prevented by a feeling of dread from asking him why he wears the veil. Even a delegation is unable to question him, for that piece of crape seems "to hang down before his heart, the symbol of a fearful secret between him and them. Were the veil but cast aside, they might speak freely of it, but not till then" (p. 45).

Only his fiancee remains unterrified and is able to question him directly. To her he explains with a faint smile that the veil is " 'a type and a symbol' " that he is bound to wear as long as he remains on earth " 'both in light and darkness, in solitude and before the gaze of multitudes, and as with strangers, so with my familiar friends. No mortal eye will see it withdrawn. This dismal shade must separate me from the world: even you, Elizabeth can never come behind it!' " (p. 46). To her further questioning he responds, " 'If it be a sign of mourning . . . I, perhaps, like most other mortals, have sorrows dark enough to be typified by a black veil.' " When she suggests that others will suspect him of hiding from a sense of guilt, he answers, again with his sad smile, " 'If I hide my face for sorrow, there is cause enough . . . and if I cover it for secret sin, what mortal might not do the same?' " With "this gentle, but unconquerable obstinacy" (ibid.), he continues to resist all her entreaties until finally she too succumbs to the power of the veil, and trembling, turns to leave the room. He rushes to her and cries passionately, " 'Have patience with me, Elizabeth. . . . Do not desert me, though this veil must be between us here on earth. Be mine, and hereafter there shall be no veil over my face, no darkness between our souls! It is but a mortal veil—it is not for eternity! Oh! you know not how lonely I am, and how frightened to be alone behind my black veil. Do not leave me in this miserable obscurity for ever!' " To this she begs him to lift the veil just once and look her in the face. When he replies that cannot be, she says farewell and departs. As she leaves, "even amid his grief, Mr. Hooper smiled to think that only a material emblem had separated him from happiness, though the horrors which it shadowed forth, must be drawn darkly between the fondest of lovers" (p. 47).

As is so often true with Hawthorne, the highly symbolic content does not prevent one from responding both to the minister's pain and his pride or from wondering what Elizabeth might have achieved through greater patience and greater tolerance of the distance between them.

From that time on, no further efforts are made to remove the veil, and the minister goes through life without ever lifting it, even though he suffers greatly from others' continued dread and suspicion and especially from the children's fear of his melancholy figure. In fact, his own antipathy to the veil becomes so great that he never willingly passes a mirror or stoops to drink at a still fountain lest "he should be affrighted by himself." He is so enveloped in "an ambiguity of sin or sorrow . . . that love or sympathy could never reach him"; he passes through his whole life "kind and loving, though unloved" separated from "cheerful brotherhood and woman's love," and locked by that veil "in that saddest of all prisons, his own heart" (pp. 48–50). At the same time, the veil makes him, as Hawthorne so interestingly puts it, "a very efficient clergyman," one with particular power over "souls that were in agony for sin" and a particular ability "to sympathize with all dark affections" (p. 49).

On his deathbed at the end of a long and virtuous life, he is attended by a zealous young minister who begs permission to remove the veil so that no shadow should be left on so pure a life and then bends forward to lift it. At this the dying man, "exerting a sudden energy which made all the beholders stand aghast," covers the veil with his hands and cries: "Never! . . . On earth, never!" and concludes his life with this terrifying eloquence:

> "Why do you tremble at me alone?" cried he, turning his veiled face round the circle of pale spectators. "Tremble also at each other! Have men avoided me, and women shown no pity, and children screamed and fled, only for my black veil? What, but the mystery which it obscurely typifies, has made this piece of crape so awful? When the friend shows his inmost heart to his friend; the lover to his best-beloved; when man does not vainly shrink from the eye of his Creator, loathsomely treasuring up the secret of his sin; then deem me a monster, for the symbol beneath which I have lived, and die! I look around me, and, lo! on every visage a Black Veil!" (Pp. 51–52)

There are many responses, of course, to be made to such an argument and to such a prideful man, but it is instructive to remember how difficult they would be to exert at such a final separation. Inappropriately but irresistibly I find myself mumbling: "The grave's a fine and private place / But none, I think, do there embrace." Well, maybe not so inappropriately, since one could accuse the minister of exhibiting, like Marvell's mistress, a certain coyness of both the body and the heart. And I find myself thinking of those sad creatures who perform the crime labeled "exposing themselves" or their "private parts," where the self exposed is only that one small piece of self that dangles between the legs. Perhaps they are seeking to escape prisons of their own hearts where love and sympathy can never reach them. And Moslem women. But all this, I suspect, is largely some coy and nervous fumbling of my own in the face of a peculiarly frightening effort to preserve a loneliness—here even in the very act of denouncing it, and because I have so many conflicting feelings about his gesture.

I know I like his melancholy smile better than the exultant self-dramatization of isolation exhibited by Oliver Wendell Holmes when he says:

> Only when you have worked alone—when you have felt around you a black gulf of solitude more isolating than that which surrounds the dying man, and in hope and despair have trusted to your own unshaken will—then only will you have achieved. Thus only can you gain the secret isolated joy of the thinker, who knows that a hundred years after he is dead and forgotten men who have never heard of him will be moving to the measure of his thought. . . .[32]

There is, perhaps, a real pain in the isolation celebrated here and a real yearning for connection, especially in the "secret isolated joy" at his relation with others in the future; and Gotesky, who quotes the passage, sees that assertion about the future as an effort "to give a halo to this experience of isolation which unfortunately will not crown the heads of most men."[33] But in the final phrase of Holmes, I hear less an impulse toward connection than one toward power and control. Despite the light note of exultancy in his final outburst, Parson Hooper takes very little pleasure in either his public exhibition or his private prison of the heart. Clearly he dreads as much as cherishes his aloneness.[34]

I feel much sorrier for him than I do for those such as the aged narrator of Yeats's "The Circus Animals' Desertion" who are more or less satisfied at the end to rest alone "in the foul rag-and-bone shop of the heart," or those such as the wonderful isolato in Crane's "The Heart":

> In the desert
> I saw a creature, naked, bestial,
> Who squatting upon the ground,
> Held his heart in his hands,
> And ate of it.
>
> I said, "Is it good, friend?"
> "It is bitter—bitter," he answered;
> "But I like it
> Because it is bitter,
> And because it is my heart."[35]

Among his other satisfactions, it is worth observing, this desert creature has encountered a fellow creature who has some knowledge about heart-eating and who calls him friend.

I think too that Parson Hooper's exaggerated and self-defeating sense of the awfulness of separation and solitude is a necessary antidote to the many overly comfortable celebrations of those states: like James Thomson's "Hymn on Solitude," in which he speaks of "solitude" thus:

Companion of the wise and good,
But from whose holy piercing eye
The herd of fools and villains fly.
O! how I love with thee to walk,
And listen to thy whispered talk.
Which innocence and truth imparts,
And melts the most obdurate hearts.
A thousand shapes you wear with ease,
And still in every shape you please.

and begs of it:

Oh, let me pierce thy secret cell,
And in thy deep recesses dwell![36]

or like some of Thoreau's musings in *Walden,* wonderful as they are:

> Society is commonly too cheap. We meet at very short intervals, not having had time to acquire any new value for each other. We meet at meals three times a day, and give each other a new taste of that old musty cheese that we are. We have had to agree on a certain set of rules, called etiquette and politeness, to make this frequent meeting tolerable and that we need not come to open war. We meet at the post office, and at the sociable, and about the fireside every night; we live thick and are in each other's way, and stumble over one another, and I think that we thus lose some respect for one another. . . . It would be better if there were but one inhabitant to a square mile, as where I live. The value of a man is not in his skin, that we should touch him.[37]

or like this more elaborate proclamation, which I quote at some length because its terminologies reveal certain strains in such postures that greater artists obscure:

> Solitude is a return to one's own self when the world has grown cold and meaningless, when life has become filled with people and too much of a response to others. . . . The overdevelopment of socialized man, the constant need for involvement with people, is often motivated by a fear of discovering one's own real self. . . . Socialized man too often lacks the courage to become more profoundly aware, to stretch his resources to new levels, and to participate in the mystery of living, which is ineffable, unpredictable, and, in some ways, private and unsharable. The

> response to others, however meaningful or meaningless, can be broken only through solitude. . . .
>
> In solitude, man does not deal with concrete and practical realities, for being practical is simply another way of socializing. . . . The truly solitary process is not tangible and materialistic; it cannot be defined and quantified. It remains aesthetic and mystical. The moment it is studied and "understood" it becomes something else, something radically unlike the original solitude, with all its vague, diffuse visions and dreams, with all its imagining and wondering and its incomprehensible powers that sensitize and cleanse. In the process the individual often purges himself of false idols, distortions, and deceptions; he creates a new picture of reality and reaches for the truth. The moment of solitude is a spontaneous, awakening experience, a coming to life in one's own way, a path to authenticity and self-renewal.[38]

How easy to drift from this into the comfortable dialectic with which this writer ends his book:

> Loneliness is an inevitable outcome of real love, but it is also a process through which new love becomes possible. Love which is genuine is its own thing. It is unique, incomparable, true only as itself. And because real love is unique, it is inescapably lonely. In the alive person, the rhythms of loneliness and love deepen and enrich human existence. The lonely experience gives a person back to himself, affirms his identity, and enables him to take steps toward new life. The experience of love is the spark and energy of excitement and joy; it is what makes friendship a lifetime joy and what makes activity purposeful. A balance is essential. Exaggeration of either loneliness or love leads to self-denial and despair. Love has no meaning without loneliness; loneliness becomes real only as a response to love.[39]

I certainly do not wish to deny the importance of solitude, and I believe it does have very important relations to a heightened awareness of others, some of which I shall explore shortly. Nor do I want to accuse these romantics of doing precisely what is described by Robert Weiss when he says that though loneliness is entirely natural in certain situations, "it is so easy to think of it as weakness or self-indulgence, so easy to say that since one is suffering no physical pain or obvious privation, it should be possible to shrug off one's loneliness, even to label it solitude and thereupon enjoy it."[40] But rose-colored glasses and clean hands can distort as much as black veils. Neither loneliness nor attachment to others is nearly so nice as such descriptions make them. Such conditions have terrible as well as wonderful dimensions. Solitude can exert the restorative powers and provide the renewal of self described by romantics like Thoreau, Thomson, and Moustakas; it can also, as Weiss reports, cause people to feel they are not themselves[41]; it can even destroy all sense of selfhood and meaning as it does for Martin Decoud in Conrad's *Nostromo*, who kills himself to escape the void created by ten days of solitude. Loneliness can be so "frightening and uncanny," as Frieda Fromm-Reichman explains, that some of its victims "try to dissociate the memory of what it was like and even the fear of it."[42] What Moustakas finds a comfortable rhythm between loneliness and love can become the terrible tearing it was for Scobie or Miss Lonelyhearts. For some unfortunate creatures, the truth would be in Orwell's assertion that "the essence of being human" includes being "prepared in the end to be defeated and broken up by life, which is the inevitable price of fastening one's love upon other human individuals."[43]

Still, Parson Hooper is guilty of a willful suppression of sunshine, both in his own life and in others', and of flaunting his awareness of the truths of sin and separation. The word *willful* seems too strong though, when one thinks of some of Hawthorne's statements about his own twelve-year period of isolation in the middle of Salem, especially in the letter to Longfellow, in which he writes: "By some witchcraft or other—for I really cannot assign any reasonable why and wherefore—I have been carried apart from the main current of life, and find it impossible to get back again. Since we last met [at college] . . . , I have secluded myself from society; and yet I never meant any such thing. . . . I have made a captive of myself, and put me into a dungeon, and now I cannot find the key to let myself out."[44]

And yet and yet and yet—what a terrible way Parson Hooper has found to perceive his loneliness and to pronounce his simultaneous separation from, and attachment to, the rest of mankind. And to go all the way to his death behind the veil, to remain even in the grave a veiled corpse: "The grass of many years has sprung up and withered on that grave, the burial stone is moss-grown, and good Mr. Hooper's face is dust; but awful is still the thought that it mouldered beneath the Black Veil!"

Hawthorne himself at least partially escaped his dungeon through marriage and fatherhood, as well as through his writing, perhaps, and could write to his wife:

> So now I begin to understand why I was imprisoned for so many years in this lonely chamber, and why I could never break through the viewless bolts and bars; for if I had sooner made my escape into the world, I should have grown hard and rough, and have been covered with earthly dust, and my heart might have become callous by rude encounters with the multitude. . . . But living in solitude till the fullness of time was come, I still kept the dew of my youth and the freshness of my heart. . . . [45]

Having finally found a way to get a little out from under my own black veil, let me put down a few more testaments to the possibly beneficent effects of loneliness on the heart: Graham Greene's, that "in solitude, one welcomes any living thing—a mouse, a bird on the sill, Robert Bruce's spider. In complete loneliness even a certain tenderness can be born";[46] Mrs. Ramsay's feeling that when "one was alone, one leant to inanimate things; trees, streams, flowers; felt they expressed one; felt they became one; felt they knew one; felt an irrational tenderness thus . . . as for oneself";[47] and perhaps most moving of all, Elizabeth Bowen's observation in *The Death of the Heart* that "only in a house where one has learned to be lonely does one have this solicitude for *things*. One's relation to them, the daily seeing or touching, begins to become love, and to lay one open to pain."[48] I do not think it is too much a lowering of the veil to add that one of the things that makes loneliness easier to bear, or even a pleasure, is the sense one has during such experiences of the wonderfulness and meaningfulness of connection; one forgets or represses one's knowledge of its frequent emptiness or triviality. The pleasure is not unlike that of the lonely alcoholic who settles comfortably onto his or her stool at the bar at the beginning of the evening's drinking, savoring what looks like the warm haze of friendliness lying ahead. And, of course, as William James has pointed out, the alcohol will reduce the thickness of armors and will often lead to temporary states of consciousness sufficiently mystical and unifying to be included as a variety of religious experience. For certain lonely ones, as we shall see, the distance of others invests them with poignance approaching sacredness.

It is their failure to recognize all these wonderful and terrible tensions within and between self and other that most marks the victims and definers of what has been called "alienation." One of the chief symptoms of the disorder seems to be an immense obliviousness to the mystery, threat, attractiveness, complexity, and, above all, whatness of the other. And that same obliviousness seems manifest in all but a few (notably Erik Erikson and Rollo May) who have written on the subject. They convey little sense of the magicality and physicality that inheres in almost any human being or of the interestingness of all things "other." Indeed, they probably help spread the disease by their insistence upon the importance of being able to relate to abstractions such as the universe, or work, or causes, or society and by their own inability to feel the importance and drama of the relationship with particular beings and things, both real and fictional. They see bowling or gardening as escapes; they do not feel the weight of the ball on the arm, hear the crash of the pins, or see the flower one has grown in all its inconceivable presence. They do not feel the texture—flabby, horny, or firm—of the hand one holds or fails to hold, even (or especially) when it is a sticky hand. A somewhat similar blindness, I believe, afflicts most of the metaphysicians and even many of the religious existentialists who have written about "self" and "other." They too usually turn the other into an abstraction, tend to forget that we can actually touch the other or yearn to touch the other, kill the other, or have an experience like the one of Vivaldo's quoted earlier, in which "his heart began to beat with a newer, stonier anguish, which destroyed the distance called pity and placed him very nearly" in another's body.

❖

It is the existence of such dimensions and strains in our ties to one another and distances from one another, the mysteries inherent in our condition of remaining together and apart, that above all make necessary the further expansion of Auden's canvas.

On a hill above that sea into which Icarus has plunged, surely there must be someone in that heightened confusion about self and others that sometimes afflicts all of us, like Virginia Woolf's Mrs. Jarvis, the clergyman's wife, who is unhappy but "not very unhappy"; but on the moors, when "the ships on the sea below seem to cross each other and pass on as if drawn by an invisible hand; when there are distant concussions in the air and phantom horsemen galloping, ceasing; when the horizon swims blue, green, emotional—then Mrs. Jarvis, heaving a sigh, thinks to herself, 'If only some one could give me . . . if only I could give some one. . . . ' But she does not know what she wants to give, nor who could give it to her."[49]

In addition to Auden's and Bruegel's ploughman, who "may have heard the splash, the forsaken cry" but for whom "it was not an important failure," there must have been a farmworker more like the one in Robert Frost's "The Tuft of Flowers." Having come to a field to turn over the grass, this man looks and listens for the person who had mowed it earlier in the day.

> But he had gone his way, the grass all mown,
> And I must be, as he had been,—alone.
> "As all must be," I said within my heart,
> "Whether they work together or apart."

As he says this, however, a "bewildered butterfly" flies past him seeking an uncut flower to light upon. The man watches his quest sympathetically and is just about to start his work when the butterfly turns and leads his eyes to "a tall tuft of flowers beside a brook" that the mower had spared. Upon approaching the flowers and discovering they are butterfly weed, the man goes on to muse:

The mower in the dew had loved them thus,
By leaving them to flourish, not for us,

Nor yet to draw one thought of ours to him,
But from sheer morning gladness at the brim.

The butterfly and I had lit upon,
Nevertheless, a message from the dawn,

That made me hear the wakening birds around,
And hear his long scythe whispering to the ground,

And feel a spirit kindred to my own;
So that henceforth I worked no more alone;

But glad with him, I worked as with his aid,
And weary, sought at noon with him the shade;

And dreaming, as it were, held brotherly speech
With one whose thought I had not hoped to reach.

"Men work together," I told him from the heart,
"Whether they work together or apart."[50]

If one finds the poem a bit sentimental, as I do, in its easy transition from aloneness to togetherness and in the comfortable formulation at the end, one is certainly entitled to read it as a dramatic monologue of a lonely man who from the opening line is yearning for connection, and to be moved by his sympathy with the bewildered butterfly, by the way he unites himself and the butterfly into "us" and "our," and by the eagerness with which he becomes an imaginary brother of his invisible companion. If one is bothered by the narrator's insistence that the message was not intended and that the communion is over the tuft of flowers, I would suggest that is the only way certain shy and lonely ones can connect.

Somewhere on the shore, there must also be someone like Lily Briscoe, whom we have already observed as a young woman longing to become one somehow with Mrs. Ramsay. I would like to join her some years later and remain with her for a while as she engages in a more complicated effort to manage her distances and takes part in one of Virginia Woolf's most fascinating exhibitions of the intricacies by which a number of people manage that apparently necessary feat of remaining simultaneously together and apart.

On the morning in question, Lily has placed her easel on the lawn at the edge of the sea and is desperately trying to resist the appeals for sympathy of the now-widowed Mr. Ramsay. As he groans and sighs, all Lily can wish is "that this enormous flood of grief, this insatiable hunger for sympathy, this demand that she should surrender herself up to him entirely . . . should leave her, should be diverted . . . before it swept her down in its flood." At the same time, she chides herself bitterly for being "not a woman, but a peevish, ill-tempered, dried-up old maid" (p. 226). "His immense self-pity, his demand for sympathy poured and spread itself in pools at her feet, and all she did, miserable sinner that she was, was to draw her skirts a little closer round her ankles, lest she should get wet" (p. 228). Both of them become more and more enclosed in their characteristic gestures, until Lily notices the remarkable way his boots express his character and exclaims spontaneously, "What beautiful boots!" (p. 229). Ashamed of herself for praising his boots when "he asked her to solace his soul; when he had shown her his bleeding hands, his lacerated heart, and asked her to pity them," she expects and feels she deserves a sharp, ill-tempered response.

Instead, Mr. Ramsay smiles. "His pall, his draperies, his infirmities" fall away and lifting his feet to show them off agrees they are first-rate boots and discourses happily on the difficulties of getting boots made as they should be. At this she feels they have reached "a sunny island where peace dwelt, sanctity reigned and the sun forever shone, the blessed island of good boots," and "her heart warmed to him" (p. 230). Then, when he shows her the knot he has invented and has three times knotted and unknotted her laces, she is further opened to him:

> Why, at this completely inappropriate moment, when he was stooping over her shoe, should she be so tormented with sympathy for him that, as she stooped too, the blood rushed to her face, and, thinking of her callousness (she had called him a play actor) she felt her eyes swell and tingle with tears? Thus occupied

> he seemed to her a figure of infinite pathos. He tied knots. He bought boots.

She is aware "there was no helping Mr. Ramsay on the journey he was going," (a literal journey to the lighthouse but with very complex associations and also a journey toward death). But "now just as she wished to say something, could have said something perhaps," given him the word of sympathy he had seemed so much to need, his children arrive for the journey and he leaves her. When they have gone, she sighs with both "relief and disappointment. Her sympathy seem[s] to be cast back on her, like a bramble sprung across her face," and she feels "curiously divided," as if one part of her were drawn out toward the lighthouse, which "looked this morning at an immense distance," and "the other had fixed itself doggedly, solidly" on the lawn with her paints and canvas (p. 234).

She never is able literally to give him the words of sympathy he so wishes for, but during the hour or so that it takes the boat to reach the lighthouse, she experiences a very complex course of memories and thoughts that in a sense bring her and Mr. Ramsay together. These are too complex to do justice to here, for they compose one of the most intricately woven streams of consciousness I know of. But they include a terribly painful sense of loss and yearning for the dead Mrs. Ramsay and an effort, generated by her unexpended sympathy for Mr. Ramsay, to keep track of the boat and to imagine its arrival at the lighthouse.

At one point, as the boat seems to merge with the sea and sky, Lily thinks:

> So much depends . . . upon distance: whether people are near us or far from us; for her feeling for Mr. Ramsay changed as he sailed further and further across the bay. It seemed to be elongated, stretched out; he seemed to become more and more remote. He and his children seemed to be swallowed up in that blue, that distance; but here, on the lawn, close at hand, Mr. Carmichael suddenly grunted. She laughed. He clawed his book up from the grass. He settled into his chair again puffing and blowing like some sea monster. That was different altogether, because he was so near. (P. 284)

Lily is only partly right, however, for in the process of painting her picture, thinking about the Ramsays' love for one another and wanting Mrs. Ramsay, she seems to achieve some deeper sense of connection with Mr. Ramsay. "And as if she had something she must share, yet could hardly leave her easel, so full her mind was of what she was seeing, Lily went past Mr. Carmichael holding her brush to the edge of the lawn. Where was the boat now? And Mr. Ramsay? She wanted him" (p. 300).

Although she can no longer see the boat, at the very moment Mr. Ramsay does, in fact, step ashore at the lighthouse, Lily says aloud, "He must have reached it," and suddenly feels completely tired out. For the lighthouse had become nearly invisible in the blue haze, "and the effort of looking at it, and the effort of thinking of him landing there, which both seemed to be one and the same effort, had stretched her body and mind to the utmost. Ah, but she was relieved. Whatever she had wanted to give him, when he had left her that morning, she had given him at last" (pp. 308-9).

This moment of separateness and union is followed immediately by another, for as she stands there, old Mr. Carmichael joins her at the edge of the lawn, saying " 'They will have landed,' and she felt that she had been right [in her earlier feeling that he had been sharing her thoughts]. They had not needed to speak. They had been thinking the same things and he had answered her without her asking him anything. He stood there as if he were spreading his hands over all the weakness and suffering of mankind; she thought he was surveying, tolerantly and compassionately, their final destiny" (p. 309).[51]

A moment later Lily is able to complete the painting that has been giving her so much difficulty throughout the book. "With a sudden intensity, as if she saw it clear for a second, she drew a line there, in the centre. It was done; it was finished. Yes, she thought, laying down her brush in extreme fatigue, I have had my vision" (p. 310), and with this the book ends.

That line which completes the picture signifies many

things, but I think of it mostly as that harmony she felt unable to maintain earlier in the morning when she first begins to vacillate between her canvas and the seascape and feels "she could not achieve that razor edge of balance between two opposite forces; Mr. Ramsay and the picture; which was necessary" (p. 287): Mr. Ramsay with his insistent claim for sympathy representing human involvement and all the "disorderly sensations" (p. 234) these arouse in her; the picture, her escape into the pursuit of artistic wholeness and truth, which draws her "out of gossip, out of living, out of community with people," a pursuit that gives her both a kind of purpose and peace but also an emptiness and loneliness.

An odd metaphor that "razor edge of balance" in its simultaneous cutting edge and equipoise. With that kind of balance, it is understandable that Lily's unions would have to incorporate so much distance and yet so much intensity.

Most of us have a lonely enough and embittered enough part of ourselves to note, probably with mixed relish and dismay, that Mr. Ramsay is not aware of Lily's experience of union, any more than Frost's early morning reaper was aware of the sense of communion with him experienced by the farmworker who narrates the poem. Although, as I will explain shortly, Virginia Woolf leads us to far more complex awarenesses than that, she does allow such a recognition and also tinges our final glimpse of Lily with loneliness and fatigue; for in returning to her canvas, she has turned away from the sea and from Mr. Carmichael. She does not even have the sense that her vision will be shared, for she thinks that her canvas "would be hung in the attics . . . would be destroyed." And I cannot prevent myself from remembering the one occasion on which she had shared her painting—an occasion that significantly is presented in direct conjunction with the passage I quoted earlier on Lily's desire to merge with Mrs. Ramsay or to be the bee that haunted her dome-shaped hive. And that passage is associated directly with an imaginative effort of Lily's to confute Mrs. Ramsay's serene certainty that she and all other women should marry or else miss the best of life: "She would urge her own exemption from the universal law; plead for it; she liked to be alone; she liked to be herself; she was not made for that" (p. 77). The person she shares the painting with is Mr. Bankes, whom Mrs. Ramsay thinks it would be an admirable idea for her to marry (p. 109).

When Mr. Bankes first approaches her easel, Lily

> winced like a dog who sees a hand raised to strike it. She would have snatched her picture off the easel, but she said to herself, One must. She braced herself to stand the awful trial of some one looking at her picture. One must, she said, one must. And if it must be seen, Mr. Bankes was less alarming than another. But that any other eyes should see the residue of her thirty-three years, the deposit of each day's living mixed with something more secret than she had ever spoken or shown in the course of all those days was an agony. At the same time it was immensely exciting. (Pp. 80–81)

He asks some questions about her intentions and listens interestedly to her efforts to explain until, fearing to bore him, she takes the canvas off the easel and thinks:

> But it had been seen; it had been taken from her. The man had shared with her something profoundly intimate. And, thanking Mr. Ramsay for it and Mrs. Ramsay for it and the hour and the place, crediting the world with a power which she had not suspected—that one could walk away down that long gallery not alone anymore but arm in arm with somebody—the strangest feeling in the world, and the most exhilarating—she nicked the catch of her paint box to, more firmly than was necessary, and the nick seemed to surround in a circle forever the paint box, the lawn, Mr. Bankes, and that wild villain, Cam, dashing past. (P. 83)

To some extent then, despite her momentary sense of unity with Mr. Ramsay and Mr. Carmichael, Lily may be seen as a "dried-up old maid," one who is walking down that long gallery still alone and has probably missed the best of life; this even though she is able to feel as she does about Mr. Bankes because he too craves separateness for himself and permits her to maintain her private space (Mrs. Ramsay thinks they should marry in part because they "are both cold and aloof and rather self-sufficing" [p. 157]) and even though she later thinks of her failure to marry as an escape "by the skin of her teeth" and had felt an "enormous exultation" when "it had flashed upon her that she . . . need never marry anybody" (p. 262).

But Virginia Woolf has made our sense of Lily's experience at the end and our own experience more complex than I have so far suggested. Each time Lily's unexpended sympathy leads her to look toward the boat and sea, there is a break in the text and the scene shifts to the boat. These scenes are narrated by a third-person narrator and convey what are presumably the actual thoughts and actions of the characters rather than Lily's imagining of them. But this narrator is so unobtrusive and the narration so resembles some of Lily's earlier imaginings of scenes that the line between the two becomes blurred and we feel that Lily, through an exhausting outflinging of sympathy, has somehow shared the actual experiences in the boat, and thus is not merely a lonely observer. At one point, after we have witnessed directly a period of separateness, silence, and withholding of sympathy in the boat, and the narrator has turned back to Lily's mind, we read: "There he sits, she thought, and the children are quite silent still. And she could not reach him either. The sympathy she had not given him weighed her down. It made it difficult for her to paint" (p. 254).

What we and Lily have shared is a most amazing illustration of the ways in which three people—the now 71-year-old Mr. Ramsay and his two youngest children, 17-year-old Cam and 16-year-old James—contrive to keep themselves together and apart. Since this literal journey to the lighthouse is too long and intricate even to summarize effectively, I will offer here only a brief indication of how it begins and ends, a long footnote with a slightly fuller tracing of what happens in between, a ruminative note or two, and a plea for my reader to turn to the book itself. From the beginning and throughout the trip, the three family members sit apart, Mr. Ramsay in the middle, Cam alone in the bow, James in the rear, steering. The children, angry at their father's general self-assertiveness and because they feel he has forced them to make the trip against their wills, are bound in a silent compact to resist his tyranny "to the death." So they sit "one at one end of the boat, one at the other, in silence. They would say nothing, only look at him now and then where he sat with his legs twisted, frowning and fidgeting, and pishing and pshawing and muttering things to himself, and waiting impatiently for a breeze. And they hoped it would be calm. They hoped he would be thwarted. They hoped the whole expedition would fail, and they would have to put back with their parcels, to the beach" (p. 243). At the same time, of course, they are acutely aware of him. As old Macalister (who along with his son is accompanying them) talks about the great storm last Christmas, they only caught a word or two but "were conscious all the time of their father—how he leant forward, how he brought his voice in tune with Macalister's voice; how puffing at his pipe, and looking there and there where Macalister pointed, he relished the thought of the storm and the dark night and the fisherman striving there. . . . So James could tell, so Cam could tell (they looked at him, they looked at each other), from his toss and his vigilance and the ring in his voice" (p. 245) as he questions Macalister about the ships that had been driven into the bay in the storm, three of which had sunk.

Since we have Bruegel's canvas and Auden's poem to worry about as well as Lily's and Virginia Woolf's, I must note that Macalister and others had not turned away from the disaster but had launched a lifeboat in the storm to try to save the shipwrecked sailors and that Cam's compact with her brother slackens a bit as she finds herself feeling proud of her father, thinking that had he been there he would have launched the lifeboat and reached the wreck (p. 246).

Relevant also to this canvas, and perhaps to Lily's too, is the fact that this trip to the lighthouse is the completion and commemoration of one planned by the charitable and sympathetic Mrs. Ramsay many years before—a trip whose chief purpose was to bring some comforts for the lighthouse keepers,

> those poor fellows, who must be bored to death sitting all day with nothing to do but polish the lamp and trim the wick and rake about on their scrap of garden, something to amuse them. For how would you like to be shut up for a whole month at a time, and possibly more in stormy weather, upon a rock the size of a tennis lawn? she would ask; and to have no letters or newspapers, and to see nobody; if you were married, not to see your wife, not to know how your children were,—if they were ill, if they had fallen down and broken their legs or arms; to see the same dreary waves breaking week after week, and then a dreadful storm coming, and the windows covered with spray, and birds dashed against the lamp, and the whole place rocking, and not to be able to put your nose out of doors for fear of being swept into the sea? How would you like that? she asked, addressing herself particularly to her daughters. So she added, rather differently, one must take them what comforts one can. (Pp. 11–12)

And although not the dominant note at the end of the book, those gifts for the lighthouse men are much more prominent than has usually been recognized. The final paragraph describing the trip begins with Mr. Ramsay telling the children to "bring those parcels. . . . The parcels for the Lighthouse men" and ends with Mr. Ramsay springing "lightly like a young man, holding his parcel, on to the rock" (p. 308). The next paragraph is the one that ends with Lily feeling she finally had been able to give something to Mr. Ramsay.

I must also, I am afraid, add Mr. and Mrs. Ramsay to our collection of birds; for according to Lily, Mrs. Ramsay has "an instinct like the swallows for the south, the artichokes for the sun, turning her infallibly to the human race, making her nest in its heart" (p. 292). Mr. Ramsay, to himself and to the narrator perhaps, seems fated "whether he wished it or not, to come out thus on a spit of land which the sea is slowly eating away, and there to stand, like a desolate sea-bird, alone" (p. 68). To James he feels sometimes like a "fierce sudden black-winged harpy, with its talons and its beak all cold and hard, that struck and struck at you (he could feel the beak on his bare legs, where it had struck when he was a child) and then made off, and there he was again, an old man, very sad, reading his book" (pp. 273–74)—a book, I wish I had not noticed, with covers "mottled like a plover's egg" (p. 273). To

Cam, "with his great forehead and his great nose, holding his little mottled book firmly in front of him, he escaped. You might try to lay hands on him, but then like a bird, he spread his wings, he floated off to settle out of your reach somewhere far away on some desolate stump" (p. 302).

But since they are not birds, they must go on to the end with their human flutterings toward and away from one another, and we watch for some twenty-five pages as the three, sometimes imaginatively, sometimes with actual verbal and physical gestures, perform their advances and retreats.[52]

The journey ends with Mr. Ramsay giving to James what he has desperately wished for all of his life, a word of praise, immediately after which Cam gives us this marvellous bridging and maintenance of space:

> There! Cam thought, addressing herself silently to James. You've got it at last. For she knew that this was what James had been wanting, and she knew that now he had got it he was so pleased that he would not look at her or at his father or at anyone. There he sat with his hand on the tiller sitting bolt upright, looking rather sulky and frowning slightly. He was so pleased that he was not going to let anybody share a grain of his pleasure. His father had praised him. They must think that he was perfectly indifferent. But you've got it now, Cam thought. (P. 306)

And then this one, as Mr. Ramsay, holding his parcel, ready to land, sits looking back at the island:

> What could he see? Cam wondered. It was all a blur to her. What was he thinking now? she wondered. What was it he sought, so fixedly, so intently, so silently? They watched him, both of them, sitting bareheaded with his parcel on his knee, staring and staring at the frail blue shape which seemed like the vapour of something that had burnt itself away. What do you want? they both wanted to ask. They both wanted to say, Ask us anything and we will give it you. But he did not ask them anything. He sat and looked at the island and he might be thinking, We perished, each alone, or he might be thinking, I have reached it. I have found it. But he said nothing.
>
> Then he put on his hat.
>
> "Bring those parcels," he said, nodding his head at the things Nancy had done up for them to take to the Lighthouse. "The

> parcels for the Lighthouse men," he said. He rose and stood in the bow of the boat, very straight and tall, for all the world, James thought, as if he were saying, "There is no God," and Cam thought, as if he were leaping into space, and they both rose to follow him as he sprang, lightly like a young man, holding his parcel, on to the rock. (Pp. 307-8)

As I read these final passages in the context and movement of the book, I experience, and think I am meant to, a sense of hope and exultation, especially so, I suspect, because I am old enough to need my children to forgive my self-indulgences and mannerisms and the space I keep around myself. Younger readers might feel, despite Mr. Ramsay's gift of praise, that Cam and James had given in too easily, especially since Mr. Ramsay's final words to them are commanding ones, precisely the kinds of words that leagued them against him to start with. Even such readers, though, would have to share something of the children's sudden yearning to give him something and their pride in his straight, tall youthfulness as he springs ashore.

A moment later, however, I feel something like Lily's exhaustion from my "effort of looking at it and the effort of thinking of him landing there" as well as a degree of Lily's exhaustion I share through empathy. And upon reflection, I become more sharply aware not only of the extent to which the unions are consummated within the separate skulls of the characters but of the extent to which the characters' imaginings about one another may or may not be correct or remain unverified. The children do not know what their father wants or what he is thinking. Lily's looking and thinking may or may not have been a sharing of the experiences in the boat or of our experience of them. She does not know that Mr. Carmichael has, in fact, been thinking the things she has, and there is evidence in the book that he probably has not. I am not suggesting that these uncertainties invalidate the connections. That would be not only simpleminded about the possibilities of ever knowing others accurately, it would be callous, for we must connect as we can. And certainly even wondering what another is thinking is a kind of connection. But I am left with an acute sense of the distance that remains between the characters even as they unite, and a sense that their effort to imagine or wonder about the experience of another is, again, as for so many others, as much a way of preserving aloneness as it is of overcoming it. Also, despite considerable involvement in their efforts to connect, I feel a surprising degree of detachment from them. Even from Lily. I think she would be glad of that. At the same time, I see her very distinctly in all her selfhood and otherness.

Lily and Icarus? I suppose one could say she keeps her distance from him too. But she does not turn leisurely away.

Before leaving this already absurdly overcrowded and anachronistic seascape, I must add two more figures. Their lonely embrace is of a sort that more properly belongs to the next chapter, but they need to be here too along with Frost's farmworker and Lily Briscoe and all those other figures who do not wish to become one with the ocean or their fellows, but stand at the edge, at once together and apart. One of the figures we have already encountered as a younger man listing his various addresses in the universe. It is, of course, no accident here, or for Joyce, that his name is Stephen Dedalus, which makes him a sort of Icarus or brother to him, and Stephen is aware of his mythological father's feats of aeronautical engineering, though not of our particular drowning boy. The other figure becomes, among other things, another kind of bird. Stephen has for some time been pursuing an idealized female image he calls Mercedes (from *The Count of Monte Cristo*) and has felt that an encounter with that image in the real world would transfigure him and cause all his weakness, timidity, and inexperience to fall away. Now, having wandered to the seaside, he stands in a rivulet in the strand.

> A girl stood before him in midstream, alone and still, gazing out to sea. She seemed like one whom magic had changed into the likeness of a strange and beautiful seabird. Her long slender bare legs were delicate as a crane's and pure save where an emerald trail of seaweed had fashioned itself as a sign upon the flesh. Her thighs, fuller and softhued as ivory, were bared almost to the hip where the white fringes of her drawers were like featherings of

soft white down. Her slateblue skirts were kilted boldly about her waist and dovetailed behind her. Her bosom was as a bird's soft and slight, slight and soft as the breast of some darkplumaged dove. But her long fair hair was girlish, and touched with the wonder of mortal beauty, her face.

She was alone and still, gazing out to sea; and when she felt his presence and the worship of his eyes her eyes turned to him in quiet sufference of his gaze, without shame or wantonness. Long, long, she suffered his gaze and then quietly withdrew her eyes from his and bent them towards the stream, gently stirring the water with her foot hither and thither. The faint noise of gently moving water broke the silence, low and faint and whispering, faint as the bells of sleep; hither and thither, hither and thither: and a faint flame trembled on her cheek.

Heavenly God! cried Stephen's soul, in an outburst of profane joy. (P. 171)

VIII ❖ The Lonely Embraces of Artists

WITH STEPHEN DEDALUS'S VISUAL AND VERBAL EMBRACE OF the wading girl and the spiritual ejaculation that culminates it, we have fully arrived at one of the most fascinating and important ways that some of us have found to remain simultaneously together and apart. It is a way that is especially attractive to artists and that reveals much about the nature and consequences of their loneliness. It is fascinating because, depending upon the perspective and mood from which it is viewed as well as upon inherent qualities, it can be seen as an act that is predominantly worshipful or predominantly exploitative, as being akin to mystical experience or mostly to voyeurism, as exhibiting the maturest sort of recollection in tranquillity or the crudest sort of adolescent self-indulgence, as reflecting mainly the loneliness of the observer or mainly his arrogance. It is important because it touches so closely those awesome general issues of the ethics of any imaginative seizure and the appropriate relations for any subject and object.

Although I think these comments are true enough to excuse their pretentiousness, it is also true that I am fascinated by such lonely verbal embraces because they have so many reverberations off my own relinquished and remaining areas of adolescence, and because I believe that despite their inevitable element of voyeurism, such embraces can sometimes be an important way of acknowledging the autonomy, inviolateness, even sacredness of the other, of recognizing that even love may sometimes properly take on, perhaps require, the look of distance.

Unlike those poor divided creatures of Plato's *Symposium*, Stephen Dedalus does not rush toward this other incomplete creature he has been yearning to be united with. He does not fling his arms around her neck hoping somehow to be rolled back into one with her. He does not, like many sixteen-year-olds might, even sidle obliquely in her direction hoping to manage a casual encounter. Instead "he turn[s] away from her suddenly and set[s] off across the strand," his cheeks "aflame," his body "aglow," his limbs "trembling." "On and on and on he strode, far out over the sands, singing wildly to the sea, crying to greet the advent of the life that had cried to him" (p. 172). As we read what follows, shall we think of the girl as left behind, intact, exquisite, inviolate in the space surrounding her, or as used, ingested, transformed into catalyst and food for Stephen's present excitements and future growth?

> Her image had passed into his soul for ever and no word had broken the holy silence of his ecstasy. Her eyes had called him and his soul had leaped at the call. To live, to err, to fall, to triumph, to recreate life out of life! A wild angel had appeared to him, the angel of mortal youth and beauty, an envoy from the fair courts of life, to throw open before him in an instant of ecstasy the gates of all the ways of error and glory. On and on and on and on![1] (P. 172)

Before long she seems to vanish completely as Stephen lies down in a lonely nook on the beach so that "the peace and silence of the evening might still the riot of his blood." There he feels above him "the vast indifferent dome and the calm processes of the heavenly bodies; and the earth beneath him, the earth that had borne him, had taken him to her breast" (p. 172). He closes his eyes, falls asleep with strange and lovely images that fuse the motions of world, colors, lights, and flowers, and awakes recalling not the girl but "the rapture of his sleep."

But how shall we regard his treatment of the girl? Without that young artist to paint her so exquisitely, to worship her with his eyes (however voyeuristically, however much the worship derives from self-adulation), she might never have become distinguishable from all the other children on the beach—in another sense, would never have gained existence at all. It is the intensity of his awareness of her that has marked her off so distinctly, etched her so sharply in our memories and provided the music that helps make her so lovely. True, he has transformed her into a bird; but it is also true that the birdhood is part of the essence by which we know her and by which she gains her memorableness.

Her distinctness and impact depend also upon her separateness from Stephen, upon the distance between them. The separateness allows space for the experience to echo in, within Stephen and the reader both. An actual encounter would have broken the space and the spell. (I am especially glad for her sake that he did not actually go to her, for then she would have had to deal with the [for her] flesh-and-blood young man who does not know how to behave very well toward actual young women. He might, as in his encounter with Emma at the end of the book, have acted in such a way as to deliberately confuse her, and then feeling "sorry and mean" have turned off "that valve at once and opened the spiritual-heroic refrigerating apparatus, invented and patented in all countries by Dante Alighieri" and talked rapidly of himself and his plans [p. 252].)

What has always struck me most, however, about Stephen's experience with the wading girl is the loneliness that suffuses the entire episode. Always a rather lonely young man, he has recently decided not to enter the priesthood as he had always thought he would; and on the day the episode occurs, while his father is in a pub talking with a tutor trying to get information for him about the university, he has walked off alone toward the sea. On his walk he passes a group of Christian Brothers and experiences a sense of his difference and separateness from them and then meets a group of swimming schoolmates with whom he banters a little. But soon he leaves them behind too, feeling "apart from them and in silence" (p. 168), and makes his way alone farther along the strand. Immediately before he sees the girl, he has asked himself "Where was he?" and answered: "He was alone. He was unheeded, happy and near to the wild heart of life. He was alone and young and wilful and wildhearted, alone amid a waste of wild air and brackish waters and the sea harvest of shells and tangled and veiled grey sunlight and gayclad lightclad figures of children and girls and voices childish and girlish in the air" (p. 171).[2] The girl too is depicted in the opening sentence of the paragraph that introduces her as standing "alone and still," and the same phrase opens the second paragraph about her. Even if one views this emphasis chiefly as a technique for freezing the moment, stopping the camera, so to speak, to give impact and importance to the event, the loneliness and separateness are deeply there; for there can be no connection, not even the possibility of it, when the camera stops and the people are frozen into place. Immediately after his vision, as we have seen, Stephen wanders off alone and spends many hours in what appears to be both terrestrial and cosmic solitude.

At the end of the book, he is preparing to leave his friends, his country and his home. In a final conversation with his friend Cranly he pronounces bravely:

> Look here, Cranly, he said. You have asked me what I would do and what I would not do. I will tell you what I will do and what I will not do. I will not serve that in which I no longer believe whether it call itself my home, my fatherland or my church: and I will try to express myself in some mode of life or art as freely as I can and as wholly as I can, using for my defence the only arms I allow myself to use—silence, exile, and cunning. (Pp. 246–47)

A moment later he adds: "I do not fear to be alone or to be spurned for another or to leave whatever I have to leave." When Cranly responds, "—Alone, quite alone, You have no fear of that. And you know what that word means? Not only to be separate from all others but to have not even one friend," Stephen says he "will take the risk" (p. 247).

Much of what both drives Stephen into his aloneness and helps sustain him in it, of course, is his dream of becoming a great artist; and by what is not merely a curious coincidence, in view of his name and the affinity birds seem to have for this book, he thinks of his quest in terms that are already perhaps too familiar. As he passes his schoolmates shortly before his vision of the wading girl, they call out to him "—Stephanos Dedalos! Bous Stephanoumenos! Bous Stephaneforos!" and his strange name seems more than ever a prophecy to him.

> Now, at the name of the fabulous artificer, he seemed to hear the noise of the dim waves and to see a winged form flying above the waves and slowly climbing the air. What did it mean? Was it a quaint device opening a page of some medieval book of prophecies and symbols, a hawklike man flying sunward above the sea, a prophecy of the end he had been born to serve and had been following through the mists of childhood and boyhood, a symbol of the artist forging anew in his workshop out of the sluggish matter of the earth a new soaring impalpable imperishable being? (P. 169)

A moment later "a wild spirit passed over his limbs as though he were soaring seaward . . . and his soul was in flight . . . soaring in an air beyond the world. . . . An ecstacy of flight made radiant his eyes and wild his breath and tremulous and wild and radiant his windswept limbs" (p. 169). Joyce interrupts this flight and his own rhetorical one with a sudden

> —One! Two! . . . Look out!
> —O, cripes, I'm drownded!
> —One! Two! Three and away!
> —Me next! Me next!
> —One! . . . Uk!
> —Stephaneforos!

But Stephen remains aloft. His throat aches "to cry aloud, the cry of a hawk or eagle on high, to cry piercingly of his deliverence to the winds. . . . Yes! Yes! Yes! He would create proudly out of his freedom and power of his soul, as the great artificer whose name he bore, a living thing, new and soaring and beautiful, impalpable, imperishable" (pp. 169–70). (What a distance from that little boy who early in the book hid under a table listening to his mother say, "O, Stephen will apologise," and Dante say, "O, if not, the eagle will come and pull out his eyes" [p. 8]).

The book ends with these chords in Stephen's diary:

> 16 *April:* Away! Away!
>
> The spell of arms and voices: the white arms of roads, their promise of close embraces and the black arms of tall ships that stand against the moon, their tale of distant nations. They are held out to say: We are alone. Come. And the voices say with

> them: We are your kinsmen. And the air is thick with their company as they call to me, their kinsmen, making ready to go, shaking the wings of their exultant and terrible youth.
>
> 26 *April:* Mother is putting my new second hand clothes in order. She prays now, she says, that I may learn in my own life and away from home and friends what the heart is and what it feels. Amen. So be it. Welcome, O life! I go to encounter for the millionth time the reality of experience and to forge in the smithy of my soul the uncreated conscience of my race.
>
> 27 *April:* Old father, old artificer, stand me now and ever in good stead.

Whatever else one wants to think about Stephen's and Joyce's flight—whether or not one feels they have paid sufficient attention to their drowning brother below, even if one has, like myself, drowned in *Finnegans Wake* and sometimes thinks it a kind of forgery that will lead all fiction to a watery grave, even if one is angry or crude enough to attribute, as I do not, Joyce's actual blindness to his having flown too close to the sun—one cannot deny that this Icarus, unlike Auden's and Bruegel's, has made a fine flight.

I do not think I have anything very useful to say about the trajectory of the flight itself, but I would insist that it is not sustained, as Stephen says, only by the "arms" of "silence, exile, and cunning," or by the kind of eaglehood implied when Stephen seems to celebrate the artist who "like the God of creation, remains within or behind or beyond or above his handiwork, invisible, refined out of existence, indifferent, paring his fingernails" (p. 215). It is sustained also by the "arms" and "embraces" he notes in his diary on 16 April and the kind of verbal embrace he has been able to give the wading girl. I would argue also that although each epiphany leaves Stephen lonelier than the last, as Harry Levin has noted, it is also true that his loneliness helps produce the epiphanies, that they assuage his loneliness, and that, as for many artists, they are the kind of embrace he seems to thrive on. Moreover, as was true of those lonelinesses described earlier by Graham Greene, Mrs. Ramsay, and Elizabeth Bowen, Stephen's has generated a tenderness that he can more easily express in his epiphanies than in his actual encounters. Along with all the self-indulgence of his own flight, his embrace of the girl is perhaps most marked by such tenderness.

Let me turn to another romantic young man, William Wordsworth, and to an embrace embodied in a somewhat different form—a poem: "The Solitary Reaper."

Behold her, single in the field,
Yon solitary Highland Lass!
Reaping and singing by herself!
Stop here, or gently pass!
Alone she cuts and binds the grain,
And sings a melancholy strain;
Oh listen! for the Vale profound
Is overflowing with the sound.

No Nightingale did ever chaunt
More welcome notes to weary bands
Of Travellers in some shady haunt,
Among Arabian sands;
A voice so thrilling ne'er was heard
In springtime from the Cuckoo bird,
Breaking the silence of the seas
Among the farthest Hebrides.

Will no one tell me what she sings?—
Perhaps the plaintive numbers flow
For old, unhappy, far-off things
And battles long ago;
Or is it some more humble lay,
Familiar matter of today?
Some natural sorrow, loss, or pain,
That has been, and may be again?

Whate'er the theme, the Maiden sang
As if her song could have no ending;
I saw her singing at her work,
And o'er the sickle bending—
I listened, motionless and still;
And, as I mounted up the hill,
The music in my heart I bore,
Long after it was heard no more.[3]

It is a lovely poem, probably too fragile to withstand the kind of questions I cannot keep from giving it, most of which are embraced by the general question whether the poem might not be more accurately titled "The Solitary Reaper and the Solitary Gleaner." No more than Stephen does this apparently solitary observer approach the girl; in fact, the embrace is even less reciprocal, for unlike the wading girl who is aware of Stephen's gaze and gazes back at him, this girl remains oblivious of her observer, who watches and listens, motionless and still, and then departs, carrying away her music in his heart. Again I wonder to what extent I have been involved in an act in which an other has been honored and left inviolate in her private space and to what extent an act in which she has been spied upon and exploited for the excitation of her beholders. And more than in Stephen's case I am implicated, for the narrator has urged me to "Behold her," "to stop here, or gently pass," and to "listen." Even if he had been less explicit, his tone of intimacy would produce a similar effect. He assumes my identification with him. I am not supposed to feel, as I am with Stephen, that the artist's response is at all egotistic or excessive. I can take comfort, of course, in the fact that we have been gentle and respectful voyeurs, more ruminative than sensual. We have not snapped her photo for an advertisement—for a brewery or the Scottish Tourist Agency. Still, she is unaware of being observed and listened to. I am not at all sure she would like it if she knew.

What shall I make of the fact that the narrator does not know what she is really singing about? I do not want him to go up to her with a tape recorder as do some modern hunters of rural songs. I do not like to think of him approaching and saying: "Pardon me, young lady. Are you singing of 'old, unhappy, far-off things' or 'some more humble lay' about your 'natural sorrow, loss, or pain' of today?" But I wish he were not quite so nonchalant about the issue, which from her point of view may matter a great deal. She may not share the narrator's ability to take comfort from suffering, to turn "melancholy" and "plaintive" strains into "welcome notes" and to find a voice carrying such tones "thrilling." This is probably somewhat unfair, especially in view of his

"Mount[ing] up the hill," and of his use of the word "bore" in the next-to-the-last line, which do suggest he is carrying some weight; but I cannot overcome my uneasiness about Wordsworth's ability "to find / strength . . . In the soothing thoughts that spring / Out of human suffering." It is fair to say that the poem does turn painful and unhappy things into a lovely music, both hers and the poet's. And even if I do not let myself be thrilled, I am coaxed into accepting that transformation. One cannot quite say that her song and his have become euphemisms for suffering, but they are a form of unguent and anodyne.

Again, much of the impact of the scene comes from the aloneness of the participants—despite my presence, alone at the beginning, alone throughout the embrace, and alone at the end as he wanders off. Were he not alone, neither she nor her music would have the same space to reverberate in. The narrator does not say he is lonely in his aloneness, but one feels quite sure that it is largely his loneliness that so heightens his awareness of her, sharpens her poignance for him, and perhaps even adds a touch of tenderness toward her.

In this poem he is more explicit:

> I wandered lonely as a cloud
> That floats on high o'er vales and hills,
> When all at once I saw a crowd,
> A host, of golden daffodils;
> Beside the lake, beneath the trees,
> Fluttering and dancing in the breeze.
> Continuous as the stars that shine
> And twinkle on the milky way,
> They stretched in never ending line
> Along the margin of a bay;
> Ten thousand saw I at a glance
> Tossing their heads in sprightly dance.
>
> The waves beside them danced; but they
> Outdid the sparkling waves in glee;
> A poet could not but be gay,
> In such a jocund company;
> I gazed—and gazed—but little thought
> What wealth the show to me had brought:

For oft, when on my couch I lie
In vacant or in pensive mood,
They flash upon that inward eye
Which is the bliss of solitude;
And then my heart with pleasure fills,
And dances with the daffodils.[4]

Here the poet has achieved two kinds of lonely embraces (three if one counts the writing of the poem), first gazing and gazing at the "crowd," the "host" of daffodils, gay in their "company," and then using them often when in vacant or in pensive mood as company for his heart to dance with. The inward eye provides the bliss of solitude in part because it can bring such company, in part because it can do so without sacrificing the solitude.

I want to be mean enough to suggest that even here there is a kind of exploitation: the daffodils have been made into dancers and a "show" for him and brought him "wealth"; and he uses them to brighten his life.[5] But of all the kinds of exploitation done to flowers, it is surely among the least pernicious, for he has not cut them, dug them, hybridized them, forced them into bloom on his window sill, or planted them in his own garden. He has not even taken possession of them as he does of the little Celandine[6] or given it the responsibility of engendering thoughts that lie too deep for tears.[7] He is not, as I am doing here, planting his flowers partly to take their place in a later bouquet.

Again it is the aloneness, and loneliness, that heightens the awareness of the other and permits the closeness of the embrace. Wordsworth has said that poetry "takes its origin from emotion recollected in tranquillity" and involves a contemplation of the emotion until the tranquillity disappears and the emotion itself actually comes to exist in the mind. When he engages in that activity, the poet is also and again alone, embracing not an other but only his own emotion, the figure or flower that generated it, present only at the distance of a flash upon an inward eye.

So far the embraces have been relatively uncomplicated. The lonely artist has gazed at his object, seized some of the wealth it has had to offer, and gone off alone with his plunder. A more puzzling encounter is the one in Virginia Woolf's story "An Unwritten Novel," the title of which seems both an invitation and a warning. The story begins with the sentence "Such an expression of unhappiness was enough by itself to make one's eyes slide above the paper's edge to the poor woman's face—insignificant without that look, almost a symbol of human destiny with it."[8] The setting, we soon learn, is the compartment of a train on its way to the seaside resort of Eastbourne, and the woman is sitting opposite the narrator, who is observing her from behind a newspaper. She reports that the woman "shuddered, twitched her arm queerly to the middle of her back and shook her head" and that she moved her head from side to side "with infinite weariness." The narrator's *Times* is "no protection against such sorrow as hers. . . . She pierced through my shield; she gazed [how the lonely ones love that word] into my eyes as if searching any sediment of courage at the depths of them and damping it to clay. Her twitch alone denied all hope, discounted all illusion" (p. 9). When the other passengers have all left, there are a few moments of literal encounter as the "unhappy woman" speaks of "stations and holidays, of brothers at Eastbourne, and the time of year" and then, looking out the window, mutters several fragmentary thoughts including "My sister-in-law." This last is spoken with a bitterness of tone "like lemon on cold steel," and as she spoke "she fidgeted as though the skin on her back were as a plucked fowl's in a poulterer's shop-window" (p. 10). When she falls into silence, seeming again "the most unhappy woman in the world," the narrator tries to prompt her with the phrase "Sisters-in-law," "for if there were a reason [for her unhappiness], and if I knew the reason, the stigma was removed from life."

The woman responds only by pursing her lips and rubbing hard with her glove at a spot on the window pane "as if she would rub something out forever—some stain, some indelible contamination." The spot remains, however, and she sinks back in her seat "with the shudder and the clutch of the arm I had come to expect."

At this point, how fully or literally, how much from empathy or identification, it is hard to tell, the narrator repeats the woman's actions. "Something impell[s]" her to rub at a speck on her window with her glove, a speck that remains:

> And then the spasm went through me; I crooked my arm and plucked at the middle of my back. My skin, too, felt like the damp chicken's skin in the poulterer's shop-window; one spot between the shoulders itched and irritated, felt clammy, raw. Could I reach it? Surreptitiously I tried. She saw me. A smile of infinite irony, infinite sorrow, flitted and faded from her face. But she had communicated, shared her secret, passed her poison; she would speak no more. Leaning back in my corner, shielding my eyes from her eyes, seeing only the slopes and hollows, greys and purples, of the winter's landscape, I read her message, deciphered, reading it beneath her gaze. (Pp. 10–11)

Immediately following this, the narrator leaps into vivid imagining of what the woman's experience is going to be when she arrives in Eastbourne, or, to be more accurate, renders her own stream of consciousness as she invents the story. "Hilda's the sister-in-law. Hilda? Hilda? Hilda Marsh—Hilda the blooming, the full bosomed, the matronly," she begins and develops events in considerable detail as the woman, whom she names Minnie, arrives alone by taxi at Hilda's house, is patronized by her sister-in-law, is greeted stiffly by Hilda's children, and climbs to a little bedroom looking out over the roofs of Eastbourne where she unpacks "a meagre nightgown" and "furred felt slippers," "avoid[s] the looking-glass," and finally sighs and sits by the window (pp. 11–12). After some uncertainty as to what she is thinking about—"(Let me peep across at her opposite; she's asleep or pretending it; so what would she think about sitting at the window at three o'clock in the afternoon? Health, money, bills, her God?)"—the narrator has her pray and perhaps "rub the pane too, as though to see God better" and decides she is praying because she believes she has committed some crime, perhaps dallying to look at some ribbons twenty years ago and rushing home, "but too late. Neighbors—the doctor—baby brother—the kettle—scalded—hospital—dead—or only the shock of it, the blame? Ah, but the detail matters nothing! It's what she carries with her; the spot, the crime, thing to expiate, always there between her shoulders. 'Yes,' she seems to nod to me, 'it's the thing I did' " (p. 13).

The narrator traces Minnie's consciousness as she takes a walk, feels herself stared at, decides to return to her sister-in-law's by a back way, and begins to feel that everything she sees is somehow saying her name, when suddenly Minnie fools her by thinking "Eggs are cheaper," and the narrator comments, "That's what always happens! I was heading her straight for madness, when, like a flock of dream sheep, she turns t'other way and runs between my fingers. Eggs are cheaper. Tethered to the shores of the world, none of the crimes, sorrows, rhapsodies, or insanities for poor Minnie Marsh; never late for luncheon; never caught in a storm without a mackintosh; never utterly unconscious of the cheapness of eggs. So she reaches home—scrapes her boots" (pp. 14–15).

Then there follows this most interesting passage, interesting not only in its metaphors of flowers and flight (so unlike, and yet not totally unlike, Vittorio Mussolini's flight above the rose) and in its emphasis upon the narrator's aloneness, but also in her odd sense of separateness and connection with Minnie ("I, too, on my flower").

> Have I read you right? But the human face—the human face at the top of the fullest sheet of print holds more, withholds more. Now, eyes open, she looks out; and in the human eye—how d'you define it?—there's a break—a division—so that when you've grasped the stem the butterfly's off—the moth that hangs in the evening over the yellow flower—move, raise your hand, off, high, away. I won't raise my hand. Hang still, then, quiver, life, soul, spirit, whatever you are of Minnie Marsh—I, too, on my flower—the hawk over the down—alone, or what were the worth of life? To rise; hang still in the evening, in the midday; hang still over the down. The flicker of a hand—off, up! then poised again. Alone, unseen; seeing all so still down there, all so lovely. None seeing, none caring. The eyes of others our prisons, their thoughts our cages. Air above, air below. And the moon and immortality. . . . [author's ellipsis] Oh, but I drop to the turf! Are you down, too, you in the corner, what's your name—

> woman—Minnie Marsh; some such name as that? There she is, tight to her blossom; opening her hand-bag, from which she takes a hollow shell—an egg—who was saying that eggs were cheaper? You or I? Oh, it was you who said it on the way home, you remember. . . . (P. 15)

Most fascinating of all, perhaps, is that sudden metamorphosis from butterfly to hawk—a bit of a Robinson Jeffers's hawk, celebrating its aloneness and freedom from human entrapment ("None seeing, none caring. The eyes of others our prisons; their thoughts our cages'); a bit of a voyeuristic Goethe eagle, who carries his prey into the realm of the good, the noble, and the beautiful; a hawk that finally drops to the turf, a bit shaken by her flight, to rejoin her human companion.

The narrator then goes on with her story of Minnie Marsh. She gets her back to Hilda's house, has her open the door and put her umbrella in the stand and then becomes sidetracked by a need to invent in some detail a commercial traveler named James Moggridge who takes his meals with the Marshes on Thursdays and is hidden behind the aspidistra in the living room as Minnie enters. The narrator goes so far as to set in motion a Moggridge household and tries to create a wife for him but fails—or decides not to—that she describes with wonderful whimsy: " . . . and his wife a retired hospital nurse—interesting—for God's sake let me have one woman with a name I like! But no; she's of the unborn children of the mind, illicit, none the less loved. . . . How many die in every novel that's written—the best, the dearest, while Moggridge lives. It's life's fault" (p. 17). A moment later, however, the narrator accepts the claims of life and art and enters Moggridge with a strangely Whitmanesque sort of penetration: "I come irresistably to lodge myself somewhere on the firm flesh, in the robust spine, wherever I can penetrate or find foothold on the person, in the soul, of Moggridge the man. The enormous stability of the fabric; the spine tough as whalebone, straight as oaktree; the ribs radiating branches; the flesh taut tarpaulin; the red hollows; the suck and regurgitation of the heart; while from above meat falls in brown cubes and beer gushes to be churned to blood again—and so we reach the eyes" (pp. 17–18). Having reached his eyes, she has them look through the aspidistra at Minnie, who strikes him as a "wretched, elderly female," but he responds to her twitching with a bit of sympathy. Moggridge soon rushes off, however, despite the narrator's attempt to hold on to him, at which point there is a curiously sober passage that perhaps indicates something of the importance these verbal embraces actually have for Virginia Woolf.[9] Just after Moggridge departs, she writes, "We shall never meet again. Moggridge, farewell!" (p. 18), and postpones her imaginative flight back to the top of the house where Minnie is waiting, to think:

> How the mud goes round in the mind—what a swirl these monsters leave, the waters rocking, the weeds waving and green here, black there, striking to the sand, till by degrees the atoms reassemble, the deposit sifts itself, and again through the eyes one sees clear and still, and there comes to the lips some prayer for the departed, some obsequy for the souls of those one nods to, the people one never meets again.
>
> James Moggridge is dead now, gone forever. (P. 19)

With this she returns to Minnie, who is sobbing over the emptiness of her life and feeling that she can face it no longer. But the narrator then remembers some of Minnie's smaller consolations and has her pick up her glove with the worn thumb and begin darning it. From this point until the train arrives in Eastbourne, the narrator is very much attached to Minnie and on her side. She comments on how firm her stitches are and on how proud she must be of her darning; she wants nothing to disturb her as she darns. When Minnie has finished her mending, and with pursed lips and chin held high seems to be preparing to go downstairs to have things out with her sister-in-law, she writes: "Here's the crisis! Heaven be with you! Down she goes. Courage, courage! Face it, be it! For God's sake don't wait on the mat now! There's the door! I'm on your side. Speak! Confront her, confound her soul!" (p. 20).

Suddenly the train is at Eastbourne and the narrator is

startled out of her imagining by the presence of the "actual" woman ("Oh, I beg your pardon! Yes this is Eastbourne"). She helps the elderly woman with her luggage, and chats with her, thinking, "But Minnie, though we keep up pretences, I've read you right—I'm with you now"; and when the luggage is all on the platform, "But why do you look about you? Hilda won't come to the station, nor John; and Moggridge is driving at the far side of Eastbourne" (pp. 20–21). The woman says she will wait by her bag, " 'that's safest. He said he'd meet me. . . . Oh, there he is! that's my son' " (p. 21; author's ellipsis), and the two walk off together. At first the narrator is confounded: "Surely, Minnie, you know better! A strange young man. . . . Stop! I'll tell him—Minnie! Miss Marsh! . . . Oh, but it's untrue, it's indecent. . . . Look how he bends as they reach the gateway. She finds her ticket. What's the joke? Off they go, down the road, side by side. . . . " Then she is dismayed: "Well, my world's done for! What do I know? That's not Minnie. There never was Moggridge. Who am I? Life's bare as bone" (p. 21).

And then there is this remarkable paragraph with which the story ends, remarkable, in part, because again one can hear in this so very English lady's voice so much of what Whitman liked to think of as his own American voice.[10] But remarkable for many other reasons including what strikes me as a note of nervousness, even desperation, along with the whimsy and elation of its tone.

> And yet the last look of them—he stepping from the kerb and she following him around the edge of the big building brims me with wonder—floods me anew. Mysterious figure! Mother and son. Who are you? Why do you walk down the street? Where tonight will you sleep, and then, tomorrow? Oh, how it whirls and surges—floats me afresh! I start after them. People drive this way and that. The white light splutters and pours. Plate-glass windows. Carnations; chrysanthemums. Ivy in dark gardens. Milk carts at the door. Wherever I go, mysterious figures, I see you, turning the corner, mothers and sons; you, you, you. I hasten. I follow. This, I fancy, must be the sea. Grey is the landscape; dim as ashes; the water murmurs and moves. If I fall on my knees, if I go through the ritual, the ancient antics, it's you, unknown figures, you I adore; if I open my arms, it's you I embrace, you I draw to me—adorable world! (P. 21)

Obviously this is a story that will support a wide variety of interpretation and rumination, especially about its commentary on the relations between art and life, fiction and reality. It can, after all, be viewed as a story by a real author about a fictional author who is writing a novel about a woman with whom she is sharing a train compartment, a woman who is fictional to the first author and real to the second, whose fictional re-creation of her turns out to be incorrect—and so on. With enough ingenuity one could play the mirror images against one another in a way to dazzle oneself with one's own cleverness. Those who know Virginia Woolf's essay "Mr. Bennett and Mrs. Brown" may find it hard not to relate the story to the concerns she expresses there about the problems of character portrayal. And those who know her story "The Looking Glass" might wish to compare the two stories, particularly in relation to the way the two narrators react to their incorrect imaginings and to the change in the second narrator's feeling about her imaginative seizure—from an impatient sense that her "quarry" concealed so much that "one must prize her open with the first tool that came to hand—the imagination" to the view that such talk of " 'prizing her open' as if she were an oyster" is "impious and absurd."[11]

What interests me most here, however, is the spaces between all the women, the ways both authors (Virginia Woolf and her fictional narrator) have accomplished their embraces from a distance, and the ways the other person (object?) is handled and mishandled. To some extent, perhaps more than I have conveyed in my summary, the story is playful, both in tone and plot, in many respects a traditional comedy. It is built on error that is corrected by a sudden reversal, and both characters achieve happy unions, the woman with her son, the narrator with her unknown figures and adorable world. But it has its darker side, one that I believe is not only the product of my own less than rose colored glasses.

The woman in the carriage looks to the narrator like "the most unhappy woman in the world." She seems to move her head with "infinite weariness." And she does suffer apparently from a highly visible and unpleasant twitch. She makes a small effort to close the distance between herself and the narrator by chatting "palely and colourlessly," but then subsides with a twitch into silence, which apparently lasts until they arrive at Eastbourne.

The narrator seems even less able to close the space between herself and the other passenger. At first she folds her newspaper into a " 'shield,' impervious even to life." Before she and the woman are left alone in the carriage, the other travelers in the compartment have left one by one except for one man. As the train enters the Three Bridges station, she wonders, "Was he going to leave us? I prayed both ways—I prayed last that he might stay" (p. 9). She apparently has nothing to say to her companion, whose conversation seems pale and colorless, except to prod her once with the phrase "sisters-in-law" in an effort to learn the reason for her unhappiness—not with any eye to give her sympathy, to say nothing of assistance, but because, as she puts it, "If there were a reason, and if I knew the reason, the stigma was removed from life" (p. 10).

When the woman does not respond, she leans back in her corner, shields her eyes from the woman's eyes and in her aloneness, like artists and lonely children do, she invents imaginary beings to occupy her thoughts. By such an act, she does, in one way, people her world and reduce her isolation; but in the very act, she at the same time lengthens the distance between herself and the flesh-and-blood (though fictionally so for us) woman who actually shares her compartment. One cannot even say that her imagining has been a kind of connection with that woman or valid act of sympathy or empathy, for as the story makes so patently clear, the Minnie she has invented is not the woman who has been sitting opposite to her. At the end of the story, the narrator is elated, full of readiness for new verbal embraces (of the incorrect sort we have just witnessed?); but she is still alone. No one seems to have met *her* at the station.

Not only is the narrator's connection with her imaginary figures greater than with her traveling companion, but she has greater sympathy and concern for them. She seems far more upset by the departure of Moggridge or even of his wife ("that unborn [child] of the mind") from her life than she does by the departure of the woman. She is able to join and cheer for the fictive Minnie Marsh when she has imagined her into confronting her sister-in-law. But when her companion, whom she had thought perhaps one of the loneliest and unhappiest women in the world, turns out to be lucky enough to have a son to laugh with and walk down the road side by side with, she seems incapable even of a moment of pleasure for her, not even a glimmer of it. All she seems capable of feeling is distress at the dissolution of her imaginary figures and momentary collapse of her fictive world. When she does cheer up, there is still no sympathetic pleasure for the woman; the excitement is about the potentiality for creating and embracing new imaginary people.

In a way what I am doing here is absurd and unfair. Her quiet withdrawal when the woman refuses to tell her story is surely far better than Miss Lonelyhearts' response when he twists the arms of the old gentleman who refuses to tell his. Far better even if one thinks of her imaginings mostly as a form of voyeurism in which she is using the woman for purposes of emotional and intellectual self-excitation. I do not really wish her to be a Scobie, determined at all costs to be her sister's keeper. I do not even think she can be accused of turning "quite leisurely away from the disaster." But, at the same time, I have no satisfactory way of explaining to myself why the narrator, the author, and I myself have been permitted to move with quite so much ease, even pleasure, from an expression of unhappiness so great it seemed to announce the most unhappy woman in the world to the adoration of unknown figures in an "adorable world." It is possible that Virginia Woolf wants the reader to worry about this, but I do not think so. At the same time, however, I am not sure that I hope she did, for much about her life and death suggests those verbal embraces helped keep her alive so long as she was able to imagine them.

Whatever the form of these artists' embraces, whether sharp and sudden epiphanies like Stephen's or more extended observations like Wordsworth's or Virginia Woolf's, whether tinged with adolescent sexuality or more sober passions recollected in tranquillity, they seem marked by a peculiar aura of loneliness, a peculiar degree of fascination with the imaginary creations and a peculiar degree of distance from them. The artist cannot ever really touch those phantom creatures. Yet without them "life is bare as a bone." And something similar is true of the verbal embraces of countless other artist figures, ranging all the way from such youthful dreamers as Thomas Wolfe's Eugene Gant or Sherwood Anderson's George Willard[12] to such aged ones as Thomas Mann's Gustave Aschenbach, who dies in the midst of such a lonely embrace.

None of this is surprising when we remember that art, especially writing, is a peculiarly lonely profession. The writer must do his work alone in a room, except for imaginary companions who cannot return his embraces, and who sometimes, like those of Baldwin's Vivaldo Moore, do not even seem to trust him and refuse to surrender their privacy.[13] Real people and real connections quite literally threaten to deprive the writer of his imaginary ones. One need not give that predicament quite so desperate a cast as Sherwood Anderson does in his story called "Loneliness," where the child-man artist figure gives up his wife and children to live with his imaginary friends and, when deprived of them by another real person, whimpers and complains, " 'I'm alone, all alone here. . . . It was warm and friendly in my room but now I'm all alone.' "[14] One can put it as E. M. Forster does when he writes: "Estimable is mateyness, and the man who achieves it gives many a pleasant little drink to himself and others. But it has no traceable connection with the creative impulse and probably acts as an inhibition on it. The artist who is seduced by mateyness may stop himself from doing the one thing which he, and he alone, can do—the making of something out of words or sounds or paint or clay or marble or steel or film which has internal harmony and presents order to a permanently disarrayed planet."[15] Or one can put it as lightly as Walter Ong does when he writes that "the person to whom the writer addresses himself normally is not present at all. Moreover, with certain exceptions . . . he must not be present. I am writing a book which will be read by thousands. So, please, get out of the room. I want to be alone. Writing normally calls for some kind of withdrawal."[16] The wives and children of most writers could give powerful though not quite so happy testimony about this very elementary condition—that writing is a solitary activity, to perform which the writer must cut himself off from actual people and spend a good part of his life with imaginary ones. I sometimes think one could almost define writers as being people who have made a profession out of loneliness,[17] have continued into adult life and occupation the lonely child's talent for making up imaginary companions. At the very least, they have converted loneliness into solitude. Not all feel quite so isolated as Hawthorne, whose testimony we read earlier, or as Joyce, who describes his youthful counterpart Stephen Hero as "very lonely," as living a "strange life—without help or sympathy from anyone," and as feeling "different from others," "happy only when he was . . . alone or in the company of phantasmal comrades." But I have never known a writer or read of one whose childhood was not marked by some special intimacy with loneliness.

Many writers, I believe, would assent to this revealing formulation of Rilke's, assent with respect both to the origins of their need to become artists and their highest hopes for their art. Immediately preceding the passage in question, Rilke has been speaking, somewhat as Bertrand Russell did in "A Free Man's Worship,"[18] of the foreignness and indifference of Nature, a Nature who "knows nothing of us . . . whatever men may have achieved, no man has been great enough to cause her to sympathize with his pain, to share in his rejoicing." And he continues:

> The ordinary man, who lives with men, and sees Nature only in as far as she has reference to himself, is seldom aware of this prob-

lematic and uncanny relationship. He sees the surface of things, which he and his like have created through the centuries, and likes to believe that the whole earth is concerned with him because a field can be cultivated, a forest thinned, a river made navigable. His eye focused almost entirely on men, sees Nature also, but incidentally, as something obvious and actual that must be exploited as much as possible. Children see Nature differently; solitary children in particular, who grow up amongst adults, foregather with her by a kind of like-mindedness and life within her, like the smaller animals, entirely at one with the happenings of forest and sky and in innocent, obvious harmony with them. But just because of this, there comes later for youth and maiden that lonely period filled with deep, trembling melancholy, when they feel unutterably forlorn, just at the time of their physical maturing; when they feel that the things and events in Nature have *no longer* and their fellow men have *not yet,* any sympathy for them. Spring comes, even when they are sad, the roses bloom, and the nights are full of nightingales, even though they would like to die. . . . And, on the other hand, they see people, equally strange to them and unconcerned, with their business, their cares, their successes and joys, and they do not understand it. And finally, some of them make up their minds and join these people in order to share their work and their fate, to be useful, to be helpful . . . whilst the others, unwilling to leave the Nature they have lost, go in pursuit of her and try now, consciously and by the use of their concentrated will, to come as near to her again as they were in their childhood without knowing it. It will be understood that the latter are artists: poets or painters, composers or architects, fundamentally lonely spirits who, in turning to Nature, put the eternal above the transitory . . . and who, since they cannot persuade Nature to concern herself with them, see their task to be the understanding of Nature, so that they may take their place somewhere in her great design. And the whole of humanity comes nearer to Nature in these isolated and lonely ones. It is not the least and is, perhaps, the peculiar value of art, that it is the medium in which man and landscape, form and world, meet and find one another. In actuality they live beside one another, scarcely knowing aught of one another, and in the picture, the piece of architecture, the symphony, in a word, in art, they seem to come together in a higher, prophetic truth, to rely upon one another, and it is as if, by completing one another, they become that perfect unity, which is the very essence of a work of art.

From this point of view the theme and purpose of all art would seem to lie in the reconciliation of the Individual and the All, and the moment of exaltation, the artistically important Moment, would seem to be that in which the two scales of the balance counterpoise one another.[19]

Although the passage speaks eloquently enough for itself, I would underline its description of the adolescent sorts of forlornness and yearnings that help shape the artist and usually remain a part of his consciousness, what Weiss has called "loneliness's diffuse driving restlessness, its compulsion to locate an intimate other whose identity may as yet not be known," "that condition of objectless pining, of pining for a kind of relationship rather than for a particular person."[20] That condition we have witnessed already in some of the verbal embraces of Joyce, Wordsworth, and Virginia Woolf, that "desolation of loneliness" of Richard's in *The Morning Watch* that found so delicious the "sad and soaring weight" of the images and meanings of Christianity. The passage illuminates also some of the consequences of the artist's loneliness for art itself, which I shall want to touch on shortly—the extent to which it defines experience in terms of drama and polarities, to which it is informed by yearnings for connection and unity, and to which such connection or "reconciliation" is presumably achieved in a "moment," a moment and reconciliation, we should notice, that is in virtually the same breath spoken of as a "perfect unity" and a balancing of counterpoised scales. The passage also, though more delicately than is often true, reveals one of the more ugly consequences of the artist's lonely origins and later separateness, his contempt for ordinary life and the ordinary man.[21]

Perhaps equally illuminating, if not more so, in the unselfconsciousness of its adolescent egotism, is this effusion of Moustakas:

> I want to begin with the lonely child in *me*. Standing alone. Walking on the edge of darkness. Entering the night. Sitting quietly in the sunlight. I can remember and I can feel the sense of being separate, of wanting to be separate and know me. Sometimes the only way was to escape into the woods, a woods sparsely populated with dwarfed, shaggy trees. Yet when I closed my eyes and sat silently, I could feel the wind; I could hear the chirping of the birds; and I could imagine the beauty of the forest, the mountains, and the sea. Sometimes I watched the movements of the clouds and, through my own self, created images, shapes, and forms that brought a sense of wonder into my life. In that solitude, a spirit arose, a passionate urgency to be who I am—in poetry, in dance,

> in story and song. It was not only my own unfolding, my own destiny that was at stake, not only my own listening to me, but it was also my awareness of misfortune—the poverty, sickness, and death in the world—and my fervor to create a truly human, full life everywhere. I wanted to laugh, to create joy, to plunge into the moment fully, to savor everything; but I was also aware of how long it takes to finally make it, to fully encounter life. I felt I would have to wait forever. I was impatient to live now, but there were always barriers to overcome and caution on all sides.
>
> Then somehow the exciting moment arrived and at last I entered wanting to remain there forever. For a time I experienced the enduring nature of life and felt the timeless quality of love and its spontaneity and freedom; I felt reborn into a real knowledge of myself and others. That was it—to have the serenity and the passion all at once. . . . [22]

"To have the serenity and the passion all at once," the simultaneous possession of the self and others. Put so it sounds intolerably greedy. But that is what Stephen Dedalus, Wordsworth, and Virginia Woolf's narrators wanted in the episodes we have viewed, and found a way of getting through their lonely embraces. Probably it is what most writers have sought, and to some degree received, from their art. And readers too.

There has been more than enough talk already of the alienation of the artist in this century, but I do not think enough recognition has been given to the inevitable isolation and separateness of any artist, even the most gregarious and socially integrated, and to the effects of such aloneness upon the works of art themselves. The bare fact that writers are people who have chosen a peculiarly lonely profession and are engaged in a verbal and imaginative seizure of the world more than in an actual one would, alone, suggest that there would be profound biases in the ways they think, feel, and write about nearly all the crucial aspects of human experience.

Many of these effects I have already touched upon, perhaps belabored: the attractiveness of verbal and imaginative embraces with their affinities on the one hand with voyeurism in which the other is used essentially to excite the observer and, on the other, with a respectful, sometimes tender or even reverential maintenance of distance in which the other retains a kind of inviolability; the attraction of the unknown other who can be embraced without consequences and the ease with which others are abandoned; the way in which the embraces serve both to alleviate and preserve the aloneness; the tendency of some artists to be more concerned with their own consciousnesses and internal dramas than with the external events that they are witnessing or participating in.

Let me wallow briefly in some further speculations. To what extent does the artist's loneliness account for his frequent reliance upon epiphanies and *moments* of connection or unity? In his fine study of the epiphany in the modern novel, Morris Beja explains the increasing reliance on the epiphany as due in part to the "contemporary preoccupation with the sense of isolation, the despair of ever having true contact with another human being, the fear of always remaining an outcast and stranger among the rest of mankind," and goes on to say that "no one theme is more important than this in the epiphanies experienced by such outsiders as Marcel, Stephen Dedalus, Joe Christmas, Eugene Gant, and Septimus Warren Smith (or the six characters in search of an end to loneliness in *The Waves*).[23] But I do not think he sees quite how fully the epiphany suits the condition and needs of any writer. Since that condition is one of separateness, the connections established are likely to be no more than matters of moments—moments felt as possessing peculiar intensity not only because of their brevity but because they break the loneliness and are in such startling contrast to it. The loneliness also provides the space and quiet in which the revelation can reverberate and the time and space for it to be savored. The "moment," itself, is separated and isolated—lonely, so to speak—insofar as it is a moment thrown out of connection with the flow of time or even separated out from oblivion. Epiphanies also have the advantage of usually not requiring any action. From a certain point of view, they can be seen as helping artists avoid the complexities and responsibilities of connection. They carry off their rich emotions with no possibility of real intrusion by a real other, and they can indulge themselves, as a Thomas Wolfe or a Virginia Woolf so often do, in the sense of the ephemerality of the connection—which they much more than life or time have manufactured. Like writing itself (and reading also), such moments offer a safe and separated kind of connection. Stephen need not worry about what to say to the wading girl. Thomas Wolfe's young heroes can embrace their fellow men from behind the insulation of a moving train. I am being unfair, I know, but I cannot forget how easy it is to have epiphanies. There is a kind of lonely adolescent (I was one of them) who requires only a little darkness, a setting where he is on the outside looking in, or inside looking out, and an unknown other, and no possibility of actual involvement, to feel a sense of profound kinship with that other or even all mankind, and to tremble with pride at his capacity for heightened awareness. Beja notes the extent to which the epiphanies of Thomas Wolfe and his heroes are self-deceiving, self-congratulatory, and unconvincing, his compassion "more rhetorical than real,"[24] but he does not seem to see that what they are exhibiting is only a peculiarly transparent form of an activity at which many writers and adolescents excel.[25]

I wonder too about the extent to which the loneliness and separateness of the writer is responsible for certain kinds of distinctness gained by the other in most epiphanies and moments of connection. I am thinking of the sharpness and clarity of the wading girl in *Portrait,* or the way Mr. and Mrs. Ramsay and two of their children appear to Lily Briscoe in *To the Lighthouse* during a sudden moment in which they have taken on special meaning and weight: " . . . There was a sense of things having been blown apart, of space, of irresponsibility as the ball soared high and they followed it and lost it and saw the one star and draped branches. In the failing light they all looked sharp-edged and ethereal and divided by great distances" (pp. 110–11), or of the kind of distinctness that, as we shall see later, nearly everyone and everything has for Agee in *Let Us Now Praise Famous Men,* a distinctness that surely is gained in part by his sense of the profundity of the gap between himself and the tenant farmers. Without the spaces in these encounters, the other would not appear so sharp and clear; the loneliness, especially of the adolescent sort, adds the sharpness and poignance, and sometimes a sensory distinctness that must come from that sexually tinged longing that is so much a part of the adolescent's "deep trembling melancholy." It is the adolescence, also, that often helps fuse the sexual and religious poignancies, as occurs when Stephen encounters the wading girl or when Sally Seton kisses Clarissa Dalloway on the lips and there is a "radiance," a "revelation," a "religious feeling" (*MD*, pp. 52–53).

I wonder too if there are not connections to be discovered between the kinds of distinctness produced by the artist's states of separateness and connection and the kinds of transfigurations of nature William James describes as occurring in the eyes of melancholics and those who have undergone conversion experiences and entered the faith or "assurance state," a state often preceded by a melancholy sense of separateness and isolation: for the newly enlightened "an appearance of newness [that] beautifies every object; the precise opposite of that other sort of newness, that dreadful unreality and strangeness, which is experienced by melancholy patients"[26] where the world "looks remote, sinister, uncanny. Its color is gone, its breath is cold, there is no speculation in the eyes it glares with."[27] That religious kind of newness and beauty seems present in Stephen's vision of the wading girl, whom he does after all regard with worshipful eyes and who causes his soul to cry out "Heavenly God!" though the outburst is one "of profane joy." Something very like that other dreadful strangeness characterizes the opening scene of the next chapter in which he is sitting unhappily in his kitchen draining "his third cup of watery tea to the dregs" and "chewing the crusts of fried bread that were scattered near him, staring into the dark pool of the jar. The yellow dripping had been scooped out like a boghole and the pool under it brought back to his memory the dark turfcoloured water of the bath in Clongoes" (p. 174).

I wonder whether there is not a relation between the kind of space the writer occupies and the kind he sometimes gives his characters. Is it not likely that those whose temperament and profession require a fairly large inviolable space around themselves would view others as possessing a similar sort of space and therefore even a kind of sanctity. And would not that aura of inviolability also make the viewing of the other more exciting, more voyeuristic, since one is looking into a private space. I should think the writer would have a special anxiety about this also because like other lonely people he would himself both want his space to be violated and dread it. For those like Hawthorne, Virginia Woolf, and Agee, for whom both the other and the self seem particularly inviolate and mysterious, I imagine such relations work with special force.

It would seem likely, in fact, that the temperamental and professional aloneness of writers would have a profound effect on the ways they treated all matters involving separateness and connection and lead to a deep preoccupation with those matters. One might expect that the loneliest (Hawthorne? Melville? Conrad? James? Kafka? Joyce? Woolf?) would define their fictional worlds largely in terms of those dimensions. One might expect many writers to place an exaggerated emphasis both on the dangers of connection and upon the value of imaginative connection. It would seem likely that their stories and novels would be informed with marked ambiguities and ambivalence with respect to this issue, that both loneliness and connection would be shown as damaging, and that they would dramatize connections revealing odd mixtures of satisfaction and dissatisfaction. It is not surprising that a reading of all the fiction written since the Victorian period and even including much before then would probably lead a Martian to conclude that nearly all connection between humans was extremely difficult, that it nearly always involved great pain or brought disastrous consequences, and that it was best achieved in the imagination when there was no actual encounter between the parties.

Nor is it surprising that so many writers exhibit a fear of action and a bias in favor of contemplative over active people. It is understandable that they write books like *Miss Lonelyhearts, The Secret Agent, Nostromo, Heart of the Matter,* and *The Idiot,* to say nothing of *Don Quixote,* where efforts to intervene in the lives of others are shown to be disastrous, or books like *The Plague* and *Diary of a Country Priest* where those who do help others in meaningful ways are destroyed in the process. Even George Eliot's Dorothea Brooke, who does eventually learn to give without destroying others or herself, is shown, finally, both as a failed Saint Teresa and a failure in curious ways of her own.

And one would expect to find, as we so clearly do, a great many artists attacking the world and ordinary life—as repressive, stultifying, dishonest, prison-like, injurious to sensitive selves. This has been so persistent and obvious a phenomena, expressed with everything from the violence of a Jeffers to the passionate aplomb of Wordsworth's "The world is too much with us," that illustration is hardly necessary. But let me offer one; a passage from a letter from Flaubert to Louise Colet:

> Humanity hates us; we do not minister to it and we hate it because it wounds us. Therefore, we must love one another in Art, as the mystics love one another *in God,* and everything must grow pale before that love. Let all life's other lamps (which stink, one and all) vanish before that great sun. In an age when common bonds are snapped, and when Society is just one huge brigandage (to use official parlance) more or less well organized, when the interests of flesh and spirit draw apart like wolves and howl in solitude, one must act like everyone else, cultivate an ego (a more beautiful one naturally) and live in one's den. The distance between myself and my fellow men widens every day. I feel this process working in my heart and I am glad, for my sensitivity towards all that I find sympathetic continually increases, as a result of this very withdrawal.[28]

Such a diatribe requires no answer perhaps, apart from the observation that such distance also led Flaubert—if one is to ponder over his "Madame Bovary, c'est moi"—into a curiously close (incestuous? hermaphroditic? masturbatory?) verbal embrace.

I think that the questions and observations I have been making in the past several pages or so are valid and worth further exploration, but I am also uncomfortable about them, and feel that I have been engaged in an unsympathetic sort of exercise in which the writer has become a subject of study, potentially statistical, rather than a human, and his loneliness and disconnection a causative factor rather than a condition of a person. For most writers, writing is a way of connecting, of easing a loneliness that may be in part self-imposed and treasured, but also painful. Probably they would not write if they had no desire for connection.

Many writers—perhaps most—also see their writing as something that may help reduce the loneliness and separateness of others. Too many have expressed such a hope to give other than the briefest sampling. Of the most modest such statements I know of, I like especially E. M. Forster's "only connect" and Anderson's quiet "Perhaps I was vain enough to think that these stories told would, in the end, have the effect of breaking down a little of the curious separateness of so much life, these walls we build up about us."[29] Of the more famous and grandiloquent ones—by Blake, Shelley, Whitman, and Faulkner, among others, I think I am at least put off by the rhetoric of Conrad's statement that, confronted by the enigmatic spectacle of life,

> the artist descends within himself, and in that lonely region of stress and strife, if he be deserving and fortunate, he finds the terms of his appeal. His appeal is made to our less obvious capacities: to that part of our nature which, because of the warlike conditions of existence, is necessarily kept out of sight within the more resisting and hard qualities—like the vulnerable body within a steel armor. . . . He speaks to our capacity for delight and wonder, to the sense of mystery surrounding our lives; to our sense of pity and beauty and pain; to the latent feeling of fellowship with all creation—to the subtle but invincible conviction of solidarity that knits together the loneliness of innumerable hearts,

> to the solidarity in dreams, in joy, in sorrow, in aspirations, in illusions, in hope, in fear, which binds men to each other, which binds together all humanity—the dead to the living and the living to the unborn.[30]

Of all such statements, I am most moved by this quiet one by Eudora Welty, which grows richer each time I read it and whose final sentence expresses what to me usually seems the best of all possible wishes:

> We come to terms as well as we can with our own lifelong exposure to the world, and we use whatever devices we may need to survive. But eventually, of course, our knowledge depends on the living relationship between what we see going on and ourselves. If exposure is essential, still more so is the reflection. Insight doesn't happen often on the click of the moment, like a lucky snapshot, but comes in its own time and more slowly and from nowhere but within. The sharpest recognition is surely that which is charged with sympathy as well as with shock—it is a form of human vision. And that is of course a gift. We struggle through any pain or darkness in nothing but the hope that we may receive it, and through any term of work in the prayer to keep it.
>
> In my own case, a fuller awareness of what I needed to find out about people and their lives had to be sought for through another way, through writing stories. But away off one day up in Tishomingo County, I knew this, anyway. That my wish, indeed my continuing passion, would be not to point the finger in judgment but to part a curtain, that invisible shadow that falls between people, the veil of indifference to each other's presence, each other's wonder, each other's human plight.[31]

I hope, finally, to be able to say something directly about the capacity of writing—and reading—to realize such hopes of crossing distance. But first I must face, or at least turn toward, the way in which art may seem to keep at a distance what needs to be close, its power to translate suffering into beauty or at the very least into some tolerable form.

Part Three

IX ❖ Singing about Suffering

One of the most curious omissions, perhaps, in both Bruegel's canvas and Auden's poem is that no writers, readers, or painters are apparently on the scene. Bruegel is painting it and Auden is writing about it, but no one within the frames is doing any such thing. And yet, whether one regards such activities as a turning away from suffering or a facing of it, unquestionably a most enormous quantity and quality of human effort has been devoted to them. It is probably no exaggeration to say that the single most common subject of art is some form of human suffering. It is possible also that the single most recurrent image in all of Western art is the one of that single sufferer who did presumably take upon himself the pain of all mankind. One hesitates to imagine in how many churches and museums, by how many roadsides, on how many warm breasts that figure has gone on writhing in metal, wood, or paint, on crosses large and small, or in how many poems, stories, plays, tracts, and sermons that figure has been invoked. One hesitates even to think of the number of styles that have been used to contain that suffering and to render it near or distant.

It is possible also that one or another form of tragedy has been turned to even more often than athletics for what has variously been labeled catharsis, instruction, and delight. Even if we exclude all myths, folk tales, poems, novels, plays, operas, movies, soap operas, and comic strips that contain material that might be considered tragic by the man, woman, or child in the street and consider only those works that would fall under a strict definition of the term, the attention given such sufferings is staggering to contemplate. The man- and woman-hours that have been given over to witnessing the pain of Oedipus or Hamlet alone must number in the many millions—in the billions perhaps—if one includes all the schoolchildren and others who have only read the plays. Willy Lohman of *Death of a Salesman* and Blanche DuBois of *A Streetcar Named Desire* paraded their pain for 1,600 performances on Broadway alone, and something close to a million separate people thought to gather there to watch their suffering and in some form to share it. I doubt the most rabid French terrorist would blow up a statue of Corneille or Racine. Far from turning leisurely away, generation after generation have paid admission to place themselves in formal rows to face reproductions (imitations? reenactments? beautifications?) of one or another dreadful martyrdom or forsaken cry. I want to leave them there for a while, unexplained, unjudged, and turn to a much smaller victim and a single human response.

The victim is a dog (for not all "dogs go on with their doggy lives"), and the response is that of William Carlos Williams in a poem entitled "To a Dog Injured in the Street." It is not a poem I feel I understand as well as I should. But that is probably as good a way as any of entering a territory about which too many—poets as well as critics and aestheticians—have been overconfident. And about which Grecian urns have been overconfident, if one is to assign to the urn the final line of Keats's poem: "Beauty is truth, truth beauty, that is all / Ye know on earth, and all ye need to know." This poem directly quotes Keats's "Ode to a Nightingale," but I think it is also meant to echo as well against the "Ode on a Grecian Urn."

IT IS MYSELF
        not the poor beast lying there
                yelping with pain
that brings me to myself with a start—
        as at the explosion
                of a bomb, a bomb that has laid
all the world waste.
        I can do nothing
                but sing about it
and so I am assuaged
        from my pain.
A DROWSY NUMBNESS drowns my sense
        as if of hemlock
                I had drunk. I think
of the poetry of René Char
                        and all he must have seen

and suffered
        that has brought him
                to speak only of
sedgy rivers
        of daffodils and tulips
                whose roots they water,
even to the freeflowing river
        that laves the rootlets
                of those sweet scented flowers
that people the
        milky
                way.
I REMEMBER *Norma*
        our English setter of my childhood
                her silky ears
and expressive eyes.
        She had a litter of pups one night
in our pantry and I kicked
        one of them
                thinking, in my alarm
that they
        were biting her breasts
                to destroy her.
I REMEMBER also
        a dead rabbit
                lying harmlessly
on the outspread palm
        of a hunter's hand
                As I stood by
watching
        he took a hunting knife
                and with a laugh
thrust it
        up into the animal's private parts.
                I almost fainted.
WHY SHOULD I think of that now?
        the cries of a dying dog
                are to be blotted out
as best I can.
        René Char,
                you are a poet who believes
in the power of beauty
        to right all wrongs.
                I believe it also.

With invention and courage
we shall surpass
the pitiful dumb beasts,
let all men believe it,
as you have taught me also
to believe it.[1]

I choose this poem in part because it haunts me but mainly because its complexity and allusiveness seem adequate to that of the issue it addresses. For whatever else is true of the poem, its conversion of suffering into beauty is no simple translation of exploded Ethiopian horsemen into the unfolding of a rose, nor does the narrator's singing seem to go very far toward assuaging his pain. And whatever it does with the cries of the dying dog, it can hardly be said simply to blot them out—for either the narrator or reader.

It may be that it is the narrator's self that brings him to himself with a start, in any of the senses one wishes to give to self, but there is much that compels us to attend to the dog. The title is directed to him, the "not" that precedes "the poor beast lying there yelping with pain" does more to sharpen than negate our awareness of the suffering of the beast, "the cries of [the] dying dog" are still audible late in the poem even as he speaks of blotting them out, and "pitiful dumb beasts" make up the final image in the poem.

The narrator is singing to assuage his pain, but it is he who has imagined for himself and us that bomb which has laid the world waste, he who is remembering the violences of the hunter toward the "harmless" rabbit and the watching boy.

The reverberations of the "drowsy numbness" with Keats's poem are too extensive to confine in any reasonable space, but it is worth remarking that Keats's drowsy numbness also seems more of a wish than a reality and that his poem too is full of reminders of the suffering world that lies on this side of the nightingale's song. In the final stanza, he concludes that "the fancy cannot cheat so well as she is famed to do." With Williams the drowsy numbness is belied not only by the ugly memories but by his immediate thought of René Char's suffering and his certainty that it was the suffering that led that poet to his deep immersion in beauty. I do not know what to make of the fact that my own limited knowledge of the poems of René Char reveals a far less beauty-immersed poet than Williams suggests. I do not think that Williams means to be ironic, but neither can I believe that he was blind to the ugliness and harshness of some of Char's images.

The beginning of the final stanza is open to at least three opposed, though perhaps not entirely irreconcilable, readings. When the narrator asks himself, "Why should I think of that now?" (referring to the hunter's brutality and perhaps his own kicking of the pup as well), one can read the lines that follow as an answer to the question. That is, he is thinking about (singing about) those memories and pain in order to blot out the suffering immediately before him. Or one can read the lines as a part of a question, in effect—Why should he think of that now when the cries of the dying dog, after all, are to be blotted out as best he can. Or one can read the lines as a sort of floating introduction to the leap back to René Char; that is, since one is to blot them out as best one can, he will blot them out with a willed acceptance of the beliefs of René Char. Perhaps Williams is content with such multiplicity. I am not entirely so. But however one reads the lines, they do not suggest that the narrator is doing too good a job of blotting out the cries, nor do they reduce the disturbing quality of the remaining lines of the poem.

In part those lines seem a non sequitur, for the poem has not been concerned with the power of beauty to right wrongs or of man to surpass beasts. Nor does it seem to have had much to do with the value of all mankind's believing such things. It helps a little if we remember that the narrator early in the poem emphasized all that René Char must have seen and suffered and read the last three lines as expressing a wish for all men to believe it *in the same way* (through the same experience) that he has been taught to believe it rather than to believe it *just as* he has come to believe it. But this still does not resolve the extent to which we are to see the ending as a necessary leap or an evasive one, and to the extent it seems the latter, whether the evasiveness is Williams's or that of a narrator whose evasiveness he wishes us to recognize. I cannot decide also how much, if any, importance to attach to his capitalization of his memories and lower-casing of his belief ("I REMEMBER . . . I REMEMBER . . . I believe").

My greatest discomfort, however, is that I am unable to blot out a Robinson Jeffers-like perspective that would seem to force a savage irony into the expression of belief that we shall surpass the pitiful dumb beasts, we who kick them while they are nursing, shoot them and then happily fuck them with a knife. And surpass "dumb" beasts? When the poem has been about a beast "yelping with pain" and "the cries of a dying dog." Surpass them by *singing!* I do not think Williams intends such a reading or that the poem can support it, for it too deeply undermines a narrator who in too many other ways is shown sympathetically and seems to be a close relation of Williams himself. Perhaps he intends to say that we should surpass the beasts with "invention and courage" as *opposed to* kicking, shooting, and knifing them. And I can believe, if not what he has asked me to, that both Williams and his narrator have surpassed the dumb beasts—not by their invention and courage or even primarily by their singing but by their capacity for sympathy and self-examination. Still this does not quite blot out my memory of those happy hunters of Jeffers's who surpassed the beasts with invention and courage by trapping a mammoth in a pitfall, by thinking to use fire when their sticks and stones could not hurt him, and watched happily as they "roasted the living meat slowly to death." Nor does it quite blot out that other image of man's invention that Williams himself has put in my head at the beginning of the poem—the image of "a bomb that has laid all the world waste." I am quite sure he means us to understand that he can do nothing but sing about that too and thereby assuage his pain. I wish I were more sure that he meant me to notice the full extent of the narrator's difficulties as he tries to sing away his pain, and the extent to which his song does finally both begin and end as a song about himself.

Having said all this, I am still uneasy about my own reading of the poem and feel there is something I have missed, perhaps a note of bitterness and self-contempt, something that would reduce the ambiguity a little. Only a little though, for there should be ambiguity and confusion when one sings about suffering and listens to such songs.

I must add a final note, one that helps me feel better about some of the possible evasiveness in the poem. William Carlos Williams was a doctor as well as a poet, and René Char between 1940 and 1945 was "Captaine Alexandre," the regional head of a partisan group in the Resistance movement in France during World War II. That should not make a difference, and I think I can give all the arguments why it should not. But it does. It matters to me that those singers were not—shall we say—stool pigeons, experimental vivisectionists, or Lord High Executioners.

What is to be said about the pleasure I take in reading, and wanting others to read, the passages I am about to present. They are all descriptions by D. H. Lawrence of crucifixes along the old imperial road from Munich across the Tyrol, through Innsbruck and Bozen to Verona, over the mountains.[2] If it can happen without reducing their important specificity, I would like them to represent as well all the aesthetic transformations of suffering performed by art. Here is one:

> It was an old shrine, the wood-sculpture of a Bavarian peasant. The Christ was a peasant of the foot of the Alps. He had broad cheek-bones and sturdy limbs. His plain rudimentary face stared fixedly at the hills, his neck was stiffened, as if in resistance to the fact of the nails and the cross, which he could not escape. It was a man nailed down in spirit, but set stubbornly against the bondage and the disgrace. He was a man of middle age, plain, crude, with some of the meanness of the peasant, but also with a kind of dogged nobility that does not yield its soul to the circumstance. Plain, almost blank in his soul, the middleaged peasant of the crucifix resisted unmoving the misery of his position. He did not yield. His soul was set, his will was fixed. He was himself, let his circumstances be what they would, his life fixed down. (P. 5)

And another:

> And in a little glass case beside the road sat a small, hewn Christ, the head resting on the hand; and he meditates, half-wearily, doggedly, the eyebrows lifted in strange abstraction, the elbow resting on the knee. Detached, he sits and dreams and broods, wearing his little golden crown of thorns, and his little cloak of red flannel that some peasant woman has stitched for him.
>
> No doubt he still sits there, the small, blank-faced Christ in the cloak of red flannel, dreaming, brooding, enduring, persisting. There is a wistfulness about him, as if he knew that the whole of things was too much for him. There was no solution, either, in death. Death did not give the answer to the soul's anxiety. (P. 10)

And another:

> . . . In the cold gloom of the pass hangs the large, pale Christ. He is larger than life size. He has fallen forward, just dead, and the weight of the full-grown, mature body hangs on the nails of the hands. So the dead, heavy body drops forward, sags, as if it would tear away and fall under its own weight.
>
> It is the end. The face is barren with a dead expression of weariness, and brutalized with pain and bitterness. The rather ugly passionate mouth is set forever in the disillusionment of death. (P. 12)

And another, "very elegant, combed and brushed and foppish on his cross" yet with something "brave and keen in it, too . . . the pride and satisfaction in the clean, elegant form, the perfectly trimmed hair, the exquisite bearing . . . more important than the fact of death or pain" (p. 14). And several others, more "weak and sentimental," in which "the carved Christs turn up their faces and roll back their eyes very piteously, in the approved Guido Reni fashion. They are overdoing the pathetic turn. They are looking to heaven and thinking about themselves, in self commiseration" (pp. 14–15). Others are "beautiful as elegies. It is dead Hyacinth lifted and extended to view, in all his beautiful, dead youth. The young, male body droops forward on the cross, like a dead flower. It looks as if its only true nature were to be dead. How lovely is death, how poignant, real, and satisfying!" (p. 15). Still others are "ordinary, factory made Christs . . . null as the Christs we see represented in England, just vulgar nothingness. But these figures have gashes of red, a red paint of blood, which is sensational" (p. 15). And there are some "with great gashes on the breast and knees of the Christ figure, and the scarlet flows and trickles down, till the crucified body has become a ghastly striped thing of red and white, just a sickly thing of striped red" (p. 15) Then one sitting by the grave whose "naked, strong body has known death, and sits in utter dejection, finished, hulked, a weight of shame. . . . What remains of life is in the face, whose expression is sinister and gruesome, like that of an unrelenting criminal violated by torture. The criminal look of misery and hatred on the fixed, violated face and in the bloodshot eyes is almost impossible" (pp. 16–17). And one more, a fallen Christ

> armless, who had tumbled down and lay in an unnatural posture, the naked, ancient wooden sculpture of the body on the naked living rock. It was one of the old uncouth Christs hewn out of bare wood, having the long, wedge-shaped limbs and thin flat legs that are significant of the true spirit, the desire to convey a religious truth, not a sensational experience.
>
> The arms of the fallen Christ had broken off at the shoulders, and they hung on their nails, as ex-voto limbs hang in the shrines. But these arms dangled from the palms, one at each end of the cross, the muscles, carved sparely in the old wood, looking all wrong, upside down. And the icy wind blew them backwards and forwards, so that they gave a painful impression, there in the stark, sterile place of rock and cold. Yet I dared not touch the fallen body of the Christ, that lay on its back in so grotesque a posture at the foot of the post. I wondered who would come and take the broken thing away and for what purpose. (Pp. 18–19)

I had hoped by now—in this book, in my life—to have some answers to the questions raised by these renditions of suffering: but essentially the questions remain. Does Lawrence's rhetoric seduce us too far from the suffering and too much into the loveliness of his language? Does that final line I have quoted—"I wondered who would come and take the broken thing away and for what purpose"—do enough to remind himself and us that the agony is not yet finished and that we have some relation to it?—a relation Margaret Atwood has defined in this single awesome equation: "Anything that suffers and dies instead of us is Christ."[3] He says he dared not touch it. I did not want him to, nor would I have dared touch it myself. I have let it touch me. For what purpose? I can comfort myself (and Lawrence) by thinking of the extent to which the writing and reading of such passages require the exercise of sympathy, exercise in all senses, and even of that in some ways closer bond, empathy. I can turn for support to the tidy formula of Yeats's "Easter 1916"—"A terrible beauty is born." Still, I think my pleasure as I read the passages is too great, though obviously I do not think so enough to give it up.

How shall I regard that special distance granted because, like Auden's poem, Lawrence's art is a depiction of other works of art that are themselves depictions of legendary or mythic suffering? Does he sufficiently cross that distance by his continual reminders of the living inhabitants of the valleys and mountains whose postures, spirits, and burdens are rendered in the images of Christ that line their roads? To what extent does a passage like this cross that distance and take us with it to confront the peasants in their own skins, and to what extent does it co-opt peasant and readers alike into a rhetoric of alliterative language and repetitive rhythm, to say nothing of Lawrentian philosophy?

> [The peasant] and his wife and the children worked on till dark, silent and intent, carrying the hay in their arms out of the streaming thunder-rain into the shed, working silent in the soaking rain. . . . The body bent forward towards the earth, closing round on itself; the arms clasped full of hay, clasped round the hay that presses soft and close to the breast and the body, that pricks heat into the arms and the skin of the breast, and fills the lungs with the sleepy scent of dried herbs: the rain that falls heavily and wets the shoulders, so that the shirt clings to the hot, firm skin and the rain comes with heavy, pleasant coldness on the active flesh, running in a trickle down towards the loins, secretly; this is the peasant, this hot welter of physical sensation. And it is all intoxicating . . . almost like a soporific, like a sensuous drug, to gather the burden to one's body in the rain, to stumble across the living grass to the shed, to relieve one's arms of the weight, to throw the hay on the heap, to feel light and free in the dry shed, then to return again into the chill hard rain, to stoop again under the rain, and rise to return again with the burden.
>
> It is this, this endless heat and rousedness of physical sensation which keeps the body full and potent, and flushes the mind with a

> blood heat, a blood sleep. And this sleep, this heat of physical existence, becomes at length a bondage, at last a crucifixion . . . at last it drives him almost mad, because he cannot escape. (Pp. 5–6)

In a moment I want to turn again to that most strenuous effort to render peasant suffering into language, the one by the man who descended from the boy we earlier watched as he struggled on Good Friday to keep his mind on Christ rather than upon his own dreams of saintliness—and who, incidently, said of Lawrence, "He seems to me somewhat crazy all right, and certainly a man of genius, and I am at present convinced one of the greater and more nearly saintlike of people"[4]—James Agee's *Let Us Now Praise Famous Men.* But first—and this seems a necessity rather than an indulgence—we must read in its entirety one more description of Christ and one more response, the one by the sickly and despondent Ippolit in Dostoevsky's *The Idiot.*

> The picture represented Christ who has only just been taken from the cross. I believe artists usually paint Christ, both on the cross and after He has been taken from the cross, still with extraordinary beauty of face. They strive to preserve that beauty even in His most terrible agonies. In Rogozhin's picture there's no trace of beauty. It is in every detail the corpse of a man who has endured infinite agony before the crucifixion; who has been wounded, tortured, beaten by the guards and the people when He carried the cross on His back and fell beneath its weight, and after that has undergone the agony of crucifixion, lasting for six hours at least (according to my reckoning). It's true it's the face of man *only just* taken from the cross—that is to say, still bearing traces of warmth and life. Nothing is rigid in it yet, so that there's still a look of suffering in the face of the dead man, as though he were still feeling it (that has been very well caught by the artist). Yet the face has not been spared in the least. It is simply nature, and the corpse of a man, whoever he might be, must really look like that after such suffering. I know that the Christian Church laid it down, even in the early ages, that Christ's suffering was not symbolical but actual, and that His body was therefore fully and completely subject to the laws of nature on the cross. In the picture the face is fearfully crushed by blows, swollen, covered with fearful, swollen and blood-stained bruises, the eyes are open and squinting: the great wide-open whites of the eyes glitter with a sort of deathly, glassy light. But, strange to say, as one looks at this corpse of a tortured man, a peculiar and curious question arises; if just

> such a corpse (and it must have been just like that) was seen by all His disciples, by those who were to become His chief apostles, by the women that followed Him and worshipped Him, how could they believe that that martyr would rise again? The question instinctively arises: if death is so awful and the laws of nature so mighty, how can they be overcome? How can they be overcome when even He did not conquer them, He who vanquished nature in His lifetime, who exclaimed, "Maiden arise!" and the maiden arose—"Lazarus, come forth!" and the dead man came forth? Looking at such a picture, one conceives of nature in the shape of an immense, merciless, dumb beast, or more correctly, much more correctly speaking, though it sounds strange, in the form of a huge machine of the most modern construction which, dull and insensible, has aimlessly clutched, crushed and swallowed up a great priceless Being, a Being worth all nature and its laws, worth the whole earth, which was created perhaps solely for the sake of the advent of that Being. This picture expresses and unconsciously suggests to one the conception of such a dark, insolent, unreasoning and eternal Power to which everything is in subjection. The people surrounding the dead man, not one of whom is shown in the picture, must have experienced the most terrible anguish and consternation on that evening, which had crushed all their hopes, and almost their convictions. They must have parted in the most awful terror, though each one bore within him a mighty thought which could never be wrested from him. And if the Teacher could have seen Himself on the eve of the crucifixion, would He have gone up to the cross and died as He did? That question too arises involuntarily, as one looks at the picture.[5]

Although the passage surely speaks for itself, I must make a few observations: first, far from being a "torturer's horse rubbing his innocent behind against a tree" as it is in Auden's poem or a pitiful creature to be surpassed by man's invention and courage as it is in William's, here the "dumb beast" so far surpasses man as to become that merciless universe of Bertrand Russell; second, that of all those Christ-lovers we have seen, only Scobie envisioned some such punch-drunk, swollen-faced figure; and finally, that my own response to this ugly Christ in his garment of ugly prose contains more aversion or disgust than sympathy or even pity. Where Lawrence draws me toward the tortured figure, this passage makes me want to turn away, though not "quite leisurely." I am not sure what conclusions should be drawn from this. Suffering in actuality *is* ugly, repulsive, not attractive. It *is* too easy to empathize with the suffering of beautiful figures and to let beauty blot out pain. Yet ugliness can produce numbness and a turning off of feeling; revulsion too can blot out pain. And though beauty may not have the power, as William Carlos Williams and René Char would like to believe, "to right all wrongs," it can soften and offer a way of remembering.

Now to what seems to me one of the most wonderful and maddening books ever written—*Let Us Now Praise Famous Men.* I give it as much attention as I do here not only because it so deeply illustrates—and confronts as well—the problems of turning suffering into beauty but because it also illustrates and confronts so many other of the issues I have been worrying about, especially those of voyeurism and self-indulgence of both writer and reader, and the autonomy of the subject of their scrutiny. It is also one of the few instances where a romantic has confronted his subjects in the flesh and has had to face the problem of his own relation to them and their sufferings, in his life as well as in his imagination and his art. For Agee lived among the tenant farmers he writes of for about six weeks, in the home of one of the families, sharing its food and bedding and vermin, though not its labor, and came to care for some of the people very much, as they did him.

Even more than most books, this one resists description, and it is almost impossible to convey to someone who has not read it more than the crudest idea of its nature, much less of its full ranges and complexities of content and tone. In a prefatory attempt to say what the book is, Agee writes that the "nominal subject is North American cotton tenantry as examined in the daily living of three representative white tenant families. Actually the effort is to recognize the stature of a portion of unimagined existence, and to contrive techniques proper to its recording, communication, analysis, and defense. More essentially, this is an independent inquiry into certain normal predicaments of human divinity."[6] He goes on to say that the authors are trying to deal with the subject "not as journalists, sociologists, politicians, entertainers, humanitarians, priests, or artists, but seriously" (p. xv) and that "it is an effort in human actuality, in which the reader is no less centrally involved than the authors and those of whom they tell" (p. xv).

The book opens with sixty-one untitled photographs by Walker Evans of tenant farmers and their children, individually and in family groups, of their houses, outside and inside, and of the surrounding countryside and nearby villages. They include close-ups of the faces and bodies of most of the people and, among other things, of their beds, bureaus, stoves, privies, porches, shoes, and gravestones. Since the photographs precede the prefatory material and even the title page, one encounters them before anything else, and they take on a special autonomy and weight. Agee explains in the preface that the "photographs are not illustrative. They, and the text, are coequal, mutually independent, and fully collaborative" (p. xv). They are quiet pictures that resist the kind of drama, pathos, and blatancy that Agee hates so much in the photographs of a similar world by Margaret Bourke White in *You Have Seen Their Faces*. Perhaps they are best described in the terms Agee uses in his "Notes for a film of Andre Malraux's *Man's Fate*, when he says that the "various head groupings, faces, etc., would not be 'composed' and romantic but literalness intensified to become formal out of its own substance."[7] And in the terms he uses in an early story to describe a "form and rhythm and melody of existence" out of which emerges "an enormous clear chord" through which "the whole commonplaceness of existence is transfigured—becomes monstrously powerful, and beautiful, and significant." He supposes "the essentials of which this music is compounded are the facts as they are, tempered by sternness and pity and calm."[8] These three qualities go far toward defining the special quality the pictures have; and if one omits the juvenile straining of "monstrously," one can say they do reveal a power, beauty, and significance by which the commonplaceness of existence is transfigured. But they reveal at the same time a poverty so awful and so awful an injury in the eyes and mouths of most of the people that one wonders by what right one looks at the pictures and wants to go on looking at them.

The remainder of the book, which is dedicated "To those of whom the record is made. In gratefulness and in love," is composed of hundreds of fairly short sections in which Agee uses almost every method he can think of to convey the truth and meaning not only of the lives of the three families but of his own relation to them and of his own writing about them. There are lists of persons and places; outlines for sections of the book both written and unwritten; Whitman-like catalogues; precise factual descriptions of people, houses, rooms, furniture, foods, clothing and other objects and exquisitely lyrical descriptions of many of the same things; ruminations about nearly every aspect of the tenant farmers' lives from the most individual and specific to the most generic and general (as in the passage on families quoted earlier on page 120). There are poems, biblical passages, and quotations from Blake, Shakespeare, and other writers; there are tirades against intellectuals, fashionable radicals, professional revolutionaries, bureaucrats, publishers, and others. There are endless apologies for doing what he is doing and plea after plea to the reader to understand that he is writing about actualities and not to view his work as art. There are infuriatingly long, circuitous, and self-conscious explanations of what he is about to attempt and why; there are moments when he falls so deeply under the spell of his own rhetoric that the effect is nearly comical; but there are also pages and pages of prose whose power and loveliness are unsurpassed anywhere. The book as a whole, I believe, despite all its self-consciousness and posturing, leaves us with a profound and indelible sense of the lives of the tenant farmers. I think it is true for the reader, as Walker Evans says was true for those who knew Agee, that "after a while, in a round-about way, you discovered that, to him, human beings were at least possibly immortal and literally sacred souls" (p. xi). I even think Agee's friend and teacher Father Flye may not be going too far when he writes to Agee after reading the book: "I find in it a sympathy, a love, a care for human beings, which make me think of our Lord; and I call it in a true sense deeply religious"[9] although I must at the same time share some of

Scobie's distrust of a Lord who permits such atrocities and comment that if Agee is often too mindful of his own suffering, Christ can be viewed as God's way of calling attention to his.

But I am pounding these chords too soon. First we must listen further to Agee's music. For despite his insistence that we must not view his work as art, he has transposed that "portion of unimagined existence" essentially into music. I am thinking not only of the large number of passages that sing with the rich lyricism of the two compositions I am about to present. (I shall offer them and those that follow at considerable length in the hope that along with their music they will give the reader who has not read it something of the substance and burden of the book. If that length seems excessive I can say only that to skim here is to do a further kind of violence to some people who have already been desperately hurt.)

> Just a half-inch beyond the surface of this wall I face is . . . another room, and there lie sleeping, on two iron beds and on pallets on the floor, a man and his wife and her sister, and four children, a girl, and three harmed boys. Their lamp is out, their light is done this long while, and not in a long while has any one of them made a sound. Not even straining, can I hear their breathing: rather, I have a not quite sensuous knowledge of a sort of suspiration, less breathing than that indiscernible drawing-in of heaven by which plants live, and thus I know they rest and the profundity of their tiredness, as if I were in each of these seven bodies whose sleeping I can almost touch through this wall, and which in the darkness I so clearly see, with the whole touch and weight of my body: George's red body, already a little squat with the burden of thirty years, knotted like oakwood, in its clean white cotton summer union suit that it sleeps in; and his wife's beside him, Annie Mae's slender, and sharpened through with bone, that ten years past must have had such beauty, and now is veined at the breast, and the skin of the breast translucent, delicately shrivelled, and blue, and she and her sister Emma are in plain cotton shifts; and the body of Emma, her sister, strong, thick, and white, tall, the breasts set wide and high, shallow and round, not yet those of a full woman, the legs long thick and strong; and Louise's green lovely body, the dim breasts faintly blown between wide shoulders, the thighs long, clean and light in their line from hip to knee, the head back steep and silent to the floor, the chin highest, and the white shift up to her divided thighs; and the tough little body of Junior, hardskinned and gritty,

the feet crusted with sores; and the milky and strengthless littler body of Burt whose veins are so bright in his temples; and the shrivelled and hopeless, most pitiful body of Squinchy, which will not grow:

But it is not only their bodies but their postures that I know, and their weight on the bed or on the floor, so that I lie down inside each one as if exhausted in a bed, and I become not my own weight and shape and self, but that of each of them . . . [and know] the soul and body of each of these seven, and of all of them together in this room in sleep, as if they were music I were hearing, each voice in relation to all the others, and all audible, singly, and as one organism, and a music that cannot be communicated: and thus they lie in this silence, and rest.

Burt half-woke, whimpering before he was awake, an inarticulated soprano speaking through not quite weeping in complaint to his mother as before a sure jury of some fright of dream: the bed creaked and I heard her bare feet slow, the shuffling soles, and her voice, not whispering but stifled and gentle, Go to sleep now, git awn back to sleep, they aint nothin agoin to pester ye, get awn back to sleep, in that cadence of strength and sheltering comfort which anneals all fence of language and surpasses music; and George's grouched, sleepy voice, and hers to him, no words audible; and the shuffling; and a twisting in beds, and grumbling of weak springs; and the whimpering sinking, and expired; and the sound of breathing, strong, not sleeping, now, slowed, shifted across into sleep, now, steadier; and now, long, long, drawn off as lightest lithest edge of bow, thinner, thinner, a thread, a filament; nothing: and once more that silence wherein more deep than starlight this home is foundered. (Pp. 54–56)

These fields are workrooms, or fragrant but mainly sterile workfloors without the walls and with a roof of uncontrollable chance, fear, rumination, and propriative prayer, and are as the spread and broken petals of a flower whose bisexual center is the house.

Or the farm is also as a water spider whose feet print but do not break the gliding water membrane: it is thus delicately and briefly that, in its fields and structures, it sustains its entity upon the blind breadth and steady heave of nature.

Or it is the wrung breast of one human family's need and of an owner's taking, yielding blood and serum in its thin blue milk, and the house, the concentration of living and taking, is the cracked nipple: and of such breasts, the planet is thickly and desperately paved as the enfabled front of a goddess of east india.[10] (Pp. 116–17)

Nor when I say transposed into music am I thinking only of the extent to which he leaves scarcely anything untouched by some kind of song: whether a spring—"not cowled so deeply under the hill that the water is brilliant and nervy, seeming to break in the mouth like crystals, as spring water can: it is about the temper of faucet water, and tastes slack and faintly sad, and as if just short of stale. It is not quite tepid, however, and it does not seem to taste of sweat and sickness, as the water does which the Woods family has to use" (p. 118); or Mrs. Ricketts's dress:

> It is made of a coarse tan cotton I will speak of later. It is shaped like a straight-sided ball, with a little hole at the top for the head to stick through, the cloth slit from the neck to below the breasts and held together if I remember rightly with a small snarl of shoe-lace; the bare arms sticking through the holes at the sides, the skirt ending a little below the knee, the whole dress standing out a little from the body on all sides like a child's youngest cartoons, not belted, and too stiffened perhaps with dirt to fall into any folds other than the broadest and plainest, the skirt so broad away from her at the bottom that, with her little feet and legs standing down from inside it, for all their beauty they seem comic sticks, and she, a grievous resemblance to newspaper drawings of timid men in barrels labeled John Q. Public. (P. 251)

or the objects on the bureau in the Gudgers' front bedroom:

> An old black comb, smelling of fungus and dead rubber, nearly all the teeth gone. A white clamshell with brown dust in the bottom and a small white button on it. A small pincushion made of pink imitation silk with the bodiced torso of a henna-wigged china doll sprouting from it, her face and one hand broken off. A cream-colored brown-shaded china rabbit three or four inches tall, with bluish lights in the china, one ear laid awry: he is broken through the back and the pieces have been fitted together to hang, not glued, in delicate balance. A small seated china bull bitch and her litter of three smaller china pups, seated round her in an equilateral triangle, their eyes intersected on her: they were given to Louise last Christmas and are with one exception her most cherished piece of property. A heavy moist brown Bible, its leaves almost weak as snow, whose cold, obscene, and inexplicable fragrance I found on my first night in this house. (P. 146)

I am thinking also of the rhythmical spareness of passages like this one:

From March through June, while cotton is being cultivated, they live on the rations money.

From July through to late August, while the cotton is making, they live however they can.

From late August through October or into November, during the picking and ginning season, they live on the money from their share of the cottonseed.

From then on until March, they live on whatever they have earned in the year; or however they can.

During six to seven months of each year, then—that is, during exactly such time as their labor with the cotton is of absolute necessity to the landlord—they can be sure of whatever living is possible in rations advances and in cottonseed money.

During five to six months of the year, of which three are the hardest months of any year with the worst of weather, the least adequacy of shelter, the worst and least of food, the worst of health, quite normal and inevitable, they can count on nothing except that they may hope least of all for any help from their landlords.

Gudger—a family of six—lives on ten dollars a month rations money during four weeks of the year. He has lived on eight, and on six. Woods—a family of six—until this year was unable to get better than eight a month during the same period; this year he managed to get it up to ten. Ricketts—a family of nine—lives on ten dollars a month during this spring and early summer period.

This debt is paid back in the fall at eight percent interest. Eight percent is charged also on the fertilizer and on all other debts which tenants incur in this vicinity. (Pp. 106-7)

Even when he is trying desperately to make us feel how unbearable it is to pick cotton, he is incapable of not singing (the passage is long and I have already hurt it by some deletions; to skim further would be to turn leisurely away from a martyrdom that most of us who can afford to read this book have special reason to witness):

It is simple and terrible work. Skill will help you; all the endurance you can draw up against it from the roots of your existence will be thoroughly used as fuel to it: but neither skill nor endurance can make it any easier.

Over the right shoulder you have slung a long white sack whose half length trails the ground behind. You work with both hands as fast and steadily as you can. The trick is to get the cotton between your fingertips at its very roots in the burr in all three or four or five gores at once so that it is brought out clean in one pluck. It is easy enough with one burr in perhaps ten, where the cotton is ready to fall; with the rest, the fibers are more tight and tricky. . . . You would have to try hard, to break your flesh on any one burr, whether on its sharp points or its edges; and a single raindrop is only scarcely instrumental in ironing a mountain flat; but in each plucking of the hand the fingers are searched deep in along these several sharp edges. In two hours' picking the hands are just well limbered up. At the end of a week you are favoring your fingers, still in the obligation of speed. The later of the five or six times over the field, the last long weeks of the season, you might be happy if it were possible to exchange them for boils. With each of these hundreds of thousands of insertions of the hands, moreover, the fingers are brought to a small point, in an action upon every joint and tendon in the hand. I suggest that if you will try, three hundred times in succession, the following exercise: touch all five fingertips as closely as possible into one point, trying meanwhile to hold loose cotton in the palm of the hand; you will see that this can very quickly tire, cramp, and deteriorate the whole instrument, and will understand how easily rheumatism can take up its strictures in just this place.

Meanwhile, too, you are working in . . . sunlight that stands and stacks itself upon you with the serene weight of deep sea water . . . so that it can seem you are a diving bell whose strained seams must at any moment burst, and the eyes are marked in stinging sweat, and the head, if your health is a little unstable, is gently roaring, like a private blow-torch, and less gently beating with aching blood: also the bag, which can hold a hundred pounds, is filling as it is dragged from plant to plant . . . the sack heavier and heavier, so that it pulls you back as a beast might rather than a mere dead weight: but it is not only this: cotton plants are low, so that in this heat and burden of the immanent sun and of the heavying sack you are dragging, you are continuously stooped over even if you are a child, and are bent very deep if you are a man or a woman . . . but not even the strongest back was built for that treatment, and there combine at the kidneys, and rill down the thighs and up the spine and athwart the shoulders the ticklish weakness of gruel or water, and an aching that is increased in geometrical progressions, and at length, in the small of the spine, a literal and persistent sensation of yielding, buckling, splintering, and breakage. . . .

. . . There are sometime shifts into gaiety in the picking, or a brief excitement, a race between two of the children, or a snake killed; or two who sit a few moments in their sweat in the shaded clay when they have taken some water, but they say very little to each other, for there is little to say, and are soon back to it, and mainly, in hour upon hour, it is speechless, silent, serious, ceaseless and lonely work along the great silence of the unshaded land, ending each day in a vast blaze of dust on the west, every leaf sharpened in long knives of shadow, the day drawn down

> through red to purple, and the leaves losing color, and the wild blind eyes of the cotton staring in twilight, in those odors of work done and of nature lost once more to night whose sweetness is a torture, and in the slow, loaded walking home, whose stiff and gentle motions are those of creatures just awakened. (Pp. 306–11)

The book, both in its parts and as a whole, is organized more like a musical composition than any other formal structure, and Agee continually uses musical terms, references, and images to express both his own progressions and the qualities of the tenants' lives. Opening nearly at random I note "sonata," "syncopations," "orchestration," "chord," and "counterpoint." He speaks of "the hearing and seeing of a complex music in every effect and in causes of every effect and in the effects of which this effect will be part cause, and the more than reasonable suspicion that there is at all times further music involved there, beyond the simple equipment of our senses and their power of reflection and deduction to apprehend" (p. 208). On one occasion he seeks to resolve the essential elements of the Gudger house into a "chord," "the full bodily recognition" of which can "arrest the heart" (p. 166), and then explains if one can examine precisely how such a house is made and let all its relations and substances "*be, at once,* driven upon your consciousness, one center . . . there is such an annihilating counterpoint as might be if you could within an instant hear and be every part, from end to end, of the most vastly spun of fugues" (p. 166). On another occasion he says he hopes "the book as a whole will have a form and set of tones rather less like those of narrative than like those of music" (p. 220).

Perhaps his most astonishing and revealing use of music is one that closes the Preamble, in which he has tried to explain why the whole endeavor in which he has been engaged seems to him "curious, obscene, terrifying, and unfathomably mysterious" and to persuade the reader to think of the work as something more than one more book. "Above all else," he urges the reader, "in God's name don't think of it as Art"; and he goes on to argue that the "deadliest blow the enemy of the human soul can strike is to do fury honor. Swift, Blake,

Beethoven, Christ, Joyce, Kafka, name me a one who has not been thus castrated" (p. 14). To start on a cure for this "disease," he suggests a test to see how respectable Beethoven is and "by what idiocy Blake or work even of such intention as mine is ever published and sold." He admits that the test is "unfair," "untrue," "stacks all the cards," and "is out of line with what the composer intended," and then with the deliberate sort of irresponsibility that characterizes much of the Preamble, says "all so much the better" (p. 14). The test is this:

> Get a radio or a phonograph capable of the most extreme loudness possible, and sit down and listen to a performance of Beethoven's Seventh Symphony or of Schubert's C-Major Symphony. But I don't mean just sit down and listen, I mean this: Turn it on as loud as you can get it. Then get down on the floor and jam your ear as close into the loudspeaker as you can get it and stay there, breathing as lightly as possible, and not moving, and neither eating nor smoking nor drinking. Concentrate everything you can into your hearing and into your body. You won't hear it nicely. If it hurts you, be glad of it. As near as you will ever get, you are inside the music; not only inside it, you are it; your body is no longer your shape and substance, it is the shape and substance of the music.
>
> Is what you hear pretty? or beautiful? or legal? or acceptable in polite or any other society? It is beyond any calculation savage and dangerous and murderous to all equilibrium in human life as human life is; and nothing can equal the rape it does on all that death; nothing except anything, anything in existence or dream, perceived anywhere remotely toward its true dimension.
>
> Beethoven said a thing as rash and noble as the best of his work. By my memory he said: "He who understands my music can never know unhappiness again." I believe it. And I would be a liar and a coward and one of your safe world if I should fear to say the same words of my best perception, and of my best intention.
>
> Performance, in which the whole fate and terror rests, is another matter. (Pp. 14–15)

There is some silliness here, but also a profound sincerity beneath the fuss and fanfare. Both reality and the properly furious responses to it, I believe, do sometimes blast upon and surround Agee with such music, and he would wish to reach for it at times in his performance. He is not such a fool, of course, as to think he can gain that kind of impact by always keeping his own volume turned on loudly, and, as we have already seen, his own music moves through many modulations. On a few occasions, I think, it lapses into that sort of "thin sad music of humanity," which helps Wordsworth into "the soothing thoughts that spring / Out of human suffering." Spring? More often it could be described as the kind of music Agee wants to accompany some of the horrible scenes in the film he planned of Man's Fate: "a kind of formal music made only of the muted, swarming noise of suffering."[11] At his best, I believe, and through his total effort in the book, he removes enough of our padding and his own to let us hear something of that squirrel's heartbeat and of the sound of the grass growing, and something of that roar (a kind of music) on the other side of silence that George Eliot says we could die of if we had a keen enough vision and feeling.[12] Dan McCall puts it marvelously well when he says with reference to Agee's descriptions of a mule, a cow, and a kitten: "*Let Us Now Praise Famous Men* insistently enforces a kind of demented lucidity; Agee gets so close to helplessness, that both he and it are naked. 'Naked' is not really right, or enough, for the skin has been peeled away; the surface of the world has been rubbed raw. Animals are animals—accurately, patiently, and copiously described—and they are also immortal souls in pain. This is true not only of cats and cows but of trunks, beds, and bureau drawers as well."[13]

How can it be proper to turn such a "swarming noise of suffering," such a "roar," into music, to transpose such things into beauty? What right do we have to listen? By what right do I eagerly assent when he insists that much of what he sees is, in fact, beautiful:

> that a house of simple people which stands empty and silent in the vast Southern country morning sunlight, and everything which on this morning in eternal space it by chance contains, all thus left open and defenceless to a reverent and cold-laboring spy, shines quietly forth such grandeur, such sorrowful holiness of its exactitudes in existence, as no human consciousness shall every rightly perceive, far less impart to another; that there can be more beauty and more deep wonder in the standings and spacing of mute fur-

> nishings on a bare floor between the squaring bourns of walls than in any music ever made; that this square home, as it stands in unshadowed earth between the winding years of heaven, is, not to me but of itself, one among the serene and final, uncapturable beauties of existence: that this beauty is made between hurt but invincible nature and the plainest cruelties and needs of human existence in this uncured time, and is inextricable among these, and as impossible without them as a saint born in paradise. (P. 121)

Is it enough to share his verbal guilt and self-awareness as he himself wrestles with the issue:

> To those who own and create it this "beauty" is, however, irrelevant and undiscernible. It is best discernible to those who by economic advantages of training have only a shameful and thief's right to it: and it might be said they have any "rights" whatever only in proportion as they recognize the ugliness and disgrace implicit in their privilege of perception. The usual solution, non-perception, or apologetic perception, or contempt for those who perceive and value it, seems to me at least unwise. In fact it seems to me necessary to insist that the beauty of a house, inextricably shaped as it is in an economic and human abomination, is at least as important a part of the fact as the abomination itself: but that one is qualified to insist on this only in proportion as one faces the brunt of his own "sin" in so doing and the brunt of the meanings, against human beings, of the abomination itself. (P. 182)

He himself remains troubled about this, for he tells us immediately to consider the above "merely as a question raised: for I am in pain and uncertainty as to the answers, and can write no more of it here" (p. 182); and sometime later he felt impelled to add a footnote stating that "the 'sin,' in my present opinion, is in feeling in the least apologetic for perceiving the beauty of the houses" (p. 182).

Is it enough to share his anguish and accept his exquisitely fashioned burden of guilt when he wonders how he can possibly make clear the arduousness and repetitiveness of Mrs. Gudger's work and the effect of it on her body, mind, heart, and being:

> How is this to be made so real to you who read of it, that it will stand and stay in you as the deepest and most iron anguish and guilt of your existence that you are what you are, and that she is

> what she is, and that you cannot for one moment exchange places with her, nor by any such hope make expiation for what she has suffered at your hands, and for what you have gained at hers: but only by consuming all that is in you into the never relaxed determination that this shall be made different and shall be made right, and that of what is "right" some, enough to die for, is clear already, and the vast darkness of the rest has still, and far more passionately and more skeptically than ever before, to be questioned into, defended, and learned toward. There is no way of taking the heart and the intelligence by the hair and of wresting it to its feet, and of making it look this terrific thing in the eyes: which are such gentle eyes: you may meet them, with all the summoning of heart you have, in the photograph in this volume of the young woman with black hair: and they are to be multiplied, not losing the knowledge that each is a single, unrepeatable, holy individual, by the two billion human creatures who are alive upon the planet today; of whom a few hundred thousands are drawn into complications of specialized anguish, but of whom the huge swarm and majority are made and acted upon as she is: and of all these individuals, contemplate, try to encompass, the one annihilating chord. (Pp. 290–91)

Even if I can thrust enough against the music here to let that "deepest and most iron anguish and guilt" take painful and personal form, I cannot take on the never relaxed determination to make it all different and right. Especially because, as Agee is fully aware elsewhere, neither he nor I know any way of making it right.

Obviously it is not "enough"; and yet it seems something more than self-indulgence to write, read, and pass on such passages—and even this one from the Preamble:

> If I could do it, I'd do no writing at all here. It would be photographs; the rest would be fragments of cloth, bits of cotton, lumps of earth, records of speech, pieces of wood and iron, phials of odors, plates of food and of excrement. Booksellers would consider it quite a novelty; critics would murmur, yes, but is it art; and I could trust the majority of you to use it as you would a parlor game.
>
> A piece of the body torn out by the roots might be more to the point.
>
> As it is, though, I'll do what little I can in writing. Only it will be very little. I'm not capable of it; and if I were, you would not go near it at all. For if you did, you would hardly bear to live. (Pp. 12–13)

He exaggerates, of course. No matter how well he wrote or how much he was capable of, we are padded well enough to go near it and still bear to live, just as most lovers manage to live without the lovers they have sworn they could not live without; just as Agee himself did, in fact, live with the flesh-and-blood sufferers and certainly came back to tell the tale. Yet I like the passage and resist the part of me that is smirking at how easily I accept the exaggeration, how eagerly I join him in taking on the burden of guilt in place of some other burden. I resist even the less smirking knowledge that it is usually easier to carry a burden than to give up a part of oneself. Resist it in part with the knowledge that giving up parts of oneself, even whole limbs, does not necessarily heal another's mutilation.

In some respects it seems of very great significance that Agee was writing about the lives of actual rather than fictional people, and he himself places great weight on this. "In a novel," he says in the Preface, "a house or person has his meaning, his existence, entirely through the writer," whereas here "his true meaning is much huger. It is that he *exists,* in actual being, as you do and as I do, and as no character of the imagination can possibly exist. His great weight, mystery, and dignity are in this fact" (p. 11). And he goes on throughout the book trying to make us know that the most important thing about his characters is that they exist, that George Gudger "is a human being, a man, not like any other human being, so much as he is like himself . . . that he is exactly, down to the last instant, who, what, where, when, and why he is . . . living right now, in flesh and blood and breathing, in an actual part of a world in which also, quite as irrelevant to imagination, you and I are living" (p. 210).

I understand that passionate desire to make himself and his reader apprehend the flesh-and-blood reality of the suffering, and I can remember the way I once desperately pounded that note in an effort somehow to convey the enormity of what I was witnessing as a soldier in World War II. I called the poem "More Terrible Than All the Words" and over and over again felt compelled to repeat "the reality, not the words, remember." Now I think the distinction matters less. It is true that when real people are observed, to say nothing of photographed, the voyeurism takes on further ugliness, an ugliness qualified but not removed, by the reverence and sense of guilt with which he performs the act and by his frequent acknowledgments that his invasion *was* "spiritual burglary."[14] In fact, some of the people in the book are reported to have felt resentment at having been so invaded and exposed.[15] And it always matters terribly, of course, to the sufferers whether they are real or not, for fictional characters do not experience their own pain. But for the reader, whose encounter is only with the words, I do not see why it matters very much whether his compassion (or voyeurism) is directed toward a Scobie or a George Gudger, or a Jesus Christ, for that matter. Unless he knows some way to alleviate the real sufferer's pain, which is most unlikely. This is not to negate the weight of reality but rather to attest to the power of art to give to the fictional much the same "weight, mystery, and dignity" that comes from being real and to the promiscuity of our compassion, which is not as far from Scobie's as we sometimes think. I am not sure one's guilt should be greater in the face of the real suffering since it is only a single instance pulled from oceans of torment and these same oceans lie beneath the fictional instances as well.

I know I have for too long kept skittering away from the question of action—those possibilities that range all the way from saintliness to the writing of checks—and I must stay put with it for at least a few moments, even though I do not think I have anything to say directly that is either correct or useful. Virginia Woolf complains about novels that leave one feeling one ought "to join a society, or more desperately, to write a check."[16] I am a little upset by the ease with which she dismisses those possible functions and consequences of art, as I am by any who would define art's *proper* purposes, but surely she is right that there is something limited about portraits of the human condition that imply a cure by check. After reading *Let Us Now Praise Famous Men,* one probably feels more directly involved or implicated than Woolf would approve, but one does not feel like writing a check and would not know where to send it if one did, any more than one does after reading the most astonishing of all transformations of suffering into beauty—Dante's "Inferno." In fact, the poverty Agee depicts is so profound and so deeply spiritual as well as material as to make me ashamed of the checks I do send to agencies like the Highlander School and Southern Poverty Law Center that are sufficiently hopeful or foolish to attempt actions. So deep is the deprivation that it is hard to imagine what a saint could do. At the same time, the book forbids absolutely the luxuries either of complacency or despair.

With respect to the possible effectiveness of social or political action, Agee is usually tormentingly ambiguous. Although he sometimes speaks of himself as a Communist and sometimes implies that only revolution could significantly improve the tenant farmer's lot, he deeply distrusts both the Communist party and the Soviet Union and has this to say of revolutionaries: "Though there are revolutionists whom I totally respect, and before the mere thought of whom I hold myself in contempt, I go blind to think what crimes others would commit upon [the tenant farmers], and instill into them; and by every appearance and probability these latter, who for all their devotion and courage seem to me among the most dangerous and hideous persons at large, are greatly in the majority, and it is they who own and will always betray all revolutions" (p. 285). Nor is he any more hopeful about the New Deal reforms that were being attempted at the time. In general, whenever he gets close to the question of whether anything helpful can be done and if so what, he begins to vacillate nervously and often runs in several directions at once. But I am hardly the one to blame him for that. Nor do I, in fact, either for him or myself, know what other behaviors are appropriate. In the face of certain kinds of concern, no action can ever be commensurate.

I will go on sending checks, however, although I doubt they are of any more use than my guilt. I go on sending them because of what it would feel like not to send them—to acquiesce to that distance. And because they do reduce my sense of guilt a little, which may not be such a bad thing. For if the absence of guilt turns humans not into innocent beasts but monsters, too much can turn into profitless self-laceration and rage; even murderous rage as it does in this passage where Agee's answer to the murder he detests seems to be only a murderousness of his own.

> . . . I believe that every human being is potentially capable, within his "limits," of fully "realizing" his potentialities; that this, his being cheated and choked of it, is infinitely the ghastliest, commonest, and most inclusive of all the crimes of which the human world can accuse itself; and that the discovery and use of "consciousness," which has always been and is our deadliest enemy and deceiver, is also the source and guide of all hope and cure, and the only one.
>
> I am not at all trying to lay out a thesis, far less to substantiate or solve. I do not consider myself qualified. I know only that murder is being done, against nearly every individual in the planet, and that there are dimensions and correlations of cure which not only are not being used but appear to be scarcely considered or suspected. I know there is cure, even now available, if only it were available, in science and in the fear and joy of God. This is only a brief personal statement of these convictions: and my self-disgust is less in my ignorance, and far less in my "failure" to "defend" or "support" the statement, than in my inability to state it even so far as I see it, and in my inability to blow out the brains with it of you who take what it is talking of lightly, or not seriously enough. (P. 279)

I do not want to go on quoting Agee, for no quotes can convey the ranges of either his seriousness or his rage, or the extent to which his book demonstrates the possibilities of consciousness as deceiver and cure. I want everyone who can to read his book, and however irritated they become at its excesses, to read it to the end. I can imagine a reader deciding then that language is the deadliest enemy of the oppressed—that one bandage, one gift of a mule, yes, even one horrid standardized prefabricated house or one revolutionary gesture, however futile or self-inflating, would be more decent and valuable than all of Agee's exertions, than all the humming of all the poets. I can imagine a reader thinking this and then remembering it was Agee's words that led him to feel so, and not knowing how to get beyond that paradox. I can imagine a reader who decides from it to become a writer or a teacher of literature. I can even imagine a reader who somehow is left with all those responses whirling around in his mind, doing little more than jostling one another. As is true for me until I remember to read again a passage like this one in which he tells of the photographing of the Ricketts family, and know without question that, whatever its harmfulness, the translation of suffering and sympathy into music can sometimes be a sufficient way to bear witness.

> You [Mrs. Ricketts] realized what the poor foolishness of your husband had let you all in for, shouting to you all to come out . . . all to stand there on the porch as you were in the average sorrow of your working dirt and get your pictures made; and to you it was as if you and your children and your husband and these others were stood there naked in front of the cold absorption of the camera in all your shame and pitiableness to be pried into and laughed at; and your eyes were wild with fury and shame and fear, and the tendons of your little neck were tight, the whole time, and one hand continually twitched and tore in the rotted folds of your skirt like the hand of a little girl who must recite before adults, and there was not a thing you could do, nothing, not a word of remonstrance you could make, my dear, my love, my little crazy, terrified child; for your husband was running this show, and a wife does as she is told and keeps quiet about it: and so there you stood, in a one-piece dress made of sheeting, that spread straight from the hole where the head stood through to the knee without belting, so that you knew through these alien, town-dressed eyes that you stood as if out of a tent too short to cover your nakedness: and the others coming up: Ivy, blandly, whom nothing could embarrass, carrying her baby, her four year old child in a dress made of pillowsack that came an inch below his navel; he was carrying a doll; Pearl, with her elegant skin, her red-brown sexy eyes; Miss Molly; and Walker setting up . . . the camera; stooping beneath cloak and cloud of wicked cloth, and twisting buttons; a witchcraft preparing, colder than keenest ice, and incalculably cruel: and at least you could do, and you did it, you washed the faces of your children swiftly and violently with rainwater, so that their faces were suddenly luminous stuck out of the holes of their clothes, the slightly dampened hair swept clean of the clear and blessed foreheads of these flowers; and your two daughters, standing there in the crowding porch, yielding and leaning their heads profound against the pulling and the entanglements, each let down their long black hair in haste and combed and rearrayed it (but Walker made a picture of this; you didn't know; you thought he was still testing around; there you all are, the

mother as before a firing squad, the children standing like columns of an exquisite temple, their eyes straying, and behind, both girls, bent deep in the dark shadow somehow as if listening. . . .): and we, the men meanwhile, Woods and George and I (Fred was in the lineup, talking over and over about being in the funny papers and about breaking the camera with his face, and laughing and laughing and laughing), we were sitting at the roots of a tree talking slowly and eating one peach after another and watching, while I was spreading so much quiet and casualness as I could; but all this while it was you I was particularly watching, Mrs. Ricketts: you can have no idea with what care for you, what need to let you know, oh, not to fear us, not to fear, not to hate us, that we are your friends, that however it must seem it is all right, it is truly and all the way all right: so, continually, I was watching for your eyes, and whenever they turned upon me, trying through my own and through a friendly and tender smiling (which sickens me to disgust to think of) to store into your eyes some knowledge of this, some warmth, some reassurance, that might at least a little relax you . . . but your eyes upon me, time after time, held nothing but the same terror, the same feeling at the very most, of "if you are our friend, lift this weight and piercing from us, from my children" (for it was of them and of your husband that you had this care, at all times; I don't believe one could ever persuade you such a thing can exist as a thought for yourself); and at length, and just once, a change, a softening of expression; your eyes softened, lost all their immediate dread, but without smiling; but in a heartbroken and infinite yet timid reproachfulness, as when, say, you might have petted a little animal in a trap, beyond its torn toothed fierceness, beyond its fear, to quiet, in which it knows, of your blandishments: you could spring free the jaws of this iron from my wrist; what is this hand, what are these kind eyes; what is this gentling hand on the fur of my forehead: so that I let my face loose of any control and it showed you just what and all I felt for you and of myself: it must have been an ugly and puzzling grimace, God knows no use or comfort to you; and you looked a moment and withdrew your eyes, and gazed patiently into the ground, in nothing but sorrow, your little hand now loosened in your dress. (Pp. 331–33)

I suppose there may be some who can dismiss such a passage with a phrase like "elevated pathos," and others who will feel Agee is still too absorbed in the deliciousness of writing exquisitely about pain. And I have known moods of distance and coldness that can resist its music. But mostly it seems to me a magnificent illustration of what Eudora Welty must mean by parting that curtain, that "veil of indifference to each other's presence, each other's wonder, each other's human plight," and I would like to begin my final chapter by remaining with it for awhile.

X ❖ With Respect to Voyeurism

IF I WERE MRS. RICKETTS (I CANNOT SAY "IN HER SHOES," FOR she wears no shoes in her picture and Agee says he never saw her in shoes—the other women normally wear their husbands' cast-off work shoes), I think I might be glad to have been written of so, to have been recognized once in my life as a creature whose feelings were worth careful acknowledgment, even though it meant a further awful exposure. I say "think" and "might" in part because Mrs. Ricketts could not read the passage. She "can neither read nor write. She went to school one day in her life and her mother got sick and she never went back" (p. 276). Even if she knew how to read at the best level attained by any of the tenant farmers, most of the passage would be beyond her understanding.[1] I also say "think" and "might" because Agee has made so uncompromisingly clear that I am not, and never could be, her and that even my effort to put myself in her shoelessness is a mark of my own privilege and infinite distance from her. Still, if she could have read and understood, I think she might have been glad—even though some of the ways I am about to look at the passage involve luxuries far beyond her means.

Whatever the self-concern in the passage, Mrs. Ricketts has the same kind, and even degree, of reality for Agee that he has for himself. Perhaps he patronizes her a little, perhaps should have resisted his "my dear, my love, my little crazy terrified child." But he has not been guilty of that nearly universal blindness that someone once measured as the difference in the way it feels to pick one's own nose and the way it feels to watch another do so. A nicer and fuller definition is this one by Josiah Royce: "What, then, is thy neighbor? Thou hast regarded his thought, his feeling as somehow different from thine. Thou hast said, 'a pain in him is not like a pain in me, but something far easier to bear.' He seems to thee a little less living than thou; his life is dim, it is cold, it is a pale fire beside thy own burning desires. . . . So, dimly and by instinct hast thou lived with thy neighbor, and has known him not, being blind. Thou hast made [of him] a thing, no self at all."[2] Agee makes perfectly clear that Mrs. Ricketts's pain hurts her just as much, more perhaps, than his hurts him.

At the same time, he recognizes and makes us know that she is a distinct, separate person from himself, with her own space, gravity, and laws of being. His sympathy is directed not only toward her circumstances but toward what one writer on sympathy has called "the center of self-awareness and self-respect in the other's personality."[3] Perhaps his sympathy is enough to allow the word "love," which the same writer has said "calls explicitly for an understanding entry into the individuality of *another* person *distinct in character* from the entering self, by him accepted as such, and coupled, indeed, with a warm and whole-hearted endorsement of 'his' reality as an individual, and 'his' being what he is."[4] That the "other" is both equivalent to oneself in degree of reality and yet a distinct and different self may seem too obvious to belabor and buttress with such weighty pronouncements, but most preaching and much loving, including Scobie's and even Mrs. Ramsay's, has leaned one way or the other. (Perhaps Shylock would have done better to plead his differences as well as his identity in breath and bleeding.) Agee seems most rare to me in the extent to which he seeks both to treat (and feel about) others as he would wish to be treated (and felt about) himself and to cherish them for what they are in and of themselves. It is, in part, this combination of recognitions that makes Agee so cautious about action and social reform, so tears him between a wish somehow to repair the damages done to others and to celebrate them as they are in all their crippled glory, between feeling that much of what he has witnessed is an "abomination" that we should have a never-relaxed determination to make different and right, and believing in those lines of Blake with which he ends the penultimate section of his book: "Everything that is is holy" (p. 418).

Although it means moving even further from anything

Mrs. Ricketts has the means to understand, I want to turn to a rather fancy way of talking more about the quality of Agee's compassion for her, and the other tenant farmers as well, and about his sense of responsibility in relation to them.

In some respects I can understand him best as the "attentive man" described by Martin Buber, whose description of our normally padded condition has such echoes of George Eliot's "roar," Auden's hardness of hearing, and Agee's "annihilating chord" that he must have meant it to be used here. Each of us, he writes,

> is encased in an armour whose task is to ward off signs. Signs happen to us without respite, living means being addressed, we would need only to present ourselves to perceive. But the risk is too dangerous for us, the soundless thunderings seem to threaten us with annihilation, and from generation to generation we perfect the defence apparatus. All our knowledge assures us, "Be calm, everything happens as it must happen, but nothing is directed at you, you are not meant; it is just the world. . . . Nothing is required of you, you are not addressed, all is quiet."
>
> Each of us is encased in an armour which we soon, out of familiarity, no longer notice. There are only moments which penetrate it and stir the soul to sensibility. And when such a moment has imposed itself on us and we then take notice and ask ourselves, "Has anything particular taken place? Was it not the kind I meet everyday?" Then we may reply to ourselves, "Nothing particular, indeed, it is like this every day, only we are not there every day."
>
> The signs of the address are not something extraordinary, something that steps out of the order of things, they are just what goes on time and time again, just what goes on in any case, nothing is added by the address. The waves of the aether roar on always, but for most of the time we have turned off our receivers.[5]

Whatever else is true of him, Agee is one of those who has presented himself and feels something is required of him. What that requirement is, however, is most difficult to know, for when something is "really said" to someone in Buber's terms, the sayer is not an "object" merely to be denoted or described. The listener has "got to do with him. Perhaps I have to accomplish something about him; but perhaps I have only to learn something, and it is only a matter of my 'accepting.' It may be that I have to answer at once, to this very man before me; it may be that the saying has a long and manifold transmission before it, and that I am to answer some other person at some other time and place, in who knows what kind of speech, and that it is now only a matter of taking the answering upon myself" (p. 10).[6] Even to know what has been said is terribly difficult to define or reveal, "for it has never been said before nor is it composed of sounds that have ever been said . . . it is not a *what* at all, it is said into my very life; it is no experience that can be remembered independently of the situation ["the reality not the words, remember!"], it remains the address of that moment and cannot be isolated, it remains the question of a questioner and will have its answer." It "remains the question" because the "speech" never gives "information or appeasement." The "emergency structures of analogy and typology are indispensable for the work of the human spirit, but to step on them when the question of the questioner steps up to you, to me, would be running away. Lived life is tested and fulfilled in the stream alone" (p. 12). Or again, "the attentive man would no longer, as his custom is, 'master' the situation the very moment after it stepped up to him: it would be laid upon him to go up and into it. Moreover, nothing that he believed he possessed as always available would help him, no knowledge and no technique, no system and no programme; for now he would have to do with what cannot be classified, with concretion itself" (p. 16).

I think now of Agee's first effort within the photographing scene to "answer" with that deliberate "friendly and tender smiling" (which sickens him to disgust to think of) that he hopes will give Mrs. Ricketts some little reassurance but does nothing at all to reduce her terror, and of his second letting of his face loose of any control so that it showed her "just what and all I felt for you and of myself," what "must have been an ugly and puzzling grimace," but one that does relax her fear a little and her twitching hand. I think also of his response to her renewed pain when she sees a neighboring family, the Gudgers, arrive for their pictures to be taken with their children all washed and in their best clothes, a pain that remains, so that as Evans and Agee are leaving at the end of that first day, they see "the unforgiving face, the eyes, of Mrs. Ricketts at her door: which has since stayed as a torn wound and sickness at the center of my chest, and perhaps more than any other thing has insured what I do not yet know: that we shall have to return, even in the face of causing further pain, until that mutual wounding shall have been won, and healed, until she shall fear us no further, yet not in forgetfulness but through love" (p. 337). I think, finally, of the kind of effort to "answer"—to them, to himself, to us—that the whole book is, an effort so thoroughly informed and unformed by his knowledge of the inadequacy of his "answer" that it becomes very much what Buber suggests it may when we venture a serious response—a stammer. "We are likely to stammer," he says, "—the soul is but rarely able to attain to surer articulation—but it is an honest stammering, as when sense and throat are united about what is to be said, but the throat is too horrified at it to utter purely the already composed sense. The words of our response are spoken in the speech untranslateable like the address, of doing and letting—whereby the doing may behave like the letting and the letting like a doing" (p. 17).[7]

Perhaps this makes more understandable the structural stuttering of a book like Virginia Woolf's *The Waves,* the syntactical strainings of a writer like James Baldwin, and the literal stammer of a Stevie Verloc, whose simple mind believes that even the suffering of horses requires an answer, even the suffering of cabdrivers and charwomen who seek to ease their pain with liquor. Perhaps it would be better if Auden's humming turned sometimes into more of a stammer.

And perhaps the difficulty I am having now in knowing how to proceed is a kind of stammer induced by the seriousness of both Agee's and Buber's address.[8] For nothing I am able to think of seems adequate to the question posed by that picture-taking and by the writing about it and reading about it, and by my asking others to do so: by Agee's exquisite tenderness[9] and terrible ruthlessness; by his very real pain and sense of guilt and his obvious pleasure in being able to write of it so deliciously; by the sincerity of his wish to heal his and

Mrs. Ricketts's mutual wounding through "ultimate trust, through love," and my knowledge that the gap between those two people can never be so bridged for more than a moment, if at all; by my feeling that in reading such a passage I am performing something ugly and evasive and self-indulgent and am doing one of the best and least harmful things I know how to do.

I had planned to use (exploit) the passage to say something first about the particular quality of Agee's tenderness and to wonder whether it did not bear some relation to the "melting moods" of saints described by William James[10] and then about the balance of pity and self-pity in the passage and the book in general[11] and to show off some of the thoughts I have had about the relations between the two in other works, most notably Bellow's *Seize the Day* and Tolstoi's "The Death of Ivan Ilych." I had planned to ruminate (hum?) a bit about the effect on readers of whether and how much authors seemed to trust and care for them and to wonder about the effects of the distances and even hostilities toward the reader of some modern authors, Beckett, for example. And I had planned to move, very cleverly, from the question of how we could know whether Agee had correctly reported Mrs. Ricketts's state of mind to ruminate about the extent to which we can ever know others without sympathy or their self-disclosure and how much it really matters whether in the role of voyeurs we know precisely what they are thinking and feeling, so long as we are imagining with care.

Now the only response that seems decent is to withhold such verbal consolations, to refuse to turn so leisurely away from Mrs. Ricketts, that lady who was forced to have her picture taken, in a dress made of sheeting, before she could properly clean her children, that lady with her eyes "wild with fury and shame and fear," the tendons of her little neck "tight, the whole time," and one hand continually twitching and tearing "in the rotted folds of [her] skirt like the hand of a little girl who must recite before adults" (p. 331). As I look at her, I am sharply aware that my looking, however much my tenderness for her or severity toward myself, does not help her one bit. Neither her nor any of her descendants or equals in suffering anywhere in the world. While looking at her, it is nearly impossible to take the usual comfort of feeling that reading about suffering, or writing about it, is somehow valuable. It is hard to take much beyond the comfort of believing that the looking is not doing her any harm. That, and knowing that though it is a kind of voyeurism, it is neither experimental nor cold-blooded. Neither on Agee's part, nor my own. I do not think we have been guilty of the kind of violations of the "sanctity of a human heart" Hawthorne so powerfully warns of in *The Scarlet Letter* and elsewhere or even of that prizing open like an oyster that the voyeur of Woolf's "The Lady in The Looking-Glass" rejects as something "impious and absurd." Perhaps in a world where manipulation and soul shucking[12] have become so commonplace that Ethan Brand[13] is nearly everybody's analyst and social engineer, such voyeurism is not so bad a thing. Not as bad as some of the possessings and engulfings I wrote of earlier. This is easier to say as I am writing down my thoughts than while I am confronting her portrait and letting myself be present at her and Agee's address. And yet even then, when her need demands that I offer something, there is a space around her and a sanctity within that makes absolutely clear the terrible presumption of venturing closer, even if I thought I knew how to help, which I do not. With her face in front of me, I remain stuck in the distance of my voyeurism and guilt. The only way of moving is to force myself to turn away from her, at least for a few moments.

Having done so, I can afford to ask some questions that can never be asked in her presence. Is there an armor, perhaps, and a deafness that blocks off an apprehension of joy. If Vittorio Mussolini is so deaf and padded that he can see in the blood and guts of exploding men and horses the unfolding of a rose, is there not a black veil or selective receiver that can prevent one from regarding a rose, even a whole garden, without tuning into the canker or the worm. When the roar becomes too loud, should there not be a little man or woman with a flower to remind one that there are happy people, that however unhappy one may be, life will sooner or later withdraw its claws, that the earth is a farm and a garden and even a playground as well as a hospital and a cemetery.

I would like to have such a person behind my door. Even if I cannot believe in a resurrection, for either Jesus or Icarus, and cannot settle for the willed optimism of a Whitman or Shelley which pretends that springtime is ultimately less far behind than winter; even if I refuse to blot out the images of those—the Ethiopian horsemen, Leda, Mrs. Ricketts, Hiroshimans—who have been fucked from the sky, or those savage images at the ends of *Gravity's Rainbow* and *Dr. Strangelove* where the nearly ultimate bomb is falling as we all sing sentimental songs, I can remember that sunshine and rain also come from above. I can remember that the same George Eliot who knows so much about the roar could write this poem—which asks the awful question but refuses to be transfixed by it:

> You love the roses—so do I. I wish
> The sky would rain down roses, as they rain
> From off the shaken bush. Why will it not?
> Then all the valley would be pink and white
> And soft to tread on. They would fall as light
> As feathers, smelling sweet: and it would be
> Like sleeping and yet waking, all at once.[14]

At the risk of appearing foolish to those who never heard Al Jolson sing this song or whose sentimentalities do not embrace popular lyrics, I must also remember how it feels to listen to him celebrating these blessings of the sky:

> Tho' April showers may come your way
> They bring the flowers that bloom in May
> So when it's raining have no regrets, regrets;
> Because it isn't raining rain you know,
> It's raining violets.
> And when you see clouds upon a hill
> Then soon you'll see crowds of daffodils,
> So keep on looking for the blue-bird
> And list'ning for his song

Whenever April showers come along.
Whenever April showers come along.[15]

Although I am unable to gain or give solace through visions like those of Dante and T. S. Eliot that absorb all pain into one unearthly rose,[16] I can remember Mrs. Dalloway's view that we can at least "decorate the dungeon with flowers"[17] and think of the great bunch of roses Richard brings her on their anniversary, buying them because he is feeling it a miracle that he is married to her and is going home in the middle of the day to tell her that he loves her: "setting off with his great bunch held against his body . . . to say straight out in so many words (whatever she might think of him), holding out his flowers, 'I love you.' Why not? Really it was a miracle thinking of the war, and thousands of poor chaps, with all their lives before them, shovelled together, already half-forgotten; it was a miracle" (p. 174). No more than ever before does he manage to say the words although he believes she understands and sits holding her hand thinking "happiness is this" (p. 180). And she does understand, so well that when he is about to leave for some committee on Armenians or perhaps Albanians and stands for a moment as if he were about to say something, she wonders "What? Why? There were the roses." It is then that she has those thoughts I quoted earlier and want to quote again about the necessary distances between people: "And there is a dignity in people; a solitude; even between husband and wife a gulf; and that one must respect, thought Clarissa, watching him open the door; for one would not part with it oneself, or take it against his will, from one's husband, without losing one's independence, one's self-respect—something, after all, priceless" (p. 181). Before he leaves, he brings her a pillow and quilt and settles her on the sofa, "looking at his roses." And she thinks how she "cared much more for her roses than for the Armenians. Hunted out of existence, maimed, frozen, the victims of cruelty and injustice (she had heard Richard say so over and over again)—no she could feel nothing for the Albanians, or was it the Armenians? but she loved her roses (didn't that help the Armenians?)—the only flowers she could bear to see cut" (p. 182). A bit later she thinks that the reason she likes giving parties so much is that what "she liked was simply life" (p. 183). And then:

> But to go deeper, beneath what people said (and these judgements, how superficial, how fragmentary they are!) in her own mind now, what did it mean to her, this thing she called life? Oh, it was very queer. Here was So-and-so in South Kensington; someone up in Bayswater; and somebody else, say in Mayfair. And she felt continuously a sense of their existence; and she felt what a waste; and she felt what a pity; and she felt if only they could be brought together; so she did it. And it was an offering; to combine, to create; but to whom?
>
> An offering for the sake of offering, perhaps. Anyhow, it was her gift. Nothing else had she of the slightest importance; could not think, write, even play the piano. She muddled Armenians and Turks; loved success; hated discomfort; must be liked; talked oceans of nonsense: and to this day, ask her what the Equator was, and she did not know.
>
> All the same, that one day should follow another; Wednesday, Thursday, Friday, Saturday; that one should wake up in the morning; see the sky; walk in the park; meet Hugh Whitbread; then suddenly in came Peter; then these roses; it was enough. After that, how unbelievable death was!—that it must end; and no one in the whole world would know how she had loved it all; how, every instant . . . (Pp. 184–85; author's ellipsis)

I can remember, along with the slaughterhouses and Agee's flayed steer who comes back to tell his tale, this poem of Robert Frost in which he ascends a little further than he did as a swinger of birches where he climbed "*toward* heaven" only till the tree could bear no more and set him down again, unlike Icarus, on earth.

Two Look at Two

Love and forgetting might have carried them
A little further up the mountain side
With night so near, but not much farther up.
They must have halted soon in any case
With thoughts of the path back, how rough it was
With rock and washout, and unsafe in darkness;
When they were halted by a tumbled wall

With barbed-wire binding. They stood facing this,
Spending what onward impulse they still had
In one last look the way they must not go,
On up the failing path, where, if a stone
Or earthslide moved at night, it moved itself;
No footstep moved it. "This is all," they sighed,
"Good-night to woods." But not so; there was more.
A doe from round a spruce stood looking at them
Across the wall as near the wall as they.
She saw them in their field, they her in hers.
The difficulty of seeing what stood still,
Like some up-ended bowlder split in two,
Was in her clouded eyes: they saw no fear there.
She seemed to think that two thus they were safe.
Then, as if they were something that, though strange,
She could not trouble her mind with too long,
She sighed and passed unscared along the wall.
"*This*, then, is all. What more is there to ask?"
But no, not yet. A snort to bid them wait.
A buck from round the spruce stood looking at them
Across the wall, as near the wall as they.
This was an antlered buck of lusty nostril.
Not the same doe come back into her place.
He viewed them quizzically with jerks of head,
As if to ask, "Why don't you make some motion?
Or give some sign of life? Because you can't.
I doubt if you're as living as you look."
Thus till he had them almost feeling dared
To stretch a proferring hand—and a spell-breaking.
Then he too passed unscared along the wall.
Two had seen two, whichever side you spoke from.
"This *must* be all." It was all. Still they stood,
A great wave from it going over them,
As if the earth in one unlooked-for favor
Had made them certain earth returned their love.[18]

I notice that the wave of love is of the earth and not the sky and only an "as if." And I am quite sure that had the proffering hand actually been stretched, the spell would in fact have been broken. There is, however, in such a mutual voyeurism about as much as I can imagine wishing for.

I must place one more poem on the side of cheerfulness even though few others may find it so, and even though, like

Virginia Woolf, its author took away her own life. The poem is the final one in Anne Sexton's volume *The Awful Rowing toward God*. The volume begins with a poem simply called "Rowing," in which the narrator has been rowing and rowing toward God, who "was there like an island I had not rowed to," and most of the poems describe how torturous a journey she found it. I do not think she would mind if I think of her as rowing out past Mr. Ramsay and his children, who are battling at once to preserve and cross the spaces between one another; out past the lighthouse keepers to whom they are bringing supplies, the supplies Mrs. Ramsay had always sent them while she was alive because she asked herself and her children "How would you like to" live with such isolation and danger; out past the open lifeboat in which Louise Rolt lay for forty days clutching her stamp album along with that orphaned six-year-old child whose survival and death Scobie finds so hard to reconcile with the love of God; out past Icarus, perhaps, and perhaps even past that "narrow raft" of Bertrand Russell which supports us on "the dark ocean on whose rolling waves we toss for a brief hour." In the final poem, the rowing ends.

THE ROWING ENDETH

I'm mooring my rowboat
at the dock of the island called God.
This dock is made in the shape of a fish
and there are many boats moored
at many different docks.
"It's okay," I say to myself,
with blisters that broke and healed
and broke and healed—
saving themselves over and over.
And salt sticking to my face and arms like
a glue-skin pocked with grains of tapioca.
I empty myself from my wooden boat
and onto the flesh of The Island.

"On with it!" He says and thus
we squat on the rocks by the sea
and play—can it be true—
a game of poker,

He calls me.
I win because I hold a royal straight flush.
He wins because He holds five aces.
A wild card had been announced
but I had not heard it
being in such a state of awe
when He took out the cards and dealt.
As He plunks down His five aces
and I sit grinning at my royal flush,
He starts to laugh,
the laughter rolling like a hoop out of His mouth
and into mine,
and such laughter that He doubles right over me
laughing a Rejoice-Chorus at our two triumphs.
Then I laugh, the fishy dock laughs.
The Absurd laughs.

Dearest dealer,
I with my royal straight flush,
love you so for your wild card,
that untamable, eternal, gut-driven *ha-ha*
and lucky love.

(Pp. 85-86)

I do not know what Icarus and some of the other highfliers in this book would make of such a horizontal ascension. I imagine they and others would find the poem too flippant and find flippant my observation that, for serious poker players like myself, five aces against a royal flush provides a far from unserious way of contemplating God's omnipotence. If the laughter, acceptance, and love at the end are shaken with more than a touch of hysteria, that seems to me at least as appropriate a response to such omnipotence as the joy or fear or trembling that other more apparently sacred souls have voiced.

I do not suppose that such rememberings as these will gladden the hearts of any but those for whom a little gladdening goes a long way. And yet I cannot quite come to rest even with them. Mrs. Ricketts and her descendents are still there—and here. And so are the truths in these two rather old-fashioned sounding paragraphs. Both are taken from an essay called "Is Life Worth Living," by William James, that sad and hopeful man I quoted earlier when he celebrated as one sea in which we can swim all those "unifying states of mind, in which the sand and grit of selfhood tend to disappear and tenderness to rule."[19] The first paragraph is in his own voice.

> When you and I, for instance, realize how many innocent beasts have had to suffer in cattle-cars and slaughter-pens and lay down their lives so that we might grow up, all fattened and clad, to sit together here in comfort and carry on this discourse, it does, indeed, put our relation to the universe in a more solemn light. "Does not," as a young Amherst philosopher (Xenos Clark, now dead) once wrote, "the acceptance of a happy life upon such terms involve a point of honor? Are we not bound to take some suffering upon ourselves, to do some self-denying service with our lives, in return for all those lives upon which ours are built. To hear this question is to answer it in but one possible way, if one have a normally constituted heart."[20]

In this paragraph he is quoting John Ruskin. It helps explain, perhaps, why that gentleman had to rely so particularly much on art to make the world habitable.

> "If suddenly in the midst of the enjoyments of the palate and lightness of heart of a London dinner-party [yes, even one of Mrs. Dalloway's], the walls of the chamber were parted, and through their gap the nearest human beings who were famishing and in misery were borne into the midst of the company feasting and fancy free; if, pale from death, horrible in destitution, broken by despair, body by body, they were laid upon the soft carpet, one beside the chair of every guest,—would only the crumbs of the dainties be passed to them; would only a passing glance, a passing thought be vouchsafed to them? Yet the actual facts, the real relation of each Dives and Lazarus, are not altered by the intervention of the house-wall between the table and the sick-bed,—by the few feet of ground (how few!) which are, indeed, all that separate the merriment from the misery."[21]

Once again the "address" of the sufferers makes me acutely aware that my attention and sympathy are of no help to them. No help to Mrs. Ricketts or to those for whom Ruskin has just removed the wall, or to any of those suffering people I have invited to the gathering within the pages of this book. Is there nothing then to justify or excuse such attentiveness apart from the fact that it does not hurt them, and the bare possibility I am sometimes able to believe in, that the mere exercise of compassion is a good in and of itself. I think there is, and that it is of great weight even though it is still a negative of sorts. It is the injury done to them, and to ourselves, when we are too little attentive "to each other's presence, each other's wonder, each other's human plight." One cannot say that all suffering is caused by the hardhearted or those who sit too comfortably within their armor or look down from too great a distance, but such complacencies do much to compel the roar and to define the shape of the cross. I have been insisting that Auden and his old masters are not quite right about the extent of our indifference. Many more of us are respectful voyeurs than they think, and that distance is not like the distance on the look of death.

Notes

Chapter I

1. For a fuller discussion of this matter, see my *With Respect to Readers: Dimensions of Literary Response* (Ithaca, N.Y.: Cornell University Press, 1970), pp. 14–16. Part of the argument there runs as follows: "For one thing, real people are not quite so real and verifiable as we pretend for most practical purposes. Large parts of the lives even of those closest to us—wives, children, friends—are forever blacked out and unverifiable, even unknowable. Parts of our own lives are similarly unverifiable. Nor can we say of ourselves and others where we begin and end, what our limits are. Essentially our sense of a real person, like our sense of a fictional one, is a construction from a relatively limited number of observations of what he says and does. For another thing, we cannot really comprehend a novel or story without giving characters at least some of the attributes of living people, for much of the information we receive about them in the text itself makes it absolutely necessary to imagine that they have ongoing lives even when we aren't watching them. If this were not true they would have to be created each time they appeared on the scene. On the most elementary level, we must imagine such a life when we are told something as simple as that Emma Woodhouse 'had lived nearly twenty-one years in the world with very little to distress or vex her' or when we are told simply that a character woke up in the morning or went to New York. In a more complex way we are encouraged to imagine a full person when we are told that a character lay awake much of the night, fitfully dreaming . . . or had a 'susceptible temperament—without any neutral region of indifference in his nature, ready to turn everything that befell him into the collisions of a passionate drama.' In fact one of the chief efforts of most novelists is to persuade us that their characters are live people."

2. *Final Harvest: Emily Dickinson's Poems*, ed. T. H. Johnson (Boston: Little, Brown & Company, 1961), p. 36.

Chapter II

1. *The Norton Anthology of Poetry*, ed. A. M. Eastman et al (New York: W. W. Norton & Company, 1970), p. 1076. For a reproduction of the painting, see the frontispiece.

2. "Squares and Oblongs," in *Poets at Work*, ed. Charles D. Abbot (New York: Harcourt Brace & Company, 1948), p. 174.

3. Ibid., p. 175. If Auden is referring to the passage in *The Confessions* I think he is (and I do not know what other it could be), he has reshaped it quite a bit. Every translation I can discover says that what Augustine held dearer than his friend was not his grief but his life. e.g. "I wept most bitterly, and found my repose in bitterness. Thus was I wretched, and that wretched life I held dearer than my friend. For though I would willingly have changed it, yet was I more unwilling to part with it, than with him; yea, I know not whether I would have parted with it even for him, as is related (if not feigned) of Pylades and Orestes, that they would gladly have died for each other or together, not to live together being worse than death" (*The Confessions of St. Augustine*, trans. E. B. Pusey [New York: E. P. Dutton & Co., 1950], p. 62).

4. Ibid., p. 177.

5. Ibid., pp. 180–81.

6. (Boston: Houghton Mifflin Company, 1956), p. 144.

7. *Voli Sulle Ambe* (Florence: G. C. Sansoni, editore, 1937), pp. 47–48. The passage reads: "Ho ancora in mente l'effetto di un gruppetti di Galla, caracollanti dietro ad uno vestito di nero, sbocciare, come una rosa, essendogli piombato in mezzo qualche tubo della mia gelatiera. Era molto divertente e si colpivano bene anche stando relativamente alti, data l'ampiezza del torreno che occupavano questi armati."

8. *The Short Stories of Ernest Hemingway* (New York: Charles Scribner's Sons, 1953), pp. 91–95.

9. *The Witch and Other Stories*, trans. by Constance Garnett (New York: Macmillan Company, 1918).

10. *The Portable Chekhov*, ed. Avrahm Yarmolinsky (New York: Viking Press, 1975), pp. 380–81. In Tolstoy's unfinished play "Light Shines in Darkness," a wealthy landowner becomes so afflicted by his awareness of the suffering of his own peasants that he actually becomes such a man with a hammer to a group of young people who have been enjoying themselves: "All you here," he scolds, "seven or eight healthy young men and women, have slept till ten o'clock, have eaten and drunk and are still eating; and you play and discuss music: while there, where I have just been, they were all up at three in the morning, and those who pastured the horses at night have not slept at all; and old and young, sick and weak, children and nursing-mothers and pregnant women are working to the utmost limits of their strength, so that we here may consume the fruits of their labor. Nor is that all. At this very moment one of them, the only breadwinner of a family, is being dragged to prison because he has cut down one of a hundred thousand pine trees that grow in the forest that is called *mine*. And we here, washed and clothed, hav-

ing left the slops in our bedrooms to be cleaned up by slaves, eat and drink and discuss Schumann and Chopin and which one of them moves us most or best cures our ennui? . . . Consider, is it possible to go on living in this way?" To which his daughter answers: "If one lets oneself think about it, one can't live" (*Plays*, trans. by Louise and Aylmer Maude [London: Oxford University Press, 1928], pp. 351–52).

11. (New York: Ballantine Books, 1969), pp. 21–22. Succeeding page references will be incorporated in the text.

12. The story goes on for another thirty-six pages to tell of Richard's further convolutions of conscience and consciousness as he and two other boys sneak off to a swimming hole, but they are similar to those we have already witnessed and I see no reason to patronize him further. This is not to say that the story itself fails to achieve a certain degree of resolution, but I do not believe it touches the issues I am concerned with. In fact, though the narrator of this particular story has gained some distance from the anguishings of his youthful counterpart, the adult Agee, as we shall see, remains afflicted by many of the same dilemmas and torments.

13. *Swann's Way* (New York: Vintage Books, 1970), p. 62.

Chapter III

1. Joseph Conrad, *The Secret Agent* (New York: Doubleday, Anchor Books, n.d.), p. 21. Succeeding page references will be incorporated in the text.

2. (New York: Doubleday, Anchor Books, n.d.), pp. 142–43.

3. Ibid., pp. 388–89.

4. *The Portable Conrad*, ed. Morton Dauwen Zabel (New York: Viking Press, 1969), pp. 694, 698.

5. Nathanael West, *Miss Lonelyhearts* (New York: New Directions, 1969), p. 1. Succeeding page references will be incorporated in the text.

6. Letter of 26 November 1937, *Letters of James Agee to Father Flye* (New York: Ballantine Books, 1971), pp. 98–99 (hereafter, *Letters to Flye*.)

Chapter IV

1. Graham Greene, *The Heart of the Matter* (New York: Viking Press, 1948), p. 59. Succeeding page references will be incorporated in the text.

2. (New York: Doubleday & Company, 1962), pp. 6–7.

3. I cannot help thinking here of the exchange between Father Paneloux and Dr. Rieux in Camus's *The Plague* after they have watched a child die in great agony. When the doctor says, "There are times when the only feeling I have is one of mad revolt," the priest answers, "I understand. . . . That sort of thing is revolting because it passes our human understanding. But perhaps we should love what we cannot understand." Against this statement the doctor summons "to his gaze all the strength and fervour he could muster against his weariness" and responds: "No father. I've a very different idea of love. And until my dying day I shall refuse to love a scheme of things in which children are put to torture" ([Penguin Books, 1977], p. 178).

4. James Agee, not surprisingly, reveals a similar perversity. In a letter to Father Flye, he describes his daughter's first day at school as "another reason I feel the year, and all of existence so far as I'm concerned, is taking a deep turn under. She's been a lovely and happy child so far; and I've felt, however foolishly, always within my sight and reach. I know that from now on will be just as before, the usual mixture of good and terrible things and of utterly indescribable things: but all I can feel is, God help her now. I begin to get just a faint sense of what heart break there must be in it even at the best, to see a child keep growing up" (*Letters to Flye*, p. 186).

5. *A Collection of Essays* (New York: Doubleday, Anchor Books, n.d.), p. 177.

6. Graham Greene, *The Heart of the Matter*; with a new introduction by the author and a passage omitted from the original edition (New York: Viking Press, Compass edition, 1974), pp. xiii–xiv.

7. *The Honorary Consul* (New York: Simon & Schuster, 1973), p. 197. There Greene speaks of an experience which "was like watching on the stage a scene, both sad and comic, from a remote seat at the back of the gallery. Distance removed the characters so far from him that he could be touched only by a formal compassion."

8. From "The Poem of Hashish," *My Heart Laid Bare and Other Writings*, quoted in *The Modern Tradition: Backgrounds of Modern Literature*, ed. Richard Ellman and Charles Feidelson, Jr. (New York: Oxford University Press, 1965), p. 931 (hereafter, *The Modern Tradition*).

9. Quoted in William James, *The Varieties of Religious Experience* (New York: New American Library, Mentor Book, 1958), p. 244 (hereafter, James, *Varieties*).

Chapter V

1. From *The Antichrist*, quoted in *The Modern Tradition*, pp. 909–10.

2. From *Beyond Good and Evil*, quoted in *The Modern Tradition*, p. 776.

3. Ibid., p. 777.

4. Ibid., p. 778.

5. *Conversations with Eckerman*, 1930, quoted in J. H. Randall Jr., *The Making of the Modern Mind* (Boston: Houghton Mifflin Company, 1940), pp. 378–79.

6. *Moby Dick* (Boston: Houghton Mifflin, Riverside edition, 1956), p. 329.

7. *Modern American Poetry, Modern British Poetry,* ed. Louis Untermeyer (New York: Harcourt, Brace & World, 1964), p. 392 (hereafter, *Modern American, Modern British Poetry*). This and all the Jeffers quotations that follow, except when otherwise noted, are from this source.

8. Melba Berry Bennett, *The Stone Mason of Tor House* (Los Angeles: Ward Ritchie Press, 1966), p. 185.

9. *The Norton Anthology of Poetry*, p. 888.

10. *The Collected Poems of W. B. Yeats* (New York: The Macmillan Company, 1951), p. 211.

11. *Selected Papers* (New York: Modern Library, n.d.), p. 3 (hereafter, *Selected Papers*).

12. Cf. chapter 3, footnote 3.

13. *Selected Papers*, pp. 11–14 *passim.*

14. Ibid.

15. (New York: Ballantine Books, 1970), p. 51.

16. Ibid., p. 54.

17. Ibid.

18. *Mrs. Dalloway* (New York: Modern Library, 1928), p. 117.

19. (New York: Viking Press, Compass edition, 1968), p. 15. Succeeding page references will be incorporated in the text.

20. *The American Tradition in Literature*, ed. Sculley Bradley et al. 4th ed. (New York: Grosset & Dunlap, 1974), p. 712.

21. *Moby Dick*, p. 408.

22. Quoted by E. M. Forster in "Virginia Woolf," *Two Cheers for Democracy* (New York: Harcourt Brace & Company, 1951), p. 257. Forster, too, speaks to that subject when he comments thus in *A Passage to India* on Fielding's and Hamidullah's response to the death of Mrs. Moore: "They both regretted the death, but they were middle-aged men, who had invested their emotions elsewhere, and outbursts of grief could not be expected from them over a slight acquaintance. It's only one's own dead who matter. If for a moment the sense of communion in sorrow came to them, it passed. How indeed is it possible for one human being to be sorry for all the sadness that meets him on the face of the earth, for the pain that is endured not only by men, but by animals, plants, and perhaps by the stones? The soul is tired in a moment, and in fear of losing the little she does understand, she retreats to the permanent lines which habit or chance have dictated, and suffers there" ([New York: Harcourt Brace & World, Harvest Books, n.d.], pp. 247–48).

23. From *The World as Will and Idea*, quoted in *The Modern Tradition*, p. 766.

24. Ibid.

25. Ibid., p. 767.

26. Ibid., p. 768.

27. Bertrand Russell, *A History of Western Philosophy* (New York: Simon & Schuster, 1945), p. 758.

Chapter VI

1. See *New York Times* 14 March (p. 26:4) and 27 March (p. 1:4) 1964. At least thirty-eight people admitted to having heard Catherine Genovese's screams for help and having done nothing as she was stabbed in three separate attacks during a period of more than thirty-five minutes. The neighbor who finally did make the call, after she was dead, first called a friend for advice as to what to do, then tried to get another neighbor to call, and when asked why he waited so long, explained, "I didn't want to get involved."

2. Walt Whitman, "Song of Myself," *Complete Poetry and Selected Prose*, ed. James E. Miller, Jr. (Cambridge: Houghton-Mifflin, Riverside edition, 1959), pp. 51–52. Succeeding references will be incorporated in the text.

3. *Letters to Flye*, p. 34.

4. "Whitman," by James Moody. The full essay is quoted in Slatoff, *With Respect to Readers*, pp. 195–207.

5. *Letters to Flye*, pp. 61–62 (author's ellipses).

6. Pp. 322–23.

7. Ibid., p. 432.

8. *Varieties*, p. 221.

9. Ibid, p. 298.

10. Ibid., p. 297.

11. *Final Harvest*, p. 25.

12. *The Norton Anthology of Poetry*, p. 671.

13. "Personal Narrative."

14. Quoted and abridged in *Varieties*, p. 320.

15. *The Short Stories of Ernest Hemingway*, p. 383.

16. *Varieties*, p. 304.

17. Ibid., p. 322.

18. Ibid., p. 165.

19. Ibid., Lectures VI and VII.

20. I am indebted for the quotation to Dennis O'Connor, who himself reports it in a quotation of Frieda Fromm-Reichman, in his "Henry James and the Language World of Renunciation," Ph. D. dissertation, Cornell University, 1975, p. 329.

21. "The Oversoul," *The American Tradition in Literature*, 6th edition, ed. George Perkins et al (New York: Random House, 1985), p. 872.

22. "Nature," Ibid., p. 792.

23. See above pp. 94-95.

24. *Emerson on the Soul*, quoted by Dan McCall in an unpublished essay entitled "Furious Angel: A Critical Portrait of James Agee," p. 153.

25. Ibid.

26. Ibid., p. 161.

27. *Letters to Flye*, p. 117.

28. *Either/Or*, quoted in *A Kierkegaard Anthology*, ed. Robert Bretall (Princeton, N. J.: Princeton University Press, 1946), p. 35.

29. "Goals in Psychoanalysis," *New Perspectives in Psychoanalysis*, ed. George E. Daniels, M.D. (New York: Grune & Stratton, 1965), p. 276.

30. *Their Eyes Were Watching God* (New York: Fawcett World Library, 1969), p. 77.

31. *Varieties*, p. 298.

Chapter VII

1. *The Symposium and Other Dialogues*, trans. Michael Joyce, Michael Oakley, and John Warrington (London: J. W. Dent & Sons, 1964), pp. 20–25.

2. From Columbia Pictures' *Funny Girl*, lyrics by Bob Merrill, music by Luke Styne, *The New York Times Great Songs of the Sixties*, ed. Milton Okun (New York: Quadrangle Books, 1970).

3. (New York: Charles Scribner's Sons, 1940), p. 232.

4. *Confessions*, bk. 4, par. ii, trans. E. B. Pusey, quoted by Laurens J. Mills, *One Soul in Bodies Twain: Friendship in Tudor Literature and Stuart Drama* (Bloomington, Ind.: Principia Press, 1937), p. 18. For Auden's reference to the passage, see above, p. 17, and chap. 2 n. 3.

5. *The Norton Anthology of Poetry,* p. 225. In "A Valediction: Forbidding Mourning" and several other poems, Donne builds even more elaborately on this conception.

6. In case someone is tempted to compile such an anthology, I must

include here two poems that should not be overlooked. One is Anne Sexton's "When Man Enters Woman."

> When man
> enters woman,
> like the surf biting the shore,
> again and again
> and the woman opens her mouth in pleasure
> and her teeth gleam
> like the alphabet,
> Logos appears milking a star,
> and the man inside of woman
> ties a knot
> so that they will
> never again be separate
> and the woman
> climbs into a flower
> and swallows its stem
> and Logos appears
> and unleashes their rivers.
> This man,
> this woman
> with their double hunger,
> have tried to reach through
> the curtain of God
> and briefly they have,
> though God
> in His perversity
> unties the knot.

(*The Awful Rowing toward God* [Boston: Houghton Mifflin Company, 1975], p. 19).

The other is George P. Elliott's "Versions," which perhaps puts the blame more where it belongs.

> *He* Because she was abashed and friendly when
> She blurted out of her clothes, because her voice
> At midnight jumped in my lap and kneaded when
> She said I was the meaning of her life,
> I watched my fingers tell her face *Don't worry,*
> *I'll be this way again*, and felt my words
> *You are my life* perch in her heart like finches
> Singing the break of day. What was her name?

> *She* Ignorant of your stillness, still desiring,
> My words *You are the meaning of my life*
> Drained me, I drank you, poured you into me.
> Your words *You are my life* became my flesh,
> That, when your blindman's fingers stroked the braille
> Of my skin, what they read there was yourself.

You stood up. I was shamed. A sudden fist
Clenched in your voice. *Goodbye*. You struck my name.
(From *Reaching* [California State University:
Santa Susana Press, 1979], unpaginated.)

7. (New York: Harcourt Brace & World, Harvest Books, n.d.), pp. 79–80.

8. *Civilization and Its Discontents*, trans. Joan Riviere, ed. James Strachey (London: Hogarth Press and the Institute of Psychoanalysis, 1975), p. 3.

9. *Modern American Poetry, Modern British Poetry,* p. 462. With respect to the matter, Auden is reported to have said: "Rereading a poem of mine, 1st September, 1939, after it had been published, I came to the line 'We must love one another or die' and said to myself: 'That's a damned lie! We must die anyway.' So in the next edition I altered it to 'We must love one another and die.' This didn't seem to do either, so I cut the stanza. Still no good. The whole poem, I realized, was infected with an incurable dishonesty—and must be scrapped" (B. C. Bloomfield, *W. H. Auden: A Bibliography* [Charlottesville: University Press of Virginia, 1964], p. viii).

10. "Thank God," says Shreve in Faulkner's *Absalom, Absalom!*, "you can flee, can escape from that massy five-foot-thick maggot-cheesy solidarity which overlays the earth, in which men and women in couples are racked like ninepins, thanks to whatever Gods for that masculine hipless, tapering peg which fits light and glib to move where the cartridge-chambered hips of women hold them fast" ([New York: Modern Library, n.d.], p. 312).

11. Thomas Wolfe, *Of Time and the River* (New York: Charles Scribner's Sons, 1935), pp. 410–11.

12. *Text and Criticism*, ed. John H. Ferris (New York: Viking Press, 1966), p. 413.

13. Ibid., p. 91.

14. Ibid., p. 379.

15. Ibid., p. 240.

16. Letter to Emanuel von Bodman, quoted in Dennis O'Connor (see chap. 6 above, n. 17) p. 129.

17. (New York, Avon Books, 1975).

18. *Final Harvest*, p. 164.

19. (New York: Harcourt, Brace & World, 1924), p. 322.

20. (New York: Dell Publishing Company, 1970), p. 358. Succeeding page references will be incorporated in the text.

21. The most recent literary assertion of this notion that I know occurs in Alison Lurie's *Only Children* when one of the characters is explaining to a friend why she did not marry a man who said things to her like " 'Marriage is the complete merging of two souls. . . . I want to know everything about you; all your thoughts, all your dreams, all your secrets. I want you to give yourself to me completely.' " She says, " 'I can't imagine anything more terrible than being completely owned by another person. Or owning them. That's what the civil war was all about' " ([London: William Heinemann, 1979], p. 64).

22. *Mrs Dalloway*, p. 181. Succeeding page references will be incorporated in the text.

23. Another of Virginia Woolf's characters, Mrs. Ramsay in *To the Lighthouse*, will never tell her husband that she loves him in so many words; but in her case it is less an inability to cross a gulf than a need to keep inviolate some space between them, to prevent him from absorbing her completely with his need for attention and sympathy.

24. *A Haunted House and Other Short Stories* (New York: Harcourt Brace & World, 1972), p. 141. Succeeding page references will be incorporated in the text.

25. (New York: Modern Library, 1950), p. 205.

26. Ibid., p. 140.

27. (New York: Random House, 1964), pp. 161–62. Succeeding page references will be incorporated in the text.

28. The Portable D. H. Lawrence, ed. Diana Trilling (New York: Penguin Books, 1980), pp. 55–56.

29. In connection with this, I think of William James's correlation between depths of melancholy and the degree of force required to reach the sufferer. For those suffering deeply from despair, he writes, "the deliverance must come in as strong a form as the complaint, if it is to take effect; and that seems a reason why the coarser religions, revivalistic, orgiastic, with blood and miracles and supernatural operations, may possibly never be displaced. Some constitutions need them too much" (*Varieties*, p. 159).

30. Robert Hershon, *Epoch* 11 (1962): 230.

31. Nathaniel Hawthorne, *Twice-told Tales* (Centenary Edition of the Works of Nathaniel Hawthorne, vol. 9 [Columbus: Ohio State University Press, 1974]), p. 38. Succeeding references will be incorporated in the text.

32. Quoted by Rubin Gotesky, "Aloneness, Loneliness, Isolation, Solitude," in *An Invitation to Phenomenology*, ed. James M. Edie (Chicago: Quadrangle Books, 1965), p. 228.

33. Gotesky, "Aloneness," pp. 228–29.

34. Something similar I think is true for the protagonist in Hawthorne's "Young Goodman Brown," the story of another good man's morbid fascination with man's sinfulness. For despite some kinship with the communicants at the Devil's Communion, Goodman Brown cannot be said to "exult" as they do (or as does the author of "Let's All Join Sticky Hands") "to behold the whole earth one stain of guilt, one mighty blood spot."

35. *Modern American Poetry, Modern British Poetry*, p. 148.

36. *Eighteenth Century Poetry and Prose*, ed. L. I. Bredvold et al (New York: Thomas Nelson & Sons, 1939), pp. 453–54.

37. (New York: Rinehart & Company, 1957), p. 112.

38. Clark E. Moustakas, *Loneliness and Love* (Englewood Cliffs, N. J.: Prentice-Hall, 1972), pp. 40–42. It is interesting to compare this passage with Virginia Woolf's so similar and yet so different description of Mrs. Ramsay's experience of solitude in the scene beginning: "For now she need not think about anybody. She could be herself, by herself. And that was what now she often felt the need of—to think; well, not even to think. To be silent; to be alone. All the being and the doing, expansive, glittering, vocal, evaporated; and one shrunk, with a sense of solemnity, to being oneself, a wedge-shaped core of darkness, something invisible to others." And ending with her decision to leave her solitude, "of her own free will" to join her husband in order to satisfy his need for her. (*To the Lighthouse*, pp. 95–100.)

39. Ibid., 145–46. There is considerable truth, of course, in such a view and in the more general notion that one can not truly encounter or connect with another without some distance or silence in which to know oneself. The trouble with Moustaka's formulation is that it is so facile and that the beloved is so thinly present, so obliterated by the author's concentration on his own states of being. Yet perhaps I should be more sympathetic, for this too may be viewed simply as one more human effort to remain simultaneously together and apart.

40. *Loneliness: The Experience of Emotional and Social Isolation*, ed. Robert S. Weiss (Cambridge, Mass: MIT Press, 1973), p. 3.

41. Ibid., p. 11.

42. Ibid., pp. 10–11. Dennis O'Connor (see chap. 6 above, n. 17) notes that neither Henry James nor his lonely characters will talk about, or even seem aware of, their loneliness.

43. *Essays*, p. 182.

44. Quoted by Austin Warren, *Nathaniel Hawthorne* (New York: American Book Company, 1934), p. xiv.

45. *Love Letters*, 1: 224-25; quoted ibid., p. xiv.

46. *The Honorary Consul* (New York: Simon & Schuster, 1973), p. 213.

47. *To the Lighthouse*, pp. 97–98.

48. (New York: Avon Books, 1979), p. 133.

49. *"Jacob's Room" and "The Waves"* (New York: Harcourt Brace & Co., Harvest Books, n.d.), p. 27; author's ellipses.

50. *The Poetry of Robert Frost*, ed. E. C. Latham (New York: Holt, Rinehart & Winston, 1969), pp. 22–23.

51. Earlier in the book, Mrs. Ramsay has such a moment with Mr. Carmichael when "to her pleasure (for it brought them into sympathy momentarily) she saw that Augustus [Carmichael] too feasted his eyes on the same plate of fruit, plunged in, broke off a bloom there, a tassel here, and returned, after feasting, to his hive. That was his way of looking, different from hers. But looking together united them" (p. 146). And this moment helps to overcome the tensions and sense of separateness which had been afflicting her and the rest of the diners.

52. Sharply condensed, they occur somewhat as follows. Shortly after Cam experiences her feeling of pride as she thinks of her father's courage, he bursts out as he often does with lines of poems and cries out loud, " 'We perished,' and then again, 'each alone' " (p. 247). For a moment "with his usual spasm of repentance or shyness," he collects himself and tries to reach Cam by pointing at, and wishing her to look toward, their house on shore, which she does reluctantly. But a moment later, looking at the house and seeing himself there alone, seeming very old and bowed, he instantly takes on in the boat "the part of a desolate man, widowed, bereft; and so called up before him in hosts people sympathizing with him," and he sighs and says "gently and mournfully," and loud enough for all to hear:

"But I beneath a rougher sea / Was whelmed in deeper gulfs than he."

Shocked and outraged, Cam moves abruptly on her seat, which rouses her father from his dream, and he exclaims, " 'Look! Look!' " so urgently that James too turns his head, and they all look at the island. Cam can see nothing and, lost in a sense of the pastness and unreality of their lives on the island, murmurs to herself, " 'We perished, each alone,' for her father's words broke again in her mind" (p. 249), upon which her father, seeing her gazing so vaguely, begins to tease her about not knowing the points of the compass. Then, troubled by her silence and a frightened expression in her eyes, he determines to make her smile at him and looks for "some simple easy thing to say to her. But what? For, wrapped up in his work as he was, he forgot the sort of thing one said" (p. 250). Then he remembers that they had a puppy and asks who was looking after it.

At this, the space between Cam and her brother widens as James thinks "pitilessly . . . now she will give way. I shall be left to fight the tyrant alone . . . watching her face, sad, sulky, yielding" (p. 250). Torn between her father's "entreaty—forgive me, care for me" and James's stern message "Resist him. Fight him," Cam breaks her silence, but sullenly, and tells him who is looking after the dog. When her father persists, asking what she was going to call him and saying he had had a dog when he was a boy, called Frisk, James feels sure she will give way. But she does not, though

> she wished, passionately, to move some obstacle that lay upon her tongue and to say, Oh yes, Frisk. I'll call him Frisk. She wanted even to say, Was that the dog that found its way over the moor alone? But try as she might, she could think of nothing to say like that, fierce and loyal to the compact, yet passing to her father, unsuspected by James, a private token of the love she felt for him. . . . For no one attracted her more; his hands were beautiful, and his feet, and his voice, and his words, and his haste and his temper, and his oddity, and his passion, and his saying straight out before everyone, we perish, each alone, and his remoteness. (Pp. 252–53)

Meanwhile her father, unaware of her struggle, gives up his effort to connect and reaches in his pocket for a book. Cam watches the reaching with an acute sense that in a moment he will have gone out of reach, but cannot forgive his tyranny and continues her silence, looking "doggedly and sadly at the shore." For a long time, Mr. Ramsay continues to read while the children go on embroidering their connection with him by thinking and thinking about him, Cam continuing to dwell on his protective, more gentle side, James developing that image of his father as a harpy and remembering his impatience and fury when his father would take his mother from him, but also remembering his increasing sense of late that he and his father were deeply alike somehow, and able finally to look at him and think that he "looked very old. . . . Like some old stone lying on the sand; he looked as if he had become physically what was always at the back of both of their minds—that loneliness which was for both of them the truth about things" (p. 301). And as the boat nears the lighthouse and he finds it no longer the "silvery, misty-looking tower with a yellow eye" (p. 276) he saw as a child but a stark tower on a bare rock, he feels satisfied for it confirms some obscure feeling about himself and about the ultimate truth of life. "It's like that," he thinks and looks at his father "reading fiercely with his legs curled tight. They shared that knowledge. 'We are driving before a gale—we must sink,' he began saying to himself, half aloud, exactly as his father said it" (p. 302). Still, a moment later when Macalister praises him for steering well, he thinks "grimly" that his father never praised him.

As they approach the island, Mr. Ramsay puts down his book and passes the sandwiches among them. "Now he was happy, eating bread and cheese with these fishermen. He would have liked to live in a cottage and lounge about in the harbour spitting with the other old men, James thought, watching him slice his cheese into thin yellow sheets with his penknife" (p. 304). And Cam keeps feeling, "This is right, this is it . . . as she peeled her hard-boiled egg. . . . Now I can go on thinking whatever I like, and I shan't fall over a precipice or be drowned, for there he is, keeping his eye on me" (p. 304).

A few moments later, Macalister tells them that they are passing over the spot where three men had drowned in the storm, and James and Cam are afraid as Mr. Ramsay looks at the spot that he will burst out with "But I beneath a rougher sea." This they feel would be so unbearable that they would shriek aloud. But to their surprise all he says is, " 'Ah,' as if he thought to himself, But why make a fuss about that? Naturally men are drowned in a storm, but it is a perfectly straightforward affair, and the depths of the sea (he sprinkled the crumbs from his sandwich paper over them) are only water after all" (pp. 305–06). Then, after lighting his pipe and looking at his watch, he says, "triumphantly: Well done! James had steered them like a born sailor" (p. 306).

CHAPTER VIII

1. Reading a passage like this, one realizes that Whitman is not quite so uniquely flamboyant as he is sometimes made out to be and that the kinships of youthful romanticism are perhaps closer than the ones of genre and nationality. Another close cousin is Paul Morel, whose epiphany at the end of *Sons and Lovers* has some remarkable affinities with Stephen's, even to the phrase "Where was he," which just precedes the passage quoted, and a similar answer: in Joyce, "Alone"; in Lawrence, "one tiny upright speck of flesh, less than an ear of wheat lost in the field" (Modern Library ed., p. 491).

2. Stephen had also been feeling particularly lonely and apart from others earlier in the book when he brooded on the image of Mercedes and yearned to meet that "insubstantial image" in the real world (pp. 64–65), a

yearning that foreshadows, and is largely appeased by, the present epiphany.

3. *The Norton Anthology of Poetry*, p. 588.

4. Ibid., p. 585

5. Not all poets find such comfort in daffodils, as is revealed in this poem by Emily Dickinson:

I dreaded that first Robin, so,
But He is mastered, now,
And I'm some accustomed to Him grown,
He hurts a little, though

I thought if I could only live
Till that first Shout got by—
Not all Pianos in the Woods
Had power to mangle me—

I dared not meet the Daffodils—
For fear their Yellow Gown
Would pierce me with a fashion
So foreign to my own—

I wished the Grass would hurry—
So when 'twas time to see—
He'd be too tall, the tallest one
Could stretch—to look at me—

I could not bear the Bees should come,
I wished they'd stay away
In those dim countries where they go
What word had they, for me?

They're here, though; not a creature failed—
No Blossom stayed away
In gentle deference to me—
The Queen of Calvary,—

Each one salutes me, as he goes,
And I, my childish Plumes
Lift, in bereaved acknowledgement
Of their unthinking Drums—

(*Final Harvest*, pp. 75–76)

6. Pansies, lilies, kingcups, daisies
Let them live upon their praises;
Long as there's a sun that sets,
Primroses will have their glory;
Long as there are violets,

They will have a place in story:
There's a flower that shall be mine,
'Tis the little Celandine.
(*The Norton Anthology of Poetry*, p. 584)

7. As in his "Ode: Intimations of Immortality," which ends:

Thanks to the human heart by which we live,
Thanks to its tenderness, its joys, and fears,
To me the meanest flower that blows can give
Thoughts that do often lie too deep for tears.
(Ibid., p. 583)

8. *A Haunted House and Other Stories*, p. 8. Succeeding page references will be incorporated in the text.

9. Though it is not really germane to this discussion, I must observe that the imagery of the passage is troublingly suggestive of Virginia Woolf's own suicidal death, a connection made even more startling when it is followed immediately by the narrator's decision to have Minnie contemplate taking her own life.

10. There is considerable evidence that Virginia Woolf did know and admire Whitman's work, evidence including a review of a book about Whitman in which she writes: "In Whitman the capacity for pleasure seemed never to diminish, and the power to include grew greater and greater; so that although the authors of this book [who visited Whitman in 1890–91] lament that they have only a trivial bunch of sayings to offer us, we are left with a sense of an 'immense background or vista' and stars shining more brightly than in our climate" (*Granite and Rainbow: Essays by Virginia Woolf* [London: Hogarth Press, 1958], p. 231).

11. *A Haunted House and Other Stories*, pp. 91–92.

12. In his lonely prowling of the streets of Winesburg, his fascination with the lonely figures whose stories he tells and his separateness from them, the ease with which he relinquishes or avoids real embraces in favor of verbal ones, and his tendency to experience a sense of brotherhood when he is feeling most detached and apart, George Willard is a particularly revealing portrait of the young artist as a lonely embracer.

13. See above, p. 166.

14. *Text and Criticism*, p. 178.

15. "Art for Art's Sake," *Two Cheers for Democracy*, pp. 92–93.

16. "The Writer's Audience Is Always a Fiction,' *PMLA*, January 1975, p. 10.

17. When Logan Pearsall Smith told Henry James of his desire to be a writer, the latter is reported to have said: "My young friend . . . and I call you young—you are disgustingly and, if I may be allowed to say so, nauseatingly young—there is one thing that, if you really intend to follow the course you indicate, I cannot too emphatically insist on. There is one word—let me impress upon you—which you must inscribe upon your banner . . . That word is Loneliness" (quoted in Stephen Donadio, *Nietzsche, Henry James, and the Artistic Will* [New York: Oxford University Press, 1978], pp. 226–27.

18. See chapter 5, pp. 117-19.

19. From "Worpswede," quoted in *The Modern Tradition*, p. 409.

20. *Loneliness,* p. 92.

21. Quite another perspective is suggested by Gotesky's notion of "survival isolation," which he defines as the "rational recognition that loneliness is essential in order to survive whether the survival is biological, psychological, intellectual, or moral. It is the recognition that if others knew us for what we are, they will seek to punish or destroy us. Criminals, espionage agents, political revolutionaries, nonconformists of all sorts—whether their opposition is moral, artistic, religious, political, or social—are frequently compelled to live in this state. They cannot usually afford to let most men know who they are and what they are doing—if they are to succeed in their objectives or even survive" ("Aloneness," p. 230). To some degree this is true for nearly all artists and for most sensitive adolescents. They face not only the outward manifestations of their difference and their sense of difference but the loneliness that comes from hiding crucial aspects of the self. (See Flaubert's letter to Colet, below, p. 227.)

22. Moustakas, *Loneliness and Love*, pp. 25–26.

23. *Epiphany in the Modern Novel* (Seattle: University of Washington Press, 1971), p. 47.

24. Ibid., p. 171. Beja comments that "despite the many moments in which Eugene or George feels an overpowering communion with other people, one's general impression is that of a bitter man more capable of abhorrence than of sympathy. For every stranger in the streets of Boston or New York to whom he feels his heart go out, there is someone, barely an acquaintance, perhaps, whom he knows and—consequently—hates, fears, and despises. As a result, the sudden insights during which he is said to fathom completely some person or object are frequently unconvincing" (p. 171).

25. It is worth observing too that the epiphany usually provides a relatively limited way of knowing and defining other people. It tends to illuminate or realize them rather than to examine or explore them, and to define them in relation to an observer rather than from their own point of view.

26. *Varieties*, p. 199.

27. Ibid., p. 129.

28. Quoted in *The Modern Tradition*, p. 19.

29. *Winesburg, Ohio: Text and Criticism*, p. 15.

30. Preface to *The Nigger of the Narcissus.*

31. *One Time, One Place* (New York: Random House, 1971), p. 8; quoted by Michael Kreyling, *Eudora Welty's Achievement of Order* (Baton Rouge: Louisiana State University Press, 1980), p. xx.

Chapter IX

1. *Pictures from Brueghel and other Poems* (New York: New Directions, 1962), pp. 86–88. I am grateful to my colleague Paul Sawyer for calling this poem to my attention.

2. *Twilight in Italy* (New York: Viking Press, 1958), p. 3. Succeeding references will be incorporated in the text.

3. *Surfacing* (London: Virago Press, 1979), p. 140.

4. *Letters to Flye*, p. 74.

5. (New York: Bantam Books, 1971), pp. 395–96.

6. P. xiv. Succeeding page references will be incorporated in the text.

7. *The Collected Short Prose*, pp. 244–45.

8. Ibid., pp. 96–97.

9. *Letters to Flye*, p. 257.

10. The most exquisite music, perhaps, is that in the passage near the end of the book describing Squinchy Gudger and his mother and then Ellen Woods, and the section "(On the Porch) 3," which ends the book.

11. *The Collected Short Prose*, p. 235.

12. Although *Let Us Now Praise Famous Men* is Agee's most sustained effort to convey that "roar," another of his works, "A Mother's Tale," is the most extreme and intense. The tale, which is repeated by a mother cow to her son and a group of other calves, is the story of a steer who somehow remains alive when he is brought into the slaughterhouse and escapes after being hung on a hook by his heels and almost completely flayed. In terrible agony, he heroically makes his way back to the ranch on which he was born to tell of his ordeal, starting with the terrifying journey in the cattle train without food or water or room to lie down, and to warn his fellow animals never to let themselves be taken by man. In that story it is as though Agee had placed himself and his chief characters and his readers in the very midst of the "roar" and in fact the story is nearly unbearable. It could be said also that both in that story and *Let Us Now Praise Famous Men* Agee makes the effort, which Conrad and others draw back from finally, to speak the unspeakable. And that in doing so he is not unlike that torn, nearly skinless, bleeding steer, who "with his desperate concern to warn us while he could . . . rolled his eyes wildly while he talked, and looked piercingly from one to another of his listeners, interrupting himself to cry out, '*Believe* me! oh, *believe* me!' for it had evidently never occurred to him that he might not be believed, and must make this last effort, in addition to all he had gone through for us, to *make* himself believed; so that he groaned with sorrow and with rage and railed at them without tact or mercy for their slowness to believe. He had scarcely what you could call a voice left, but with this relic of a voice he shouted and bellowed and bullied and insulted us, in the agony of his concern." *CSP*, p. 269.

13. P. 112.

14. He uses this phrase in a letter to Father Flye in which he explains that he tried to write the book in language anyone could read, but failed and feels guilty about that. The passage reads: "The lives of the families belong first (if to anyone) to people like them and only secondarily to the 'educated' such as myself. If I have done this piece of spiritual burglary no matter in what 'reverence' and wish for 'honesty,' the least I can do is to return the property where it belongs, not limit its language to those who can least know what it means" (*Letters to Flye*, p. 117).

15. Agee changed the surnames of the families and to a lesser degree the first names of the people, but did little else to disguise them. Not much is reliably known about the extent to which the various people became aware of the book or were able to read it, or about their attitudes toward it. It seems clear that he remained friendly with some of them and that there were exchanges of letters and gifts between him and them at least at Christmastime. It is also clear that while some of the surviving people remember Agee with fondness, at least one of the children, now grown up, feels she was unfairly used, and that there was talk from time to time in one

or more of the families of suing for some of the money the book was believed (incorrectly) to have made. Since those who have "investigated" these matters were all less scrupulous than Agee about protecting the living people, I shall not add to their exposure by citing such sources here.

16. "Mr. Bennett and Mrs. Brown."

Chapter X

1. See above, chap. 9 n. 15.

2. Quoted and abridged from Josiah Royce, *The Religious Aspect of Philosophy*, in William James, "On a Certain Blindness in Human Beings," *Selected Papers on Philosophy* (New York: E. P. Dutton & Company, 1917), pp. 8–9.

3. Max Scheler, *The Nature of Sympathy*, trans. Peter Heath (Hamden, Conn.: Archon Books, 1973), p. 138. I am indebted to my colleague Sandra Siegel for calling my attention to this book.

4. Ibid., p. 70.

5. *Between Man and Man* (New York: Macmillan Company, 1968), pp. 10–11. Succeeding references will be incorporated in the text.

6. Although I doubt Buber would fully agree, I would add that depending on the nature of the "address," the answering could be as immediate, personal, and direct as Dorothea Brooke's visit to Rosamond Vincy after the sleepless night that leads her to ask: "What should I do—how should I act now, this very day, if I could clutch my own pain, and compel it to silence and think of those three [the others involved in the painful experience]?" (George Eliot, *Middlemarch* [Boston: Houghton Mifflin Company, 1956], p. 577) or as circuitous as the pilgrimages to Hiroshima of some of those who helped build and drop the bomb. Depending on the character of the answerer, it might involve a desperate effort to understand fully another's point of view or a far more generalized warmth or melting of heart. For some it would mean a giving of self, for others a subduing or renunciation of it. On a few occasions, when no fuller encounter was possible, serious answering might even take the form of a check.

7. I do not want to press the similarities between Agee and Buber too far, but they often seem to think and feel alike and even talk alike about the ordinariness and concreteness of the sacramental communion. I can imagine it is Agee writing when Buber claims he is not concerned with the pure or with perfection but with the "breakthrough," and goes on "Whither? Into nothing exalted, heroic, or holy, into no Either and no Or, only into this tiny strictness of grace of everyday, where I have to do with

just the very same 'reality' with whose duty and business I am taken up in such a way, glance to glance, look to look, word to word, that I experience it as reached to me and myself to it. And now, in all the clanking of routine that I called my reality, there appears to me homely and glorious, the effective reality, creaturely and given to me in trust and responsibility. We do not find meaning lying in things nor do we put it into things, but between us and things it can happen" (p. 36).

8. T.S. Matthews, his editor at *Time* magazine, writes thus of Agee: "By the seriousness of his intention, a seriousness which pervades his writing as veins and arteries branch through a body, he makes us feel like the liars we are. [¶] Perhaps he was torn apart by all the things he was or might have been: an intellectual, a poet, a cineaste, a revolutionary, God's fool. A wild yearning violence beat in his blood, certainly, and just as certainly the steadier pulse of a saint. He wanted to destroy with his own hands everything in the world, including himself, that was shoddy, false, and despicable; and to worship God, who made all things" (*Remembering James Agee*, ed. David Madden [Baton Rouge: Louisiana State University Press, 1974], p. 118).

9. In this connection I think of Sainte-Beuve's listing of the qualities common to those who have received grace, which includes "an inner state which before all things is one of love and humility, of infinite confidence in God, and of severity for one's self, accompanied with tenderness for others" (quoted in William James, *Varieties*, p. 255).

10. Ibid., p. 262.

11. In one of his letters to Father Flye, Agee writes: "I imagine, though, that my mental disease, if I have one or ever collapse into one, is melancholia—in which one is distinctly too liable to self-pity, naked or in any one of its ten thousand disguises. In one way I can't see why on earth one *shouldn't* pity oneself. Nearly everything I see or can conceive of is terribly pitiable: I can't suppose I'm an exception. However, I'd rather pity myself than be pitied by others—and knowing the nasty uses to which pity can be put, think it may well be better to squirt it on oneself than on others. All the same there is something not just vitiating about it but definitely unclean—whether intrinsic, or through all but inevitable misuse, I don't know. It's the one thing that makes me weary about Stoicism (which in most other ways is so attractive—mainly because so aware of the truth; it is so often blended with, or a disguise for self-pity—a sort of self-pity with its fly buttoned)" (*Letters to Flye*, p. 199).

12. Agee writes to Father Flye that he expects he will sooner or later need some psychiatric help to deal with his drive toward self-destruction, but says he would rather die than undergo full psychoanalysis, for he sees "in every psychoanalyzed face a look of deep spiritual humiliation or

defeat; to which I prefer at least a painful degree of spiritual pain and sickness" (ibid., p. 131).

13. Ethan Brand, in a story of the same name, is Hawthorne's investigator of human nature who becomes a "fiend" when his intellect so far outstrips his heart that he loses "his hold on the magnetic chain of humanity. He was no longer a brother-man, opening the chambers or dungeons of our common nature by the key of holy sympathy, which gave him a right to share in all its secrets; he was now a cold observer, looking on mankind as the subject of his experiment, and, at length, converting man and woman to be his puppets . . . " (*Nathaniel Hawthorne*, p. 353).

14. Quoted in Lotte Günthart, *Watercolors and Drawings by Lotte Günthart* (Pittsburgh: Hunt Botanical Library, Carnegie-Mellon University, 1970), p. 121.

15. Words by B. G. De Sylva; music by Louis Silvers. Copyright MCMXXI by Harms Inc. Copyright renewed.

16. I am thinking of Dante's use of the rose throughout the Paradiso to symbolize heaven and particularly of the closing lines of Eliot's *Four Quartets*.

> And all shall be well and
> All manner of things shall be well
> When the tongues of flame are in-folded
> Into the crowned knot of fire
> And the fire and the rose are one.
> (T. S. Eliot, *The Complete Poems and Plays* [Harcourt Brace & World, 1952], p. 145).

17. See above, p. 121, and chap. 5 n. 17.

18. *The Poetry of Robert Frost*, pp. 229–30.

19. See above, p. 143.

20. *Essays on Faith and Morals*, selected by Ralph Barton Perry (Cleveland: World Publishing Company, 1962), pp. 19–20.

21. Ibid., pp. 6–7.

Index

❖